BURIED IN SHADES OF NIGHT

Buried in Shades of Night

Contested Voices, Indian Captivity, and the Legacy of King Philip's War

Billy J. Stratton

Foreword by Frances Washburn
Afterword by George E. Tinker

The University of Arizona Press
Tucson

The University of Arizona Press
www.uapress.arizona.edu

First paperback edition 2014

Printed in the United States of America
19 18 17 16 15 14 7 6 5 4 3 2

Publication of this book is made possible in part by the proceeds of a permanent endowment created with the assistance of a Challenge Grant from the National Endowment for the Humanities, a federal agency.

Library of Congress Cataloging-in-Publication Data
Stratton, Billy J., 1970–
Buried in shades of night : contested voices, Indian captivity, and the legacy of King Philip's war / Billy J. Stratton ; foreword by Frances Washburn ; afterword by George E. Tinker.
pages cm.
Includes bibliographical references and index.
ISBN 978-0-8165-3028-1 (cloth : alk. paper)
1. Rowlandson, Mary White, approximately 1635–1711. Soveraignty & goodness of God. 2. Rowlandson, Mary White, approximately 1635–1711. 3. Indian captivities—Massachusetts. 4. Indians of North America—Massachusetts—Biography. 5. Indians of North America—Massachusetts—History—Colonial period, ca. 1600–1776. 6. King Philip's War, 1675–1676. 7. Indians in literature—History and criticism. I. Title.
E87.R8S77 2013
973.2'4—dc23
2013009923

♾ This paper meets the requirements of ANSI/NISO Z39.48-1992 (Permanence of Paper).

For My Father

In a book, as in all things, there are lines of articulation or segmentarity, strata, and territories; but also lines of flight, movements of deterritorialization and destratification. Comparative rates of flow on these lines produce phenomena of relative slowness and viscosity, or, on the contrary, of acceleration and rupture. All this, lines and measurable speeds, constitutes an assemblage. A book is an assemblage of this kind, and as such is unattributable.

Gilles Deleuze and Félix Guattari

The shadows of heard stories are not bound by the measures of time and space.

Gerald Vizenor

Contents

Illustrations

Foreword

FRANCES WASHBURN

IN 1682, THE CAPTIVITY narrative of Mary Rowlandson, *The Soveraignty and Goodness of God . . .* , was published in four separate editions in both New England and London. In the three hundred and forty years since, the account has alternately been ignored and revived multiple times, but the themes of scholarly analysis have remained relatively consistent: Rowlandson's ability to adapt and survive extreme circumstances because of her Christian faith; and the triumph of good over evil, with Rowlandson and the Puritans cast in the role of the good, civilized people and the Narragansett, Pokanoket, and Nashaway/Nipmuc Indians of the mid-Atlantic woodlands as evil, bloodthirsty savages. Very little attention has been given to the accumulation of injustices perpetrated by the Puritans against the Indian tribes of the region, injustices that led Metacomet (known as King Philip to the Puritans) to war against the Puritan colonists and also led to Rowlandson's captivity. Billy J. Stratton's *Buried in Shades of Night* addresses this issue, and more, through exhaustive textual research into the circumstances surrounding the production of the original Rowlandson narrative and into the mass of documents, critical essays, and books published in relation to the original work.

Indeed, Stratton goes further. His research addresses the transatlantic history of the captivity narrative form; the religious, historical, cultural, and political situation attending Puritan New England; and the history of early American publishing and print culture, with all its vagaries and contradictions. In addition, his work considers the multiple ways the captivity genre informs the development of

American literary and popular culture to this day and the purposes and interests that the Rowlandson account and other captivity narratives have served over the past several centuries.

Buried in Shades of Night will hopefully encourage scholars and others interested in American colonial history and literature to view Indian captivity narratives in a more objective light that recalls Native experiences and brings forth questions such as: What is savagery, what is civilization, and who decides? Within the clash of colonialism, who chooses how the Other is represented? Is that representation objective, or is it only politically, self-servingly subjective? Or does it arise from either willful or unconscious ignorance?

These are some of the same questions that Edward Said addressed in his seminal text, *Orientalism*, wherein he challenged the stereotypes of Near Eastern essentialism, of the assumption the West was and is always in polar opposition to the East. Further, he argued that the West's knowledge and understanding of the East is limited by historical and literary texts that continue to reference each other in a teleological sequence that never approaches truth, but only perpetrates false, misleading, or limited information. Said sought to expose not only the relationship between power and knowledge in popular thinking but also the pervasiveness and tenacity of Orientalist constructs and representations in Western scholarship and reporting. In much the same way, Stratton seeks to expose the relations of power between the colonizer and the colonized in the Rowlandson narrative.

The process of deterritorialization and reterritorialization, as first described by Gilles Deleuze and Félix Guattari in *Anti-Oedipus: Capitalism and Schizophrenia,* is one of the approaches that Stratton employs in his analysis of the captivity narrative and colonial literature more generally. Deterritorialization is the process wherein colonial powers eliminate all referents to ownership, possession, and connections to land by the original inhabitants, replacing and reterritorializing those referents with their own ideological symbolism. Stratton argues that the Rowlandson narrative operated as a propaganda instrument of warfare, employed by colonial powers to reinscribe the very meaning of North America. Stratton excavates and sifts the evidence finely, revealing Rowlandson's narrative and the subsequent scholarship written about that text to be colonial literatures of dominance, acting as both fiction and history, serving to displace and disconnect Native Americans from their rightful heritage. As Antonio Negri and Michael Hardt wrote in *Empire*, "Native Americans could not be integrated in the expansive movement of the frontier as part of the constitutional tendency: rather they had to be excluded from the terrain to open its spaces and make expansion possible. If they had been recognized, there would have been no real frontier on the continent and no open spaces to fill."

American Indians have long read *The Soveraignty and Goodness of God*, other Indian captivity narratives, and related historical and critical works with discomfort if not resentment at the blithely racist and Eurocentric language that they contain. Until Stratton's work, few if any scholars have so thoroughly interrogated the original Rowlandson narrative or subsequent scholarship about the original text for its relation to American Indian history and subjectivity. Even in this twenty-first century, for example, modern online guides for students studying the Rowlandson story continue to emphasize and reiterate the themes of courage and faith displayed by Rowlandson while characterizing the tribes portrayed in the text as savage and inhuman. It is my hope that Stratton's work will help at long last to shed some much-needed light on the dark and misleading information that *The Soveraignty and Goodness of God* represents, while addressing the plethora of ill-informed, misguided, and factually incorrect commentaries that continue to be produced.

As a Native person, throughout my entire education from elementary school through college and graduate school, I, and other Native people, have been force-fed the metanarrative of American history, which so often negates and demonizes important historical American Indian figures such as Metacomet, Crazy Horse, Tecumseh, Geronimo, and others, while simultaneously glorifying white colonialist oppression and cultural suppression. Here at last is a scholar who writes back, who attempts to create balance and to turn the topic from a monologue into a conversation among equals. In this work, Stratton gives voice to the silenced Narragansett, Pokanoket, and Nashaway/Nipmuk people, to the much-maligned Metacomet of King Philip's War, and to all American Indian people, who only want our side of the story told objectively with grace, dignity, and respect. *Pilamaya ye.*

Acknowledgments

I WOULD LIKE TO offer my appreciation to all the friends and colleagues who provided encouragement and inspiration, read earlier drafts of this manuscript, and generously offered their feedback and suggestions as I grappled with the many difficult questions addressed throughout this work. These include friends and colleagues from the American Indian Studies Program at the University of Arizona, especially Frances Washburn, Tom Holm, Luci Tapahonso, Nancy Parezo, Tsianina Lomawaima, and Barbara Babcock. Others who have been instrumental in their assistance include John Kaiser for his valuable feedback and suggestions on chapter one, Carl Berkhout for introducing me to the rigors of descriptive bibliography and book history, and Eleanor Kauffman for insights regarding my use of Deleuze and Guattari in her reading of an earlier version of chapter one, which appeared as "Deterritorialization, Pure War, and the Consequences of Indian Captivity in Transnational Colonial Discourse" in *Rhizomes* 24 (2012). This book would certainly not be what it is without the tireless help of George "Tink" Tinker and Charlotte Quinney for their gracious insights on completed drafts of the manuscript, and Clark Davis for his support and encouragement since coming to the University of Denver. A note of appreciation also goes to Kevin Ogilvie for demonstrating the capacity of words to formulate the anguish and alleviate the pain of the human experience, and in so doing, change the world. Thanks to them, as well as the anonymous readers who also offered valuable feedback along the way, the present work is enriched in a multitude of ways I cannot even begin to describe in this limited space. Finally, I also give thanks to my family for their unyielding support and encouragement throughout my academic career.

During the course of my research, I received valuable assistance from the knowledgeable and helpful staff of the University of Arizona Library, who were instrumental in locating and maintaining uninterrupted access to the many books, manuscripts, and files central to my initial research. I would also like to thank Juan Gomez, Aaron Greenlee, and the rest of the staff at the Huntington Library for their hospitality and valuable assistance during the course of research conducted there. For their invaluable help in obtaining many of the images that supplement this manuscript, I am indebted to Stephen Tabor, Curator of Early Printed Books at the Huntington Library, as well as the staff of the Boston Public Library, including the Curator of Manuscripts, Kimberly Reynolds, Sean Casey of the Rare Books and Manuscripts Department, and Danielle Pucci, the Digital Projects Librarian. In addition, I am also indebted to Leslie Tobias-Olsen and John Minichiello at the John Carter Brown Library at Brown University for their wonderful assistance in helping me to obtain the cover image.

Finally, I am indebted to Kristen Buckles for her belief in this project and careful editorial assistance, Leigh McDonald for her brilliant work relating to design, Abby Mogollon for promotion, as well as the rest of the staff of the University of Arizona Press in their efforts to bring this manuscript to publication.

BURIED IN SHADES OF NIGHT

Introduction

IN THE WESTERN LITERARY tradition, the story of the Jewish people and their escape from enslavement at the hands of the Egyptians, as recorded in the Bible, represents an early and particularly influential captivity narrative. The arduous journey endured by B'nei Yisrael, the Children of Israel as they fled Egypt for the land of Canaan is detailed in the book of Exodus and conveys an instructive treatment of the dialectic between clemency and retribution within the context of divine providence. In this story the Israelites endure several generations of captivity under the yoke of the Egyptians before, led by Moses, they make a miraculous escape from their captivity by crossing the Red Sea. Although redeemed from captivity, the Children of Israel faced further challenges after their arrival at Mount Sinai as they struggled to overcome their collective trauma. Condemned to wander the wilderness for forty years as punishment for their lack of faith, their collective trial culminates in the establishment of a covenant between Yahweh and the Children of Israel, which allows them to finally gain entrance into the Promised Land.

The typological significance of this story in the work of seventeenth-century Puritan intellectuals such as John Cotton, William Bradford, John Winthrop, and Increase Mather, is so apparent it hardly needs stating.[1] These writers all claim inspiration from the Biblical lessons of providential suffering and perseverance, while frequently positioning Old Testament stories as models for historical explanation. In their journals, sermons, jeremiads, conversion narratives, histories, and other writings, this intertextual relationship is manifested through direct parallels between the experiences of the ancient Israelites and those of English settlers in the New England colonies. The authorized translation and interpretation of God's word—as offered forth in the Geneva Bible[2]—was accepted as an infallible source of knowledge and as a key to the understanding of historical events. Hence, the Puritan "errand into the wilderness" of North America as it was characterized by the historian Perry Miller, served to reestablish the covenant between God and the modern descendants of the Children of Israel. Consequently, the colonization of North America became an inextricable component of a world-defining metanarrative in which Native people were cast in the role of the pagan Egyptians and Babylonians, while the English settlers were self-fashioned as seventeenth-century counterparts to God's chosen people. The accumulation of texts produced by Puritan writers formed an indispensable archive of spiritual guidance and a model for proper social behavior. According to the Puritan worldview of the time, as Emory Elliott observes, "there were only two ways of doing things: God's way or the Devil's way."[3] The operation of divine providence as conceived within this stark binary was viewed as the driving force behind both the trials and triumphs of Puritan society. Although Winthrop's directive to "be all knit more nearly together in the Bond of brotherly affection,"[4] was intended to encourage social cohesion, fervid pressure was brought to bear upon the individual settlers, whose slightest transgression, it was believed, could bring providential judgment, not only on themselves but on their communities as well.

This is precisely the situation newly arrived English colonists found themselves in as they struggled to transform the "howling wildernesse"[5] of Massachusetts Bay into the gleaming "Citty on a Hill" at the center of New Jerusalem.[6] Due to the deeply ingrained cultural biases that were already well-established in European travel and exploration naratives, which will be taken up in detail in the next chapter, English settlers were not inclined to view the Indigenous inhabitants of the land—the Massachusett, Mohegan, Pokanoket, Nipmuc, Pequot, Nashaway, and Narragansett—as peoples vested with the same rights that had been granted to them by God. And although the Puritans, much like their English predecessors in Virginia and Maryland, sought to civilize and Christianize the Indians, as Roy Harvey Pearce observes about the Puritan agenda, "God had meant the savage Indians' land for the civilized English and moreover, had meant the savage state itself as a sign of Satan's power and savage warfare as a sign of earthly struggle and sin. The colonial enterprise was in all ways a religious enterprise."[7] The various Native peoples Puritan migrants encountered were perceived early on as primary obstacles to the achievement of their religio-historical vision as they planted settlements that spread like rhizomes, linked one to another, along the mid-Atlantic coast of North America. Increase Mather, presiding minister of the Old North Church in Boston, provides an articulation of this mindset in the opening pages of his work, *A Brief History of the Warr With the Indians in New-England* (1676):

> That the Heathen People amongst whom we live, and whose Land the Lord God of our Fathers hath given to us for a rightfull Possession, have at sundry times been plotting mischievous devices against that part of the English Israel which is seated in these goings down of the Sun, no man that is an Inhabitant of any considerable standing, can be ignorant.[8]

Mather's antagonistic statement is not only a self-serving expression of claims to Native lands, supported by appeals to divine providence and Biblical allegory, but also represents an implicit validation of Puritan patriarchy. Such sentiments echo the ideas found in the writings of other prominent Puritan settlers, such as Edward Johnson, who designated the English, "souldiers of *Christ*," ready to take up arms against "barbarous *Indians*, famous for nothing but cruelty."[9] As the population of English colonists continued to increase, and the wrangle for land and resources intensified, the already fragile relationship between the English and their Indian neighbors began to erode. By 1633, a mere thirteen years after the establishment of the Plymouth colony and the legendary first Thanksgiving, the combination of warfare and disease was already taking its toll. William Bradford, always eager to invoke the power of divine providence while diminishing English responsibility described the devastation of the Pequot in his journals in this way: "it pleased God to visite these Indians with a great sickness, and such a mortalitie that of a 1000. above 900. and a halfe of them dyed, and many of them did rott above ground for want of buriall."[10] Despite such assertions of God's judgment, Puritan warfare was also having a devastating effect on Native people and by 1637, the situation between the English and their Native neighbors had deteriorated into full-scale warfare. Dubbed the First Pequot War by Francis Jennings,[11] this conflict laid the groundwork for the struggle for control over the territories of the mid-Atlantic region that would extend well into the eighteenth century. The Pequot suffered devastating losses during the course of this war and were reduced to the status of second-class citizens as a result. The noted ethnologist William S. Simmons, documenting the intensity of this period of conflict, observed that "by 1676, less than sixty years after the first settlement at Plymouth and long before most of North America's Indigenous peoples had ever laid eyes on Europeans, English colonists had overwhelmed the tribes within the areas of what are now Massachusetts, Connecticut, and Rhode Island."[12] Despite the efforts of Native nations to negotiate with the English through trade and diplomacy following the establishment of colonial settlements, in the span of just three generations those Native cultures that had occupied the mid-Atlantic region for centuries had been nearly wiped out. The tragic lesson provided by the experiences of the Massachusett tribes in their interactions with English colonial settlers illustrates the way the notion of providential design would come to inform the experience of English captives.

It would be an understatement to say that descriptions of conflict with the Native people of colonial North America have been a common element in the chronicles of frontier history and early American literature. Commenting upon the fissures between historical and literary colonial discourse, Homi Bhabha has stated, "if colonialism takes power in the name of history, it repeatedly exercises its authority through the figures of farce."[13] Opening a space for emancipatory discourse and the subversion of oppressive power relations, Bhabha maintains that even the most meticulously constructed historical narratives cannot alone legitimize colonial power. While Bhabha's conception of history supplies the foundation onto which the complex array of colonial power structures are established, the resulting hegemonic configuration is maintained through a discursive array of infinitely reproducible texts. The American literary genre of the Indian captivity narrative has long served a vital position in this equation. One of the aims of this book is to untangle the complicated system of interconnected texts that operated to sublimate the disparate array of literary strategies, historical events, and asymmetrical power relations, that, together, create a unified assemblage of literary texts in the form of the Indian captivity narrative. The lynchpin of this study then lies not merely in revealing the form and character of a particular archive but by elucidating its vital function in defining the meaning and consequences of race and subjectivity, as well as nationhood and cultural negation in American history.

Flourishing in the late seventeenth century—and extending into the twenty-first century through accounts of prisoners of war such as Jessica Lynch, prisoners in Iraq and Afghanistan, and hostages taken by Somali pirates—the image of the captive remains an enduring literary figure. Narratives of captivity have proven to be essential instruments of ideology and particularly adaptive vehicles for the dissemination of hegemonic knowledge in the name of historical discourse. Much more than simply representing events as they occurred, Indian captivity narratives became a popular means by which colonial writers (re)presented the "horrors of Indian warfare"—to use the title of a popular nineteenth-century historical text—to a fervent public whose desire for Native land seemed insatiable.[14] That Wilcomb E. Washburn's encyclopedic *Garland Library of Narratives of North American Indian Captivities* (1975–1983) contains 311 separate accounts, published from the late seventeenth to the mid-twentieth century, spanning 111 volumes, is indicative of the critical role of this genre in the formation of Euro-American colonialist discourse.[15] As Annette Kolodny points out in her assessment of Washburn's compilation of Indian captivity narratives, however, he only provides a small sampling of the more than 2,500 editions, published from 1542 to 1955 that are included in John Aubrey's exhaustive bibliography of captivity texts.[16] In addition to the widespread distribution and popular appeal of Indian captivity narratives, the lurid, spectacular, and often fictionalized events described within their pages inspired the production of a considerable body of sensationalistic, illustrative art that complemented and intensified the propagandistic influence and the affective response elicited by the narratives themselves.

The fact that the earliest printed accounts of captivity set in North America, particularly those produced by Puritan authors, predated the birth of the American novel by over one hundred years is indicative of their vital role in the development of American literary culture as a medium through which colonial relationships with Native populations were circumscribed.[17] Roy Harvey Pearce, among the first scholars to address the literary significance of Indian captivity narratives, rejected the notion that the genre's relevance rested in "matters of pure historical fact and ethnological data," but instead claimed, "what is important is what the narrative was for the readers for whom it was written."[18] For Pearce, the putative significance of Indian captivity narratives rested not so much on the historical verifiability of the events themselves, but in the implicit "symbolic value" of the captivity experience.[19] Through Pearce's reading practice we are reminded that, the symbolic values, as well as those conceived simply for amusement, are not only inscribed by an author through a given captivity narrative, but that these effects can also enhance and intensify other texts that regard Native people, whether these be history or fiction. The wide influence of Indian captivity narratives in American literary history has caused the conventional lines of demarcation between fact and fiction to become severely distorted, which has most often worked to the disadvantage of Native people.

The most influential and widely read account of Indian captivity in American literature is that attributed to Mary White Rowlandson.[20] Titled *The Soveraignty and Goodness of God . . .* (1682),[21] this work presents a temporally confined and narrowly contextualized, linear narrative of events. It commences with a description of a raid, carried out by an allied Native force consisting of Nashaway, Nipmuc, Quabaug, and Narragansett people on the English settlement of Lancaster of the Massachusetts Colony, occurring in February 1676, during the opening months of the conflict known as King Philip's War. Still regarded as one of the most costly and bloody wars in North American history in terms of the relative casualty rate and valuation of property losses, this war also anticipated the end of effectual Native resistance to English colonization in New England. Triggered in June 1675 with an Indian raid on the town of Swansea and ending with the killing of the superlative leader of the

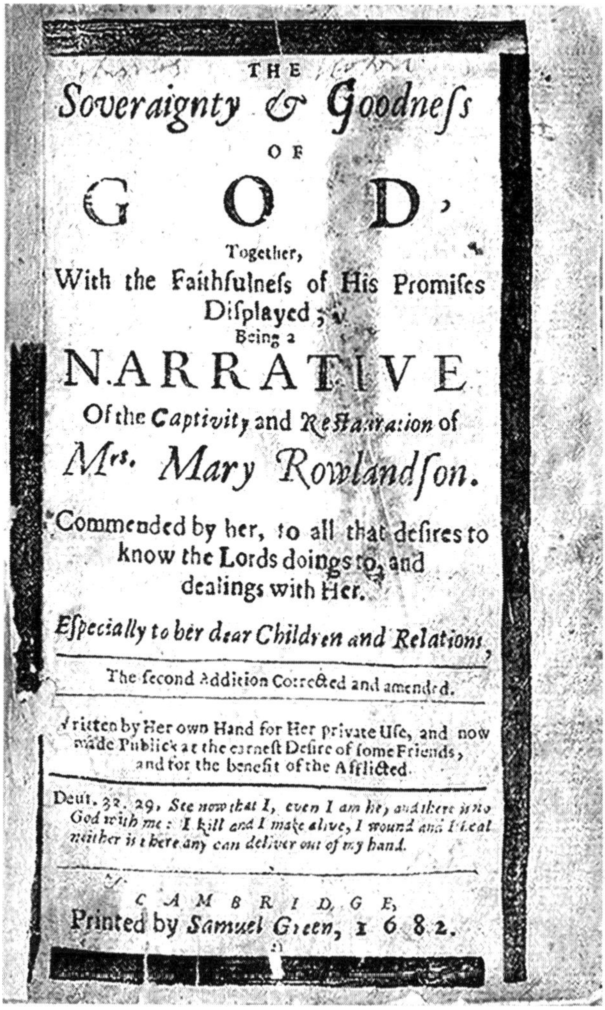

THE
Soveraignty & Goodneſs
OF
GOD,
Together,
With the Faithfulneſs of His Promiſes
Diſplayed;
Being a
NARRATIVE
Of the *Captivity* and *Reſtauration* of
Mrs. Mary Rowlandſon.
Commended by her, to all that deſires to
know the Lords doings to, and
dealings with Her.
Eſpecially to her dear Children and Relations,

The ſecond Addition Corrected and amended.

Written by Her own Hand for Her private Uſe, and now
made Publick at the earneſt Deſire of ſome Friends,
and for the benefit of the Afflicted.

Deut. 32. 29, *See now that I, even I am he, and there is no God with me: I kill and I make alive, I wound and I heal neither is there any can deliver out of my hand.*

CAMBRIDGE,
Printed by *Samuel Green,* 1682.

Figure 1. Title page of the "second Addition" of *The Soveraignty and Goodness of God,* "Corrected and amended," printed by Samuel Green, 1682. Courtesy of the Trustees of the Boston Public Library/Rare Books.

confederacy, the Pokanoket sachem, Metacomet,[22] near Mount Hope, Rhode Island, in August 1676, this war was the defining event in one of the most traumatic periods of colonial New England history. As testimony to the pervasive cultural influence of King Philip's War, English writers produced hundreds of literary texts detailing the combat. Many of these were suffused with disparaging sketches of Metacomet, who was characterized, for example, by Increase Mather, in his A *Brief History of the Warr with the Indians of New-England*, as "the perfidious and bloudy Author of the War and wofull miseryes that have thence endured."[23] A primary function of writings such as these was to validate Puritan claims and justify the prosecution of the war through the graphic chronicling of "Indian depredations"[24] and cruelties that functioned to demonize, marginalize, and effectively silence Native subjectivities.

In a speech offered as a counterbalance to colonial histories and condemnation of the practice of slavery, the Methodist Pequot minister William Apess produced one of the first narratives of Native survivance[25] with his *Eulogy on King Philip* (1836). In this text, Apess characterizes the Puritans' actions during and immediately after King Philip's War as elemental acts of racism in American history, stating, "I do not hesitate to say that through the prayers, preaching, and examples of those pretended pious has been the foundation of all slavery and degradation in the American colonies toward colored people."[26] The association Apess draws, between the fate of Native people in colonial New England with that of African peoples oppressed by the inhumanity of slavery, would go on to play a significant role in the literary development of the slave narrative as well.

As an antecedent to the anticolonial challenges leveled by Apess and subsequent Native writers, the complex literary, philosophical, and historical work performed by the Indian captivity narrative in colonial society requires further elaboration. As the daughter of John White, Lancaster's wealthiest citizen, and the wife of Joseph Rowlandson, the plantation's resident minister, Mary Rowlandson seems an ideal source for an account of a captive's experience. For in Rowlandson's narrative we are presented with the modest words of a common settler testifying to her experiences during King Philip's War, offering a rare alternative to accounts written by Puritan ministers and English government officials. The written work that resulted, *The Soveraignty and Goodness of God,* has frequently been identified as the prime or archetypal example of the Indian captivity narrative form, although information concerning the circumstances

Figure 2. Engraving of Metacomet from Benjamin Church's *The Entertaining History of King Philip's War*, by Paul Revere c. 1772. Courtesy of the Huntington Library.

of its production and subsequent publication is notably scarce. Hence, another goal of this work will be to address the conspicuous lack of historical and textual evidence in order to present a fresh reading of *The Soveraignty and Goodness of God* and the place of Mary Rowlandson within the American canon. As with all projects that seek to reclaim lost stories from the abyss of absence, I anticipate that my efforts will be hindered as I confront the ambiguities, indeterminacies, and dead ends that are a natural feature of this literary terrain. However, because of the far-reaching influence the Indian captivity narrative has had in American literature, history, and popular culture, as well as its impact on Native American people and communities, it is a project that is long overdue.

Published six years after the end of her ordeal, purportedly with the blessing and support of Increase Mather, the sensational narrative of Rowlandson's captivity became a particularly influential means by which settlers were educated about their Indian neighbors. David Mitchell and Melissa Hearn, in their insightful essay examining the function and basis of early captivity narratives, observe that in such narratives, "written under the supervision of religious elites, the survivors of captivity were expected to reassimilate themselves into the spiritual mission of the community by fashioning their stories into examples of individual redemption."[27] Of course, men such as Increase Mather were well aware of the ideological value that accounts of captivity could have in illuminating the notion of divine providence, while promoting the broader aims of colonial expansionism. Like his Puritan brethren, Mather's prolific body of work demonstrates a diligent advocacy for the strict adherence to Calvinist doctrine and political autonomy.[28] Renowned captivity scholars Kathryn Zabelle Derounian-Stodola and James Levernier help to draw critical attention to Mather's aims, noting that "in 1681, Mather had proposed to a group of Puritan ministers that they collect stories of 'special providences' concerning New England to be evaluated, sorted, and eventually anthologized."[29] While *The Soveraignty and Goodness of God* and other Puritan captivity narratives provided striking historical confirmation for the pronouncements found in the sermons and jeremiads of Mather and other ministers, the inherent iterability of these texts, like those of the Scriptures,[30] allowed them to operate as endlessly reproducible master narratives, ensuring their enduring status as indispensable tools for the extension of colonial hegemony.

One of the most important consequences of iterability, according to the French philosopher Jacques Derrida, lies in a written text's capacity "to function in the radical absence of every empirically determined addressee."[31] The implication of this observation is that although produced in a multitude of historical and social situations, in a wide range of locations, by and about settlers of diverse social classes, age, and gender, captivity narratives remained infinitely reproducible, regardless of their basis in a particular historical, social, or culturally determinable context. Aside from providing insight into the influence of Puritan dogma and social practice, the publication of *The Soveraignty and Goodness of God* on four separate occasions on three different presses and on two continents, all in 1682, proclaimed that the bloody contest over land and resources with the Native inhabitants of North America was going to be fought not only in the swamps, forests, and meadows of New England, but on the ideological battlefield as well.[32]

Because of these facts, an essential element of my investigation necessitates a close study of the discursive significance of the narrative of Rowlandson's captivity in the shaping of literary representations of Native Americans. Literary descriptions of the events relating to King Philip's War will serve as useful reference points against which subsequent depictions of Native people in American literary discourse can be examined. On another level, this analysis contributes to the recent efforts of other Native American, First Nation, Indigenous, and non-Native scholars to advance decolonization by challenging colonial histories and opening vital spaces for the recognition of marginalized subjectivities. Such an investigation is made difficult by the very nature of historical exclusion and marginalization. This includes the problems inherent in recovering Native voices that lie hidden between the lines of colonial discourse and out of the shadow of Native oral tradition. Inevitably, such an examination will also lead us to consider some of the underlying assumptions concerning the literary formulation of racial and gender distinctions in the body of contemporary critical discourse as well. In the end, it is my view that any such inquiry demands the consideration of additional issues such as the historical reliability of captivated narrators, the authorship and intentionality of accounts of Euro-American captivity, and the complex and far-reaching mimetic problems of distinguishing historical from fictive narratives within the context of American colonial discourse.

In chapter one, beyond detailing the transatlantic connections established through the publication of the Rowlandson narrative in New England and Britain, I map (literally and figuratively) the rhizomatic development of representations of the Other in European travel and exploration narratives published during the fifteenth and sixteenth centuries, as well as the dissemination of a language of othering in which demonizing, animalistic imagery came to be inextricably associated with non-Western peoples. Here, as well as in the chapters to follow, I examine the development of the Indian captivity narrative, and colonial discourse more generally, as a vehicle of what Deleuze and Guattari term: deterritorialization and reterritorialization.[33] Although the acts of dispossession and appropriation are inherent to these philosophical terms, they were chosen because they more fully engage the epistemological processes involved in the acts of dispossessing and possessing in the context of Native lands, whereby knowledge is marginalized, replaced, and in some cases, destroyed. Extending the critical foundations of Deleuze and Guattari's theoretical apparatus into the realm of colonial American history, *Buried in Shades of Night* also seeks to examine the representational systems that comprise what the Anishinaabe philosopher and novelist, Gerald Vizenor has referred to as the "literature of dominance."[34] The establishment of effective counter-discourses offers alternative ways of reading colonial texts, which act to "replace rather than to represent Indian reality."[35] The consideration of Indigenous knowledge and Native critical theory will allow us to better address the conspicuous absence and silence of Native subjectivities in captivity texts, as well as in the body of criticism concerning them.

The elaboration of the transatlantic provenance of the captivity motif in early European exploration and travel narratives in the first chapter will form the groundwork for an investigation of the various ways that adaptations of this narrative structure evolved in early American print culture and colonial hermeneutics. The tacit and ideological relationships that are revealed between European texts and those originating in colonial New England are used to more fully reveal the socio-historical and cultural contexts out of which *The Soveraignty and Goodness of God* originated.

In the second chapter, I consider the sermons and writings of John Winthrop, William Bradford, and John Cotton on the providential meaning of Puritan exile, with specific emphasis on Cotton's influential 1630 sermon, *God's Promise to His Plantation*. Here, Cotton articulates an influential conception of the geographic landscapes that were being brought under the hegemonic influence of the nascent New England colonies, and which also inform the meaning and significance of the wilderness trek Rowlandson endures during her captivity. Cotton's text is especially vital to defining the strict parameters that were to shape the form of the account of Rowlandson's captivity more than half a century later. In addition to the previously mentioned concept of deterritorialization, the nature of these connections will be further illuminated through Hayden White's notion of historical emplotment as a means of formulating an anticolonial analysis of *The Soveraignty and Goodness of God*. As such, particular attention will be paid in this study to the complex ways the description of Rowlandson's travels during her captivity were deployed to initiate the deterritorialization of an already occupied Native space as a tacit endorsement of English colonial hegemony, while acting as justification, often retroactively, for the historical disenfranchisement of Native peoples. In order to link the processes related to the act of dispossession and its literary alibi, *Buried in Shades of Night* also considers the literary and historical implications of the Indian captivity genre. By the nineteenth century, this genre included thousands of different captivity narratives, supplemented by an ever-expanding body of historical texts, frontier adventure novels, and poems. Since a comprehensive examination of the captivity narrative genre is simply not feasible given the overwhelming mass of texts at issue, I have chosen to primarily focus my attention on the position of the Rowlandson narrative, while paying special attention to the nature and circumstances of its composition and original production.

The matter of the Indian captivity narrative's function raises the thorny issue of intentionality, which is of no small concern within the context of seventeenth-century Euro-American literary discourse.

In terms of *The Soveraignty and Goodness of God* itself, as the statements of Mitchell and Hearn testify, scholars have long maintained that Increase Mather played a significant role in the publication of the text. Many even go so far as to identify him as the author of the anonymous "Preface To the Reader," which introduces Rowlandson's account. While most scholars seem to share the belief that Mather, at the very least, served in an editorial capacity during the production of the narrative, Derounian-Stodola identifies textual idiosyncrasies that are suggestive of an even more prominent role. Evidence for this claim seems particularly compelling when considering the obtrusive use of scriptural citations, which are interpolated throughout the narrative and serve as topological guideposts for Rowlandson's journey from affliction and captivity to deliverance and redemption. Although the question of Mather's influence was not originally a subject I intended to address in this manuscript, due to the inherent difficulties associated with the age of the text and the prohibitive scarcity of the primary documents available, as my research progressed it became increasingly clear that the question of authorship demanded greater attention than it had previously received. And while the product of my efforts may be met with healthy skepticism and, perhaps, even harsh criticism due to the nature of my findings, it is my hope that the conclusions reached will be judged on the merits of the case and the evidence presented. Throughout this process, my intention has been to address the Rowlandson narrative and subsequent captivities in the context of the unique and specific historical moments out of which each emerged, while being responsive to the importance of the Native perspectives that are undeniably buried within all Indian captivity narratives. I have proceeded, at times hesitantly, at times fearfully, but always where the path has lead; I realize that even now, after years of research, writing, and revision, this expedition remains deficient. Despite the inherent shortcomings of this work, it is my hope that it will nonetheless serve as a useful guide and source of encouragement for other scholars to challenge, revise, and extend the inquiry that I myself have only built upon.

In the concluding section, I move on to consider the ways marginalized writers have adopted, appropriated, and subverted its formula and style as a means of challenging deeply entrenched systems of racism and cultural oppression. This subversive strategy is perhaps most evident in the development, during the nineteenth and early twentieth centuries, of literary genres such as slave narratives and, later, Native American boarding school narratives, which demonstrated the emancipatory nature of African American and Native American literary production in powerful and compelling ways. In such texts, former slaves such as Frederick Douglass and Harriet Ann Jacobs challenged the binary oppositions operating in the Indian captivity narrative, characterizing slaveholders and their ruthless bounty hunters in the role of the barbarous savage, with the African slaves themselves assuming the privileged and sympathetic roles of victims of cruelty and oppression. The same can be said of the development of Indian boarding school narratives in the late nineteenth century that give voice to the sentiments of Native people subjected to Richard Henry Pratt's logic of deracination that was so chillingly conveyed in the directive, "Kill the Indian, save the man."

Finally, this study meditates upon the exceptional resiliency of the captivity narrative formula, which connects accounts from the ancient world, Renaissance Europe, and the Americas with contemporary narratives that emerge from the recent wars in Iraq and Afghanistan, and, no doubt, those to come. As critics such as Susan Faludi are quick to point out, the captivity narrative operates as a useful literary precursor that helps the public to make sense of current conflicts whereby the roles of good and evil, and civil and savage, can be conveniently and expeditiously revived. Many of the accounts emerging from these conflicts simply extend the demonizing function inherent in Turkish, Barbary, and Indian captivity narratives to the ubiquitous images of masked insurgents, who often seem little more than symbols of barbaric opposition to the forces of civilization, and as anachronistic barriers to the reinstatement of America's exceptionalist heritage.

As readers familiar with the Indian captivity narrative genre well know, texts such as *The Soveraignty and Goodness of God* exist in a literary realm that is fraught with ambiguity, indeterminacy, and intertextuality. At the time of original publication, such texts operated as mythico-historical master narratives to order the world in a way familiar to European settlers struggling to persevere in a foreign land. Drawing on questions that naturally arise from the narratives themselves, *Buried in Shades of Night* engages with some of the contradictions implicit in conventional means of literary and historical interpretation that all too often relegate Native peoples and their subjectivities to the margins of academic discourse, reducing them to little more than mute metaphors and tragic footnotes to American history.

1

"Like a company of sheep torn by wolves"

Transatlantic Influences on the Development of the Indian Captivity Narrative

THE LITERARY FORM OF the captivity narrative has operated as a vital circuit for transnational colonial discourse since its inception. During the Age of Discovery, accounts of captivity provided an indispensable means of connecting the European metropole to foreign lands in Asia and Africa and, later, the Americas and Australia. The development of the Indian captivity narrative within the Atlantic context functioned as a particularly effective tool for the dissemination of knowledge concerning the so-called New World and its Native inhabitants. It was, of course, through the deployment of the systems of knowledge developed in response to colonial interactions with the Other that the violent and traumatic process of dispossession was set into motion. Taking the epistemological dimension of transatlantic colonial expansionism as a primary focus in this chapter, it is useful to consider the function of the captivity form as an instrument of the process that Gilles Deleuze and Félix Guattari termed deterritorialization and reterritorialization.

The efficacy of the captivity narrative in redefining space and place was most potent after the advent of the printing press. It was only with the development of this technological advancement that the mass production and distribution of manuscripts as printed books could be achieved, transforming the written word into what Paul Virilio has conceived as a vehicle of "speed" and a manifestation of "pure war."[1] As Virilio puts it, the state of pure war is achieved when, through advances in technology, logistics comes to surpass mere strategy, producing "speed as the essence of war."[2] With the acceleration in dissemination of knowledge that the development of the printing press allowed, the captivity narrative became a vital apparatus in the logistics of colonial warfare. As a consequence, accounts of captivity became the preferred means of describing interactions between Europeans and the non-Western Other and, thus, an instrument of colonial expansionism. The unprecedented speed of the distribution of texts, describing events that often took place thousands of miles from England and Europe, led to a transformation in the utility and value of knowledge; captivity narratives emerged as among the first long-range tactical weapons.

Within the matrix of intellectual production that accompanied the Age of Discovery, Jean-Philippe Mathy has characterized the Atlantic as "a rhizomatic system of cultural exchanges."[3] Informed by the work of Deleuze and Guattari, Mathy reminds us of the dialogic nature of discourse, a quality that persists even when the subjectivities and perspectives of subaltern peoples are absent. In *A Thousand Plateaus*, Deleuze and Guattari employ the parlance of the natural sciences to describe the rhizome as a "subterranean stem," which challenges the privileged status of knowledge disseminated by writing, and printed books as standing for "the image of the world."[4] The figure of the rhizome is thus conceived to draw a distinction between systems of representation based on binary logic and a mimetic relationship with the world because, as Deleuze and Guattari note, "writing has nothing to do with signifying. It has to do with surveying, mapping, even realms that are yet to come."[5] The conception of the rhizome offers a particularly useful critical apparatus for the analysis of the Indian captivity narrative, which was vital to the physical and ideological remapping of Native North America.

For readers on both sides of the Atlantic, the Indian captivity narrative had two distinct yet complementary functions. The first, most vital, concern was to synthesize historical events within a preconceived ideological schema that served the immediate needs of the English colonists. The second was to allow for the circulation of news and information back across the Atlantic to satisfy the curiosities of English and European readers. The printing of Indian captivity narratives in locations as far away as London would have certainly appealed to those interested in what Mathy terms "the incommensurability of cultural formations" encountered by English settlers in North America.[6] The accumulation of sensationalistic images of cultural difference found in Indian captivity narratives functioned as instruments of demonization to support and justify the extension of colonial hegemony. This encapsulates the simple equation put forth by Aimé Césaire in which "colonization = thingification."[7] For Enrique Dussel, the systems of intellectual and material exchange bound up in the process Mathy and Césaire describe is what enabled the imposition of European "dominion of the *center* over the *periphery*."[8] My aim in this chapter is to bridge and extend the work of previous captivity scholars by placing representations of Native people within a transatlantic context, while considering the inherent connections of this genre to its European forerunners.[9]

Despite the clear transatlantic provenance of the captivity narrative form, critics have not shown much interest in addressing the nature of this relationship. Instead, the tendency has been to view Indian captivity almost exclusively as an expression of early American experience. Kathyrn Derounian-Stodola, for example, characterizes the Indian captivity narrative as "a discrete American literary form,"[10] while Rafia Zafar has claimed that through the Indian captivity narrative, "the British colonies had given birth to a 'simple indigenous American prose' form."[11] While reiterating this view, Brian McGinty also identifies the ideological function of this literary genre, stating, "the Indian captivity narrative was a quintessentially American form, a literary reflection of the long struggle between the European invaders and the Native peoples of North America for control of the continent."[12] More specifically, the account of Mary Rowlandson's captivity experience during King Philip's War, *The Soveraignty and Goodness of God*,[13] is commonly hailed as the archetypal example of the Indian captivity narrative. Jill Lepore, in her work, *The Name of War* (1998), identifies this text as "America's first best-seller," and "a foundational work in American literature."[14] Demonstrating the continued currency of such appraisals, while also seeming to delimit the parameters of American literary discourse, Branka Arsić goes even further, distinguishing the Rowlandson account as "the first captivity testimonial in the history of American letters."[15] As the work of these scholars testify, accounts of captivity among the Native peoples of North America have held a prominent place in American national literature, from which they exerted a powerful and enduring influence on the American psyche.

The captivity narrative of Mary Rowlandson was first printed in Boston on the press of Samuel Green, in 1682, and was soon reprinted twice more in Cambridge, Massachusetts, as well as in London during the same year. Critics have often taken this printing sequence as an indication of the text's wide popularity, although detailed information on the print runs, actual sales, and distribution is sketchy at best. Further evidence seems to throw the popular claim of best-seller status into question, since after the initial flurry of activity in 1682, the Rowlandson narrative was not published again until 1720. This date suggests that other factors may be at play, as it follows in the wake of the Yamasee War, which pitted colonial settlers of South Carolina against people of the southeastern Native nations, including the Apalachee, Catawba, Cherokee, Creek, and Yamasee, among others.

Following another lull in circulation, six more editions of the Rowlandson narrative were printed during the revolutionary period from 1770 to 1773, at which time Native nations, especially those living west of the Appalachian Mountains, fought as allies of the British. These publications were closely followed by six additional editions released in the early years of the new republic, during the American struggle for the South and the Old Northwest involving the Shawnee, Delaware, Creek and Cherokee Nations in the last decade of the eighteenth century.[16]

Considering the evolution of the captivity narrative in the eighteenth century, Greg Sieminski notes, "as the claims of Puritanism lost their force, the narratives became increasingly secular and eventually gave expression to a potent cultural myth."[17] So while the appearance of seventeen editions of the Rowlandson narrative may

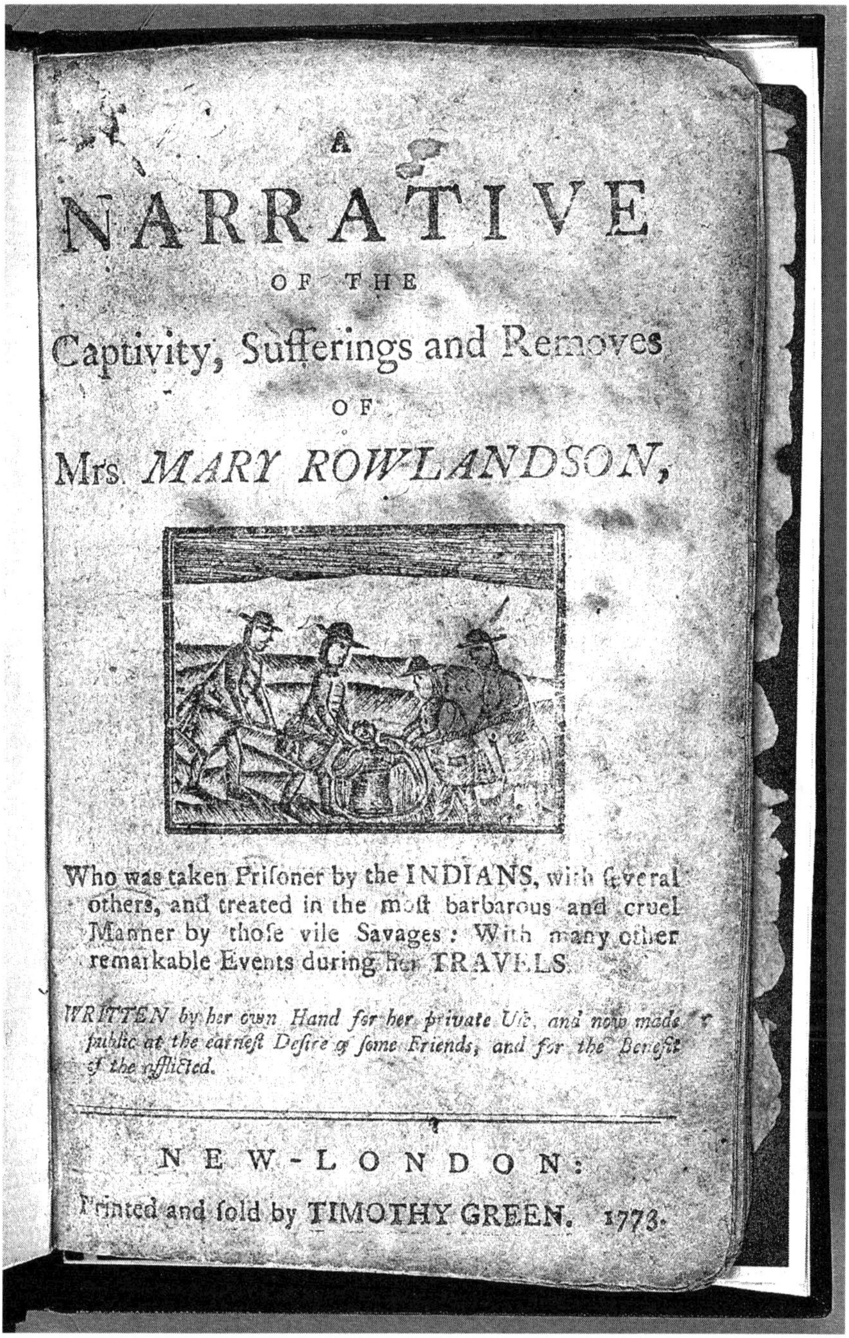

A
NARRATIVE
OF THE
Captivity, Sufferings and Removes
OF
Mrs. *MARY ROWLANDSON*,

Who was taken Prifoner by the INDIANS, with feveral others, and treated in the moft barbarous and cruel Manner by thofe vile Savages: With many other remarkable Events during her TRAVELS.

WRITTEN by her own Hand for her private Ufe, and now made public at the earneft Defire of fome Friends, and for the Benefit of the afflicted.

NEW-LONDON:
Printed and fold by TIMOTHY GREEN. 1773.

Figure 3. Title page of *A Narrative of the Captivity, Sufferings and Removes of Mrs. Mary Rowlandson*, printed by Timothy Green, 1773. Courtesy of the Huntington Library.

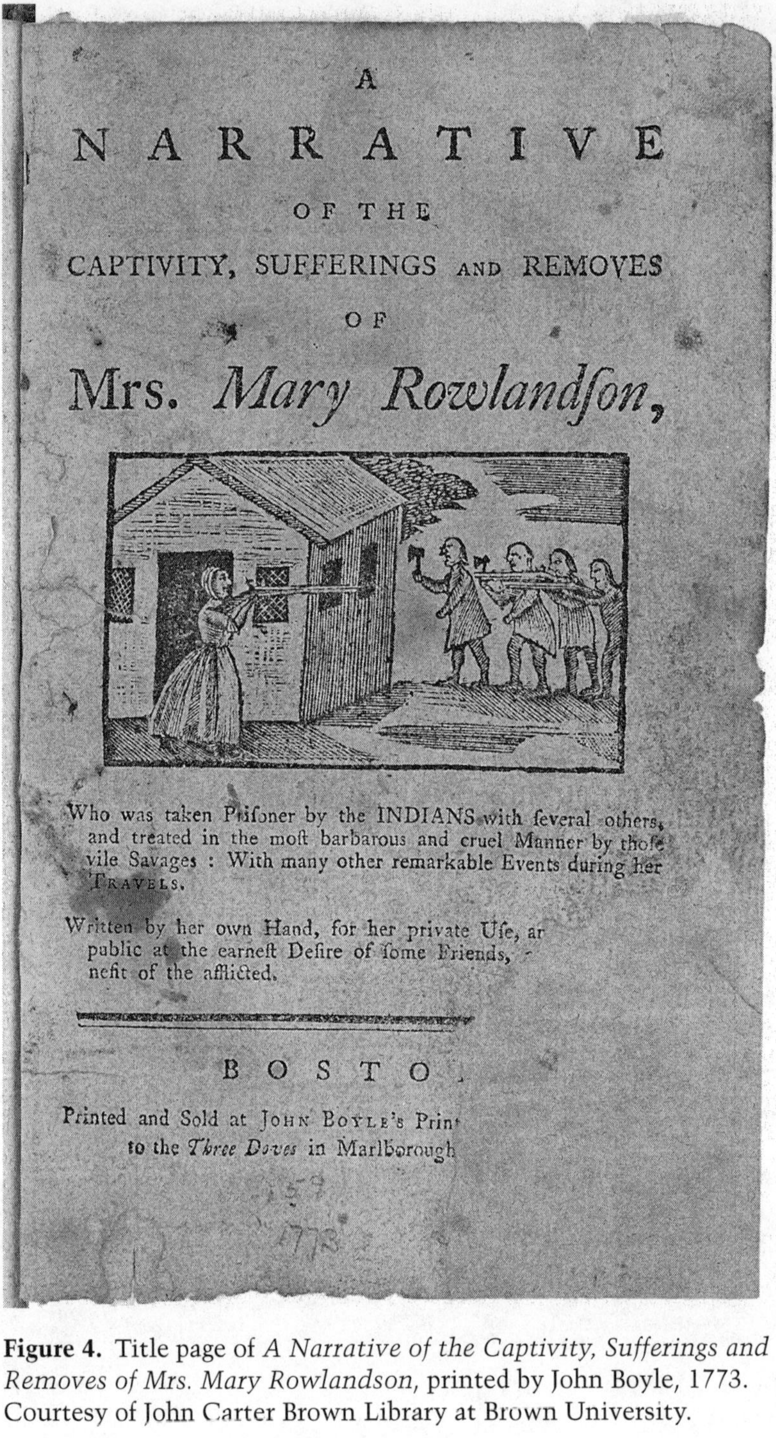

A

NARRATIVE

OF THE

CAPTIVITY, SUFFERINGS AND REMOVES

OF

Mrs. *Mary Rowlandſon*,

Who was taken Priſoner by the INDIANS with ſeveral others, and treated in the moſt barbarous and cruel Manner by thoſe vile Savages : With many other remarkable Events during her TRAVELS.

Written by her own Hand, for her private Uſe, ar public at the earneſt Deſire of ſome Friends, nefit of the afflicted.

BOSTO

Printed and Sold at JOHN BOYLE's Prin to the *Three Doves* in Marlborough

Figure 4. Title page of *A Narrative of the Captivity, Sufferings and Removes of Mrs. Mary Rowlandson*, printed by John Boyle, 1773. Courtesy of John Carter Brown Library at Brown University.

seem indicative of significant public demand for the text, when the specific conditions and historical contexts are considered, a more nuanced understanding of its place in American literary history can be ascertained. For English colonists and their American progeny, the frequent outbreaks of violence between settlers and Native peoples over land and natural resources seriously hindered the establishment of a pluralistic national culture modeled on emerging enlightenment principles of freedom, democracy, and reason.

The rhizomatic dissemination of Indian captivity narratives offered a particularly effective means of connecting English communities through the struggle against a common enemy and promoted a natural sense of social cohesion among its citizenry. In addition, the involuntary forays into the surrounding frontier by captives such as Rowlandson served to deterritorialize Native lands and provided the justification for subsequent English incursions into wilderness landscapes consecrated through the captivity experience itself. Thus, in the notes to the 1828 edition, Joseph Willard can write, "Mrs. Rowlandson speaks of steep hills, and deep swamps; but the roads now lead round the one, and over the other; and hills and swamps are the *commonest* feature in New-England scenery. The whole land is strewed with populous villages."[18]

As Americans sought to distinguish themselves from the vanquished British and their increasingly marginalized Native allies, the deployment of the Indian captivity narrative in the eighteenth century marked a transatlantic caesura in its dialectical use. The historical details of colonial warfare reveal a link between the publication history of *The Soveraignty and Goodness of God* and corresponding periods of national trauma and societal change. In the context of Euro-American/Native warfare, such trauma was manifested in borderland conflicts that include Pontiac's Rebellion in 1763, Lord Dunmore's War in 1774, and the American war against a confederacy of tribal peoples from the Ohio Valley and the Great Lakes region that culminated in the defeat of the Shawnee at the Battle of Fallen Timbers in 1794.

The tacit function of the Rowlandson reprints within this context served as an effective means of demonizing Native people, which is further implied by the subtitles used in eighteenth-century editions. In these texts, Rowlandson is identified on the title-pages as one "who was taken Prisoner by the Indians . . . and treated in the most Barbarous and Cruel manner by those vile Savages."[19] The account of Rowlandson's experiences, as well as the Indian captivity narratives of other English settlers, such as Quintin Stockwell and Hannah Dustan,[20] provided the American reading public with lurid and sensational reports of personal survival, juxtaposing acts of Indian savagery with celebrated feats of perseverance and heroism. Another consequence of the shifting meaning of the account of Rowlandson's captivity is reflected in the illustrative artwork that accompanied later editions, such as that of 1773, which bears an image that depicts Rowlandson in the role of what June Namias terms a woman of "singular prowess,"[21] with gun in hand, actively defending Lancaster and her home during the Indian attack. That Rowlandson is never described as having a gun, much less firing shots on the Indian attackers, further demonstrates the questionable historical status of Indian captivity narratives.

These details seem to dovetail nicely with Virilio's observation that "the war-machine is not only explosives, it's also communications, vectorizations. It's essentially the speed of delivery."[22] As ideological extensions of armed combat, captivity narratives came to define the nature of Euro-American/Native relations, while simultaneously serving as both an alibi for past conflict and a pretext for ongoing and future wars of aggression. The steady production and reiteration of Indian captivity narratives has acted as a means of establishing a distinctly American conception of selfhood and cultural identity within the liberal-pluralist project of nation-building predicated upon the veneration of individualism and libertarianism. As Deleuze and Guattari remind us, however, the rhizomatic nature of such texts inhibit the categorical efficacy of a privileged order, for "there is always an outside" where the rhizome can be formed with something else.[23]

As literary responses to cycles of intercultural conflict attending European conquest and settlement of North America, Indian captivity narratives do not represent a distinct literary form but rather the extension and reformulation of colonial discourses that had enjoyed a long and eminent place in the annals of Western literary history. The enduring influence of texts such as the Rowlandson narrative appears to confirm Richard Slotkin's observation that

Figure 5. Engraving of Mary Rowlandson, with rifle, as a woman of "singular prowess," from the 1770 edition of her captivity narrative printed by Nathaniel Coverly. Courtesy of the Trustees of the Boston Public Library/Rare Books.

myth has the power to "reach out of the past to cripple, incapacitate, or strike down the living."[24] Long before the publication of *The Soveraignty and Goodness of God*, however, German, Spanish, French, Dutch, and English writers had been busy composing works that purported to describe the "strange" customs and behaviors of peoples encountered by merchants, missionaries, and soldiers in voyages dating back as early as the thirteenth century.

Although early European travel and exploration narratives were widely accepted as "true" accounts of intercultural contact, designed to frighten as much as to astonish, on a deeper level, these texts served as potent cultural artifacts produced in response to a radically changing and expanding world. For today's readers, such narratives reveal considerably more about how European writers understood their place in the cosmos—their aspirations, their fears, and their biases—than they do about the peoples who were often the denigrated subjects of such works. As Deleuze and Guattari suggest, "the book is not an image of the world. It forms a rhizome with the world, there is an aparallel evolution of the book and the world; the book assures the deterritorialization of the world, but the world effects a reterritorialization of the book, which in turn deterritorializes itself in the world."[25] In European travel and exploration narratives, the convergences Deleuze and Guattari identify materialized in images of the Other, which takes the form of a monstrous cultural anomaly and looming threat to Western cultural power. Beyond peaceful coexistence, which few "men of considerable standing"[26] seriously considered, European leaders—members of the nobility, Church officials, and intellectuals—viewed non-European people as formidable obstacles to the European imperial project, who thus had to be neutralized. In addition to marshaling military forces to wage wars of conquest, the Spanish, Dutch, French, and English proved to be particularly adept in the dissemination and control of knowledge and the meaning-making techniques brought to bear most conspicuously in the form of manuscripts, broadsides, leaflets, and printed books.

On Easter Day, 1245, at the behest of Pope Innocent IV, a Franciscan friar by the name of Giovanni da Pian del Carpine departed Lyon on a journey east to convene with the ruling Khan, Güyük, regarding Mongol incursions into Eastern Europe. Although unsuccessful in his ultimate mission to convert Güyük to Catholicism, da Pian del Carpine's extensive travels resulted in the production of a manuscript titled *Historia Mongalorum quos nos Tartaros appellamus.* Composed after his return to Europe more than two years later, da Pian del Carpine's text provides one of the earliest Western accounts of the people and landscape of central Asia and became an invaluable source of information for Papal officials and military leaders throughout the medieval period. Despite the influence of da Pian del Carpine's treatise, as well as William of Rubruck's account of his own expedition as an envoy of Louis IX, however, such manuscripts remained virtually unknown outside the elite social circles of the Middle Ages. Although these works bring critical attention to the social and political organization of early European culture, their narrow influence can be attributed to the inherent limitations in the circulation and accessibility of early manuscripts and hand-printed books. In their time, accounts such as da Pian del Carpine's had significant currency with Papal authorities and the nobility in the development of foreign policy and military strategy, but their influence on the general public's perceptions of non-Western peoples was virtually non-existent. Not until the advent of printing in the mid-fifteenth century and the attendant development and expansion of the commercial book trade did such works achieve extensive circulation. As Richard Cole notes, "one of the earliest books to be printed on the Gutenberg press in 1454 was a short tract by Paulinus Chappe, which described the Byzantine struggle against the Turks and the fall of Cyprus."[27] Viewed through the historical sensitivities of fifteenth-century European readers who had just witnessed the fall of Constantinople to the Turks in 1453,[28] such texts represented an ideological extension of the Holy Crusades that had consumed Christian Europe during the previous three and a half centuries.

Comparing early printed books describing the Ottoman Turks and Moors, published from the fifteenth to the middle of the sixteenth century, with those published afterward, a distinct shift in language and style can be detected. These changes appear to correspond to the gradual expansion of the European book trade, spurred by steadily increasing literacy rates throughout Europe during this period. The contrast in literary style apparent between these texts can be discerned by comparing works composed ostensibly to provide religious leaders, military commanders, and royal administrators with "actionable intelligence," with those aimed at more general readerships throughout Europe and England. The texts produced up until the mid-sixteenth century are typified by the use of a simple and concise colonial rhetoric, being generally free of the demonizing imagery common to works published after. Viewed in terms of the affect that such texts had upon readers, those produced before the sixteenth century depend primarily on the use of illocutionary strategies for their literary effectiveness, manifested in the form of assertives, directives, expressives, and declaratives. In contrast to earlier narratives, subsequent works are distinguished by the intended perlocutionary, or psychological, effect on readers. What is significant about this shift is not simply an issue of the linguistic function of syntactic markers present in each set of texts, but the broader implications of what Deleuze and Guattari address in their criticisms of "the *abstract machine* that connects a language to the semantic and pragmatic contents of statements, to collective assemblages of enunciation, to a whole micropolitics of the social field."[29]

Hence, in a work such as William Caxton's *The Cronycles of Englond* (1482), the recent military advances of the Turks is brought to his readers' attention in a clear, unadorned manner: "aboute this tyme the cyte of Costantynople whiche was the Imperyal cyte in al grece was taken by the Turkes Infydeles."[30] The use of descriptive adjectives is kept to a minimum, the purpose of Caxton's account is simply to describe the order of factual events. For Caxton, the forthright statement that the Turks had taken Constantinople conveyed the troubling facts well enough.[31] The classification of Turks as "infydeles" may even seem redundant, given the history and nature of this long-standing conflict, and functions to reinforce a marker of cultural difference between the Oriental and the Occidental worlds. On another level, Caxton's use of this term acts as a stark reminder of the holy mission of the Crusades and as a signifier of cultural difference.

Caxton's text and those that immediately followed are generally free of the sensationalized, extravagant, and degrading depictions that were to become prominent features of subsequent literary works. In these early texts, however, the Other is primarily defined according to a limited set of marginalized cultural signifiers, which were evoked whenever writers referred to "Turkes," with the occasional use of other descriptive modifiers, such as "infydeles" and "hethen."[32] This manner of representation stands in marked contrast to texts published from the late sixteenth century on, in which writers began to employ a much more sensational literary style, designed to influence a growing public readership.

Another result of the advent of the printing press and the development of movable type, as Cole further observes, was that "culturally arrogant and ethnocentric observations of non-European peoples were given immortality in western culture by the printed page."[33] In literary depictions of Turks and Moors found in early printed books, English and European writers established an ambivalent system of cultural representation that was based not upon firsthand observation but upon a negative dialectic of cultural distinction and difference. It was precisely these earlier works that served as the stems for the rhizomatic development of the Indian captivity narrative. In European and English literary discourse, Turks and Moors and, later, Native Americans became knowable primarily through a system of representation based on the dialectic of culturally defined binary oppositions, or what the postcolonial critic Homi Bhabha has termed "the recognition of cultural and racial difference and its disavowal."[34] The establishment of this system of opposition, argues Abdul R. JanMohamed, "provides the central feature of the colonialist cognitive framework and colonialist literary representation: the Manichean allegory—a field of discursive, yet interchangeable oppositions between white and black, good and evil, superiority and inferiority, civilization and savagery, intelligence and emotion, rationality and sensuality, self and Other, subject and object."[35]

As with their North American successors, the development of Turkish and Barbary captivity narratives in early European literature represented how, in the words of Roslyn Knutson, "non-Europeans and non-Christians were . . . reinvented in texts and performances as demons, primitives, or commercial property."[36] Announcing a shift from an illocutionary to a perlocutionary rhetorical praxis, Thomas Becon, in his incendiary call to holy war, titled *The new pollecye of warre* . . . (1542), describes Ottoman Turks using terms similar to those of Indian captivity narratives, observing, "the rapacite of wolfes, the violence of lyons, the fearsenes of tygres, is nothyng in comparison of theyr furious & cruell tyranny."[37] Likewise, in *The Estate of Christians, liuing vnder the subiection of the Turke* . . . , printed in London in 1595 by John Wolfe, an anonymous author describes the condition of Christian prisoners "kept in extreame miserie, and most barbarouslie handled," during their "most lamentable captiuity."[38]

In his study of English captivity narratives in North Africa and the Middle East, Nabil Matar identifies at least ten accounts of "English captivity in the Muslim dominions" published between 1577 and 1625 in England alone.[39] Reminiscent of the animalistic descriptions of Indian people later to appear in the Rowlandson narrative, Matar discusses an account produced by Anthony Munday, *The admirable Deliverance of 266 Christians by Iohn Reynard Englishman from the captiuitie of the Turkes* (1608), in which "English heroes" are rendered in stark contrast to Turkish "bears, bulls and, rats."[40] In the sensationalistic account of the attack upon Reynard's ship in which he and his shipmates are taken captive by Turkish pirates, for instance, Munday writes, "the Turkes leapd out of their vessels, and like ratts nimbly climed vp to the taclings of the ship."[41] Such descriptions anticipate the stylistic employed to describe the attack on Rowlandson's village, in which settlers are awakened by the coming of the "savage Indians" and are soon to witness their "dear Friends, and Relations . . . stript naked by a company of hell-hounds, roaring, signing, ranting and insulting, as if they would have torn our very hearts out."[42] Viewed from within Deleuze and Guattari's rhizomatic context, the Indian captivity narrative forms "a plane of consistency" with an already deeply rooted system of transatlantic colonial representation and historical "emplotment."[43]

It should be noted that while the ten accounts Matar cites may seem slight, Carl Göllner, in his exhaustive bibliography on the

Figure 6. Engraving depicting Turkish piracy, c. 1890, from the author's private collection.

topic, identified over one thousand published imprints in Germany alone during the sixteenth century detailing the perfidy and barbarism of the Turkish people.[44] The staggering magnitude of such a profuse literary output gives modern readers a sense of the ubiquity of European writings aimed at demonizing non-Western peoples during this period. While historians such as G. V. Scammell have minimized the significance and influence of European exploration and travel narratives, stating, "national dedication to imperial enterprise was not all that it might have been,"[45] the sheer number of published imprints belies this assertion.

Although Royall Tyler's anonymously published novel, *The Algerine Captive; or, the Life and Adventures of Doctor Updike Underhill: Six Years Prisoner Among the Algerines* (1797) remains among the most well-known literary treatments of captivity in Africa, a steady stream of captivity narratives were also published throughout the nineteenth century. In his analysis of African captivity narratives, Paul Baepler estimates that during the first half of the nineteenth century alone, "American publishers issued over a hundred

American Barbary captivity editions."[46] As late as 1866, an article by a Colonel Rigby appeared in the *Proceedings of the Royal Geographical Society of London*. This sensationalized report detailed the plight of the crew of a British ship traveling from London to Bombay that had been lost off the coast of East Africa in 1855. According to other reports circulated at the time, it was believed that several members of the crew survived the shipwreck, but were later "captured by the Abghal Somalis, and carried into the interior."[47] According to Rigby, the details pertinent to this incident were deemed reliable enough to prompt "proclamations to be published in French and English offering a reward of five hundred dollars for every white man rescued."[48]

Ellen G. Friedman notes that the presence of European captives in North Africa dates back to the Middle Ages, and estimates captive populations as high as "25,000 to 35,000 by the late sixteenth century."[49] While most of these captives were abducted in the Mediterranean region, Baepler asserts that such was not always the case, stating that some "Barbary privateers began to take North American colonists as early as 1625."[50] Although details of these interactions are sketchy at best, Baepler cites an account in which "rovers had claimed two American ships and escorted them into the Moroccan harbor at Sallee."[51] In Linda Colley's work on the role of captivity in the making of the British Empire, titled *Captives*, she identifies "over a hundred printed and manuscript narratives written or dictated by Britons between 1600 and the mid-seventeenth century in response to captivity experiences in the Mediterranean and North African region, in North America, and in South and Central Asia."[52] Conditions such as these challenge conventional transatlantic emplotments that elide the agency of Native and non-Western participants in the processes of deterritorialization and reterritorialization instigated during the Age of Discovery. Given the abundance of these examples, captivity narratives emanating from colonial New England should not be viewed as a unique literary development, but rather as a natural extension and reiteration of a ready-made system of colonial representation.

Edward Said, writing in *Orientalism*, explained how Western perceptions concerning the East were established and formalized through the production of "an internally structured archive."[53] By the end of the sixteenth century, the cultural assumptions promoted by these texts—drawn from the oral and written accounts by and about captives that were found in popular stories, folklore, and the growing body of travel and exploration literature—were fixed in European thought. Based on the reiteration of demonizing imagery and the rhizomatic "lines of flight" embedded in a wide variety of texts produced in the seventeenth century and after, it is clear that such works left an indelible imprint on American perceptions of the Other. Through the maintenance of the "internally structured archive" produced from these texts, the elliptical reiteration of the sensational and exotic portrayals of people of Asia and North Africa became entrenched in historical, scientific, and ecclesiastical discourses. The depictions of non-Western people found in these works were endowed with a sense of presence, which only added to the veneer of historical legitimacy, functioning as what Hayden White refers to as a "literature of fact."[54] Like Bhabha's description of the "literature of empire" in his essay "Signs Taken for Wonders," White's observation allows us to better grasp the significance of Said's thesis.[55] Herein lies the means by which the "language, perception, and form of the encounter between East and West" came to be shaped according to the latent ideological structures found in these colonial artifacts.[56]

Building on the foundation established by Said's work, Bhabha points out that the effectiveness of the way the colonial encounter was framed in literary discourses rests in "its dependence on the concept of "fixity" in the ideological construction of otherness."[57] For Bhabha, it is not enough to simply make use of language to represent otherness "as the sign of cultural/historical/racial difference."[58] The essential power of the prevailing system of colonial representation lies in its capacity to synthesize and maintain the seemingly incongruous attributes of "rigidity and an unchanging order as well as disorder, degeneracy and daemonic repetition."[59] The conception of language Bhabha expresses here complements the notion of iterability central to Jacques Derrida's critique of communicative discourse and signification found in his influential essay, "Signature Event Context."

When Bhabha speaks about the "fixity" and "rigidity" of colonial discourse, he is addressing the ways that representations are transmitted beyond the context of their production; that is, the specific author, subject, and immediate audience of a given text. In the case of Rowlandson's captivity, this would include the ways that accounts of her experience were represented, not only as testimony to the abject savagery of the Pokanoket, Nipmuc, Narragansett, and other confederated tribes the English were fighting during King Philip's War but, more broadly, as an illustration of the bloodthirsty savage motif that continued to shape public perception long after. It is out of the discursive context created by early Indian captivity narratives that a structurally coherent, or "fixed," system of Indian representation was achieved. Bhabha's analysis illuminates the complex route by which descriptive classifications such as savage, barbarian, infidel, or pagan become naturalized, by focusing not merely on the way regimes of knowledge are established—which is one of Said's primary concerns—but also on their diachronic transmission within the discourses that support and perpetuate them. Derrida initiates his critical intervention by addressing the concept of fixity not only in terms of how it is manifested in discourse but through an analysis of what it necessarily assumes; that is to say, the process through which "one writes in order to communicate something to those who are absent."[60] If it is true that "writing *extends* the field and powers of locutionary or gestural communication," as Derrida suggests, then it follows that the European development of printing extended this field of communication, and its influence, exponentially.[61]

The creation of literary representations of the Indigenous peoples of North America was analogous to the development of representations of the Other that had circulated throughout Europe and England in previous centuries. The adoption by the English of preexisting narrative forms and literary motifs to serve colonial interests would have been a natural response for writers with a wealth of accumulated experience and shared knowledge. The development of a system of transatlantic literary exchange evident in early American writing resulted in a cartographical shift of the colonial gaze, from the dungeons and galleys of Constantinople, North Africa, and the Mediterranean to the dark, inhospitable forests of the northeastern woodlands. Given the prominence of the captivity theme in literary discourse of the sixteenth and seventeenth centuries, it should come as no surprise that the earliest descriptions of Native American people found in the works of Dutch, French, English, and, later, American writers bear many similarities to descriptions of the Moors and Ottoman Turks found in preceding texts. As with writers who depicted the horrors of Turkish captivity, a number of North American writers, seeking to represent Indian people and cultures, did so based not on their own experiences and observations but drawn from the carefully constructed array of transatlantic texts predicated on the play of intertextual regression. Jean Baudrillard has characterized this process as "an uninterrupted circuit without reference or circumference."[62] In this mythico-historical tautology, the fundamental relationship between the signifier and the signified is ideologically displaced, with Native subjects negatively defined within the categorical binaries of good and evil, civil and savage, and Christian and pagan, producing a system of correspondence that is self-constitutive, self-perpetuating, and beyond the purview of conventional modes of referentiality.

A common feature of the previously cited texts is the use of animalistic and demonic imagery to signify Otherness. From the publication of indulgences used to support ongoing wars against the Ottoman Turks and Moors and sensational accounts of barbarism that accompanied the rise of literacy and popular literature that flourished throughout the sixteenth and seventeenth centuries, to descriptions exemplified by the writings of Christopher Columbus, the exotic, lurid, and, menacing images of Indigenous people functioned to inflame the already fertile imaginations of European readers.

Hans Staden's *Geschichte eines Landes* (1557) details his captivity among the Tupinamba Indians in the Amazon basin and includes graphic descriptions of ritual torture and cannibalism.[63] Peter Hulme, in his essay, "Columbus and the Cannibals," draws specific attention to the seemingly ubiquitous representation of cannibalism attributed to Indigenous cultures of the New World. In an effort to historicize processes of colonial signification and othering, Hulme traces the term "canibale" to the journals of Columbus, in which the term was used in his description of the Caribs.[64] Through the development of the Columbian representation of "racial difference and its disavowal," Hulme identifies a "trace of that repression" that is implicit in the way Columbus's account was so readily accepted as truth.[65] Considering Europeans' lack of both reliable knowledge and cultural tolerance regarding non-European cultures during this time, it is not difficult to see how the descriptions disseminated by explorers such as Columbus would come to have such a powerful influence on the imaginations of European audiences.

As is the case with the Rowlandson narrative, Hulme points out that the "actual text on which we presume Columbus to have inscribed that name," along with the original manuscript copy, is no longer in existence.[66] The result is a system of reference with no verifiable foundation and no clear origin, which is nonetheless incessantly reinforced by subsequent writers in historical, literary, and critical texts, creating a closed system of historical citationality wherein the essential relationship between primary and secondary documentary sources is lost in labyrinthine circuits of absence, reiteration, and intertextuality. It bears mentioning that the information Columbus cites to support the claim that the Carib were, indeed, "canibales" was related to him by their admitted enemies, the Arawak. Clearly, this detail undermines the credibility of Columbus's observations. Colonial signification in the New World has also been a central concern of the work of the cultural critic Tzvetan Todorov. In *The Morals of History* (1992), Todorov questions colonial epistemological authority, dismissing Columbus's allegation of Carib cannibalism as "based on hearsay."[67] Hulme also doubts the accuracy of the testimony offered by Columbus and other explorers, while questioning the ready acceptance by historians and scholars of such claims as historical truth or accurate descriptions of Native culture. In contrast to conventional historical accounts that rely heavily on the testimony of early explorers, Hulme characterizes Columbus's account of the New World and its Indigenous inhabitants as "the first fable of European beginnings in America."[68]

Due to the wide distribution and influence of European exploration narratives, the shocking depictions of violence, cannibalism, and paganism found in the work of Staden and Columbus were reiterated in the work of colonial New England writers. In the account of the attack on Lancaster found in the opening pages of *The*

Soveraignty and Goodness of God, the innermost fears of isolated colonists are vividly depicted and provide a terrifying portrait of Indian savagery. Like many of its European and English predecessors, a first-person-present narrative voice is employed to reinforce the perceived veracity of eyewitness testimony that functions as a hegemonic instrument of historical validation. Rowlandson's narrative voice reinforces the immediacy of the frenzied attack from the perspective of a terrified settler barricaded inside a burning garrison in a way that cannot be achieved in historical texts such as those produced by William Hubbard and Increase Mather.[69] Hostilities rarely begin with a gunshot, however, as Virilio observes in his meditation on the fortified city: "war exists in its preparation."[70] The fact that Rowlandson and her fellow settlers had taken refuge in the garrison seems to confirm the validity of Virilio's claim. King Philip's War did not begin with the preceding raids on English settlements; nor with the hanging of three Pokanokets by the Puritans for the murder of the praying Indian, John Sassamon as Lepore asserts;[71] nor did it have its source in the mysterious death of Metacomet's brother, Wamsutta. King Philip's War began with the construction of the very first English fortifications in New England, which anticipated their intentions. For Virilio, the concept of pure war finds its essential presence in the "infinite preparation" that always already anticipates the conflict to come.[72]

The sense of dread and torment that Rowlandson's description of the attack evokes is palpable, interspersed as it is with flittering images of cannibal-like Indian assailants "gaping before us with their Guns, Spears and Hatchets to devour us."[73] Through such vivid accounts, Native people are dehumanized and transformed into a legion of inhuman creatures at whose hands a cruel and certain death awaited, followed by the even more dreadful fate of cannibalism. As if this imagery was not potent enough, the stylistic of the Puritan jeremiad was further utilized by framing Rowlandson's experience against a hellish backdrop of "roaring" fires and "gaping" Indians who, like their supposed animal brethren, "scornfully shouted and hallowed."[74] The attack on Lancaster is framed within an exacting historical and ideological structure through the deployment of an array of vivid and traumatic images that extend religious meaning and significance to what would otherwise be viewed, given the prevalence of Anglo-Indian conflict during this period, as a predictable, although terrifying, turn of events. Besides the allusions to Indian cannibalism found in *The Soveraignty and Goodness of God*, an array of animalistic images and motifs are also employed to further demonize Indian people. The different shades of meaning are effectively joined after Rowlandson flees the burning garrison. Overwhelmed by the attack and the carnage that she witnesses all around her, Rowlandson laments: "it is a solemn sight to see so many Christians lying in their blood, some here, and some there, like a company of Sheep torn by Wolves."[75]

Aside from the religious significance of the wolf motif, allusions to animalism are also used to invalidate the basic human rights of Native people. The means by which colonial writers were able to render Native people silent in accounts such as these is intimately related to the disavowal of Native languages as meaningless, or glossolalia. In the opening scenes of the Rowlandson narrative, there are numerous instances where Indian speech is associated with the sounds and calls of wild animals. In her description of what were likely the ceremonial utterances and songs of an Indian war party,[76] Rowlandson states, "Oh the roaring, and singing and dancing, and yelling of those black creatures in the night, which made the place a lively resemblance of hell."[77] Later, after another successful raid, this time on the settlement of Medfield, she regretfully declares, "Oh! the outragious roaring and hooping that there was . . . By their noise and hooping they signified how many they had destroyed . . . and then, Oh, the hideous insulting and triumphing that there was over some *Englishmens* scalps that they had taken (as their manner) and brought with them."[78] It is apparent that the scene described here bears little resemblance to what was taking place within the Indians' worldview. Instead, Rowlandson simply reiterates what Deleuze and Guattari term the "ready-made tracings" of the savage Other produced in the absence of knowledge about her Indian captors and their cultural practices.[79] Hence, Rowlandson's description stands as a simulacrum of an imperialist cartography—a deterritorialization and remapping—subsumed within the matrices of colonial desire in the place of Native subjectivities and knowledge that are always already marginalized and rendered incomprehensible. Despite the evocative power of Rowlandson's descriptions, which would have been fresh in the minds of many of her contemporaries, the rhetoric and imagery used to describe Native people throughout the narrative is far from unique.

In *The Soveraignty and Goodness of God*, readers often note the strong implication of cannibalism that functions as part of the text's demonizing rhetoric. Though the narrative is overflowing with invectives directed against Rowlandson's Indian captors, who are frequently described as "wolves" and "ravenous bears," not a single firsthand description of cannibalism is offered. Even when incidents intended to highlight acts of Indian savagery such as mutilation and torture are cited, they are typically offered as secondhand information passed on to Rowlandson by witnesses who are often unnamed or absent from the text. This is illustrated, for instance, in the description of the fate that befell "that poor woman," Goodwife Joslin:

> She having much grief upon her Spirit, about her miserable condition, being so near her time, she would be often asking the Indians to let her go home; they not willing to do that, and yet vexed with her importunity, gathered a great company together about her, and stript her naked, and set her in the midst of them; and when they had sung and danced about her (in their hellish manner) . . . they knockt her on head, and the child in her arms with her: when they had done that, they made a fire and put them both into it, and told the other Children that were with them, that if they attempted to go home, they would serve them in a like manner.[80]

In Rowlandson's recounting of Joslin's ritualized execution at the hands of savage Indians, she expresses ambiguity when corroborating the description, noting that the information was obtained "as some of the company told me in my travel."[81] While the veracity of this detail may be questionable, the psychological affect that it could be expected to have on readers seems certain.

The lack of historically verifiable source material concerning the accounts of torture and abuse depicted in the Rowlandson narrative is further exhibited when the subject of cannibalism is mentioned during a conversation with an Indian to whom she inquires on the

Figure 7. Female captive surrounded by Indians, c. 1880s, from the author's private collection.

whereabouts of her son, who was taken captive by a different group of Indians following the assault on Lancaster. This time, an unnamed Indian source, responds by telling Rowlandson that "his master roasted him, and that himself did eat a piece of him, as big as his two fingers, and that he was very good meat."[82] Rowlandson immediately proclaims her skepticism towards this story, "but the Lord upheld my spirit, under this discouragement; and I considered their horrible addictedness to lying, and that there is not one of them that makes the least conscience of speaking of truth."[83] Indicative of the tendency to use the Rowlandson account as a launching point for the exploration of modern philosophic concerns, Arsic´ cites from this passage in his study on the phenomenology of quietism as seeming confirmation of Indian cannibalism, but inexplicably fails to mention Rowlandson's skeptical response.[84]

In his analysis of Indian representation in accounts of captivity, "Cannibalism and Infant Killing," Colin Ramsey also considers the significance and nature of the "good versus evil binary."[85] According to Ramsey, the literary development and reiteration of the implicit binary oppositions invoked in Puritan accounts "established the paradigm for much of the subsequent development of the Indian captivity narrative form—helping to fix particular (and ethnocentric) views of the Indian in the American imagination."[86] From this foundation, Ramsey goes on to analyze "the social contexts from which captivity narratives arose, and the dubious nature of their authorship."[87] As a result of the ideological practices concentrated in the captivity narrative, Indian subjectivities are largely relegated to a historical netherworld in which viable counter-narratives are presumed to be nonexistent or inaccessible. Consequently, it is only from a standpoint attentive to Native subjectivities and perspectives that a truly comprehensive assessment of colonial literature and historiography can be achieved. The same types of allegorical and one-dimensional representations of Native people found in Rowlandson's work continue to be reiterated in film and television, as evidenced by depictions of Indigenous people in *The Missing* (2003) and *Apocalypto* (2006), as well as the AMC series *Hell on Wheels* (2011 to the most recent season 4, 2014).[88] The continued prevalence of such representations illustrates the value of recovering the absent present that is Native historical agency and subjectivity.

While *The Sovereignty and Goodness of God* displays many of the characteristics of Barbary and Turkish captivity narratives, it also acts as a counter to some of the more ambiguous depictions of Native people found in accounts of Spanish writers published throughout the sixteenth century. In the widely distributed and translated work of Bartolomé de Las Casas, *Brevíssima relacíon de la detruycíon de las Indias* (1552), Native people were portrayed in a sympathetic, if not tragic, light. Although informed by the same system of binary oppositions found in European works discussed previously, in the Spanish accounts the privilege is reversed, marking some of the earliest examples in which the Indigenous peoples of the Americas were regarded as rational human beings imbued with natural rights.

In 1583, Thomas Dawson published the first English edition of Las Casas's work in London under the title, *The Spanishe colonie, or Briefe chronicle of the acts and gestes of the Spaniardes in the West Indies. . . .* Vital to the development of *la leyenda negra*, or the Black Legend, and reprinted at the height of the Anglo-Spanish War fought for control over the transatlantic slave trade, Las Casas's manuscript was ostensibly translated and brought to press as a tool of English propaganda to publicize Spanish atrocities in the New World. Written as a treatise on Christian duty, Las Casas seeks to establish the historical veracity of his observations by frequently stating that the events he describes were witnessed "with my own eyes."[89] In subsequent English versions, such as the second edition translated by John Phillips and dedicated to Oliver Cromwell, *The tears of the Indians: being an historical and true account of the cruel massacres and slaughters of above twenty millions of innocent people, committed by the Spaniards* (1656), the translator's ideological agenda is apparent.[90] This is in keeping with Deleuze and Guattari's claim and rhetorical query that "a book exists only through the outside and on the outside. A book itself is a little machine; what is the relation . . . of this literary machine to a war machine, love machine, revolutionary machine, etc.—and an *abstract machine* that sweeps them along?"[91] As Las Casas demonstrates, the nature and manner of Indigenous representation was far from stable, with the meaning determined according to which side of the Atlantic the implied audiences of these texts resided, whether in the colonies or on European soil.

In the preface to his *Brevíssima relacíon*, Las Casas writes against the grain of the colonial archive and conventional religious symbolism established in Turkish and Barbary narratives, referring to the Indigenous people as "gentle lambs" upon whom the "Spanish fell like ravening wolves upon the fold, or like tigers and savage lions who have not eaten meat for days."[92] As illustrated in the Rowlandson narrative, this kind of demonizing language and use of animalistic imagery is a prominent, if not indispensable feature of English captivity narratives, which situate it firmly within the broader context of European colonialist discourse. However, this is not to suggest that Las Casas had renounced Western beliefs in deference to newly adopted anti-colonial subjectivities, especially considering that he continued to promote the colonial mission aimed at Christianizing and assimilating Indigenous people. As José Rabasa reminds us, "therein lies the power and seduction of their self-consciously elaborate narratives and their contribution to the culture of conquest of colonial myths and anthropological categories that still haunt much of Western ethnology, literary criticism, and fiction."[93] For the Indigenous people who were the subjects of Las Casas's sympathies, however, the results were the same. Both slavery and assimilation resulted in cultural genocide.

The tendency of European and English colonial writers to emplot their own nationalistic destinies as manifestations of divine providence is a common feature in fables of the expanding transatlantic world. The captivity narrative of Francis Knight, *A relation of seven yeares slaverie under the Turkes of Argeire* (1640), provides a useful case in point in its succinct articulation of the cultural logic of divine providence. In his description of the perilous moment of contact with the Turkes, Knight states: "On the ninth day of *December*, when it pleased *Almightie God* to give power to the *Infidels* to prevaile over me, whereby I became *Captive.*"[94] The transformation that is intimated in this passage actualizes a process of becoming, which is bound up in the physical and spiritual ordeal of captivity described in the accounts of Knight, Rowlandson, and others.

The rhizomatic network of connections extending from these liminal experiences function to trigger a process of colonial self-fashioning, which operated as a remarkably effective means of ideological and spatial appropriation throughout the Western Hemisphere. Indeed, it was precisely through the travels and sufferings of European and English captives on the frontier that the process of deterritorialization was instigated. The publication and dissemination, on both sides of the Atlantic, of narratives detailing a captive's harsh trek through the wilderness borderlands deep into Indian territory functioned as a useful vehicle by which the process of deterritorialization and cultural remapping was inscribed and codified in

American literary discourse. As is the case with Munday, Knight, Rowlandson, and many others that came before and after them, the exceptional status afforded by providential design acted as a convenient alibi for the extension of European and English claims on the Americas. Read within the broader literary history that encompasses the "rhizomatic system of cultural exchanges" inherent in the transatlantic geopolitical context, the account of Rowlandson's captivity takes on a renewed and much more evocative significance. As I have attempted to illustrate in this chapter, throughout the sixteenth and seventeenth centuries the adoption of rhetorical strategies from preceding narratives, combined with the dictates of providential design, came to attain a central position in the interpretive structure of American colonial discourse. The result of this relationship for Native people is perhaps best exemplified by Rowlandson's inadvertently ironic citation of Psalms 46:8: "*Come behold the works of the Lord, what desolations he has made in the Earth.*"[95]

2

Exile, Deterritorialization, and Intertextuality

The Cartographic Impulse of Puritan Historiography

THE PROCESSES OF DISPOSSESSION and deterritorialization typify the historical experience of Native people of the Americas following European contact in the sixteenth and seventeenth centuries. As was demonstrated in the last chapter, however, the way these processes coalesce had as much to do with the deployment of texts as it did with armed conflict. The proliferation of Indian captivity narratives in the century following the establishment of English colonies along the mid-Atlantic coast served as the ideological underpinning, not only for the subjection of Native people, but also the reterritorialization of Native space and place. With the establishment of colonies at Jamestown in 1607, Plymouth in 1620, and Massachusetts Bay in 1629, the English were well on their way to establishing colonial hegemony in New England, in much the same manner that the Spanish had in *el Virreinato de Nueva España* a century before.

In the European contest over North American land and resources, English colonial promoters sought to differentiate themselves from the infamy of *la leyenda negra* (the Black Legend) that grew out of widespread depictions of Spanish cruelties.[1] Emerging from the graphically detailed descriptions of war and conquest found in the works of historians and writers such as Bartolomé de Las Casas, Álvar Nuñez Cabeza de Vaca, Richard Hakluyt, and Daniel Defoe,[2] as well as the firsthand accounts of the conquistadors themselves, such as Hernán Cortès and Bernal Díaz del Castillo, *la leyenda negra* was well-established by the beginning of the seventeenth century. The longtime Puritan governor, William Bradford, exploits the propagandistic value of this legacy in his personal history of the Plymouth colony, published posthumously as *Of Plymouth Plantation* (1856). As a preface to his characterization of Native people as "cruell, barbarous and most treacherous, being most furious in their rage, and merciless wher they overcome; not being contente only to kill and take away life, but delight to tormente men in the most bloodie manner that may be" Bradford states, "the Spaniard might prove as cruell as the salvages of America."[3]

In his study of sixteenth-century Spanish literary discourse in North America, *Writing Violence on the Northern Frontier* (2000), José Rabasa observes that "*leyenda negra* ideologies are not content with mere denunciations of Spanish atrocities in the New World but constitute platforms for projecting and legitimating new colonial enterprises with a rhetoric of anticonquest."[4] In a deliberate attempt to capitalize on Spain's tarnished reputation, the English contrived to validate their own claims to North American land, not through military force and conquest but under the noble banners of law and divine providence. For the English, the alibi of God's establishment of what Winthrop referred to as "the citty upon the hill,"[5] combined with the postulation of Christian righteousness and *terra nullius*, laid the groundwork for the reterritorialization of Native North America. As Howard Mumford Jones has shown, however, the utilization of such strategies did not form a homogeneous textual archive in English colonial discourse. Like the array of enticements found in promotion tracts, Jones shows that colonial epistemes were often conceived for specific audiences, whose expectations differed from one generation to the next, and, at times, contradicted each other.[6]

The acceleration of English migration to North America in the first half of the seventeenth century exerted enormous pressure on the land, which became the primary source of tension and conflict between the English colonists and the Native inhabitants of New England. For Native people who were being pushed into the interior, this situation threatened to fracture their communities, with those committed to peaceful negotiations pitted against others who saw war as their best option to stop the English advance and maintain their political sovereignty. According to Emory Elliot, in the original Pauline spirit, Puritan leaders encouraged like-minded religionists from Britain to join them in New England, resulting in the influx of approximately twenty thousand new settlers during the so-called Great Migration of the 1630s.[7]

Although the contributions of John Cotton, William Bradford, John Winthrop, and Increase Mather to the English colonial mission have been well-documented, this chapter will focus primarily on the apparent influence of these writers on the captivity narrative of Mary Rowlandson, *The Soveraignty and Goodness of God*. Buttressing the views of early leaders such as Bradford and Winthrop, John Cotton was a vociferous defender of Puritan claims to North American land based on the divine right of discovery and conquest. In his influential sermon, *God's Promise to His Plantation* (1630),[8] preached at Southampton before the departure of Winthrop's fleet,[9] Cotton casts the struggles of Puritan dissenters in England and Holland in the same light as those of the ancient Israelites in Egypt. In both the subtitle and the epigraph to this sermon, Cotton cites the covenant God formed with the Israelites, found in 2 Samuel 7:10: "Moreover I will appoint a place for my people Israel, and I will plant them, that they may dwell in a place of their owne, and move no more."[10] The invocation of this verse not only acts to validate the English settlement of North America as an extension of divine providence, but also advances a religiously ordained conception of social stability to enable the colonists to cast off their status as rootless exiles, as indicated by the final clause promising that they shall "move no more." By deploying this typological apparatus as an explicit justification for English colonization and as an implicit vehicle for the reterritorialization of Native lands, Cotton could not help but affirm that Puritan settlements in New England were intended to be permanent, a point I will return to momentarily.

Cotton's sermon lays the philosophical groundwork for Puritan claims to North America, while also operating as a vital intertext with *The Soveraignty and Goodness of God*. Intertextuality is defined by Julia Kristeva as "the transposition of one (or several) sign system(s) into another," which "specifies that the passage from one signifying system to another demands a new articulation of the thetic—of enuciative and denotative positionality."[11] Much more than simply indicating relations between texts, even among those that share core ideas and common motifs, as is the case with much Puritan writing, intertextuality classifies the direct and intentional interplay of specific literary elements across multiple texts. As I endeavor to show, Cotton's sermon fulfills a significant role as an interpretive key and intertext to *The Soveraignty and Goodness of God*. The signifying system formed between these texts, supported by the additional interpolation of Biblical verse acting as a type of concordance between the two, reinforces the validity of Puritan historiography while simultaneously advancing a cohesive sense of New England congregationalism. Seeking to extend this analytic framework, this chapter examines the role of Cotton's sermon within the broader context of English settlement in New England before moving on to consider its denotative positionality within *The Soveraignty and Goodness of God*.

The symptomatic purpose of Cotton's sermon is twofold. First, it offers a seemingly irrefutable religious endorsement of Puritan voyages to North America by drawing parallels to Biblical stories about the experiences of the "Tribes of Israel"; and second, it legitimizes the appropriation of North American lands as a divinely sanctioned enterprise. Seeking to establish a framework for his conclusions, Cotton opens with a detailed exegesis on the conditions operant in the citation from Samuel, which he supplements with an array of supporting verse. According to Cotton, land for new Christian settlement is conferred "when God espies or discovers a land for a people, as in Ezek. 20.6 . . . And that is when either he gives them to discover it themselves, or heare of it discovered by others, and fitting them."[12] By placing God in the role of explorer, the correspondence to English voyages to North America is made obvious, while the text also works to assuage the fears and anxieties of pilgrims preparing to embark on a perilous transatlantic journey to a foreign land.

Once the questions of means and destination were dispensed with, Cotton lays out the conditions necessary to validate the providential claims of contemporary and future settlers. He proposes three distinct means of deterritorialization for this purpose: "First, when he casts out the enemies of a people before them by lawfull warre with the inhabitants, which God calls them unto . . . secondly, when hee gives a forreigne people favour in the eyes of any native people to come and sit downe with them either by way of purchase . . . or else when they give it in courtesie . . . thirdly, when he makes a Country though not altogether void of inhabitants, yet void in that place where they reside."[13] Through his judicious citation of Biblical verse, Cotton constructs a powerfully effective and multifaceted rationale for Puritan land claims—encapsulating the exigencies of war, treaty-making, and epidemic depopulation—that was to be reiterated time and again over the next century.

For John Winthrop, these providential instruments were essential in redefining the lands of North America as a veritable *vacuum domicilium*, whereby Native people were seen as "having only a natural right to so much land as they had or could improve, so as the rest of the country lay open to any that would and could improve it."[14] As a supplement to the New England canon, Cotton's work presents a particularly influential theological framework for military aggression against Native cultures: "when he [God] casts out the enemies of a people before them by lawfull warre with the inhabitants, which God calls them unto, as in *PS. 44.2 Thou didst drive out the Heathe before them.*"[15]

When considering Puritan colonization and expansionism, it is helpful to note Cotton's use of the phrase "lawfull warre," which is an explicit reference to the Augustinian concept of *bellum justum*, or just war.[16] The legal scholar Robert A. Williams has noted the long history Saint Augustine's concept of "just war" has had in ecclesiastical debates regarding the discovery and conquest of Native North America. He observes that just war originally referred only to "self-defense or recovery of stolen property,"[17] but in order to justify the activities of European crusaders, its meaning was subsequently extended to include preemptive military campaigns against "those people who grossly violated natural law."[18] This normalizing legal paradigm was measured, of course, against the model of Western Christian values and social practice.[19] The preference for Biblical typology among Puritan ministers, as demonstrated by the frequent interpolation of scripture in literary and historical texts, constitutes one of the primary means by which religion and historiography intersected to reterritorialize the Native lands of North America.

Similar to the Biblical subtext embedded throughout the Rowlandson narrative, readers find in Cotton's writing an analogous vehicle whereby Puritan land tenure and the doctrine of discovery were sanctioned through the citation of God's directive in Psalms to "drive out the heathen before them."[20] The ingrained mistrust of Native people encouraged by the growing archive of texts is emphasized in William Bradford's *Of Plymouth Plantation*. Writing on their imminent landing at Cape Cod, following their unsuccessful attempt to rendezvous with the Virginia Colony, Bradford laments the exile of the Puritans and extends the category of the heathen to the inhabitants of North America, stating: "It is recorded in scripture as a mercie to the apostle and his shipwraked company, that the barbarians shewed them no smale kindnes in refreshing them, but these savage barbarians, when they mette with them (as after will appeare) were readier to fill their sids full of arrows then otherwise."[21] Bradford's own foreshadowed observation, extended through history by the depictions of "barbarous cruelty" that permeate *The Soveraignty and Goodness of God* and the captivity genre in general, provided ample "legal" grounds for the English to organize punitive expeditions and wage war against Native people to ensure the protection of communities that were considered to be in imminent peril of attack.

Likewise, Cotton's second and third points regarding the rightful means of obtaining land already occupied, along with that which is "void of inhabitants," further contributes to the historical myth of benevolent English colonization that was widely disseminated through Puritan writing. Even in Nathaniel Saltonstall's account of King Philip's War that was written to justify Puritan actions, however, the integrity of Puritan land purchases is called into question, "the English took not a Foot of Land from the Indians, but Bought all, and although they bought for an inconsiderable Value, yet they did Buy it." The question of land is one of the primary issues Gayatri Spivak raises in her essay "Can the Subaltern Speak?," in which she identifies "territorial expansion" as the true motive of the English colonial project.[22] While reiterated across multiple texts, the fable of colonial rights to North American land was articulated by the English in three primary forms. First, in the presumption of necessity and providential design regarding the original settlement of New England; second, by the assertion that the land on which the first settlements were established was vacant; and third, through the belief that Native people were inherently inferior and, thus, excluded from the rights accorded by natural law.

As we have already seen, the concepts of God's "favour" on the one hand and *terra nullius* or *vacuum domicilium*, as empty land, on the other, contributes to the deterritorializing rhetoric that was elaborated in the works of John Winthrop, William Bradford, Edward Johnson, Increase Mather, and others. These notions also helped reinforce the historical distinction between the English colonial project and that carried out by the Spanish a century before. Read within its broader geopolitical context, Cotton's melding of Puritan typology and colonial ideology into a cohesive narrative whole can be seen as making a vital contribution to the cartographic impulse at the foundation of the physical and intellectual claiming of North America that underlies Puritan history.

William Bradford's recounting of the English landing at Plymouth and their initial contact with Native people depends for its meaning on the deployment of the trope of cultural negation. The story that unfolds in Bradford's journal is one where Native subjectivities are inevitably rendered absent, either by their erasure from the landscape altogether, or through the recurring motifs of disappearance and abandonment. Bradford's description of the "unknown coast" sets the tone for the formation of an English rhetoric of deterritorialization: "what could they see but a hideous and desolate wildernes, full of wild beasts and willd men, and what multituds ther might be of them they knew not."[23] The eminent historian Perry Miller seemed more than happy to perpetuate the myth of *vacuum domicilium* in his assessment of Bradford's description in which he states, "the soaring passage in which he contemplates the plight of the settlers at the moment of landing, in November, 1620, and affirms the faith in the might of which they confronted the desolate shore and the murderous climate is the masterpiece of all Puritan eloquence."[24] Miller, following Bradford's lead, seems to shirk his responsibility as a historian by taking an uncritical stance towards Puritan accounts which acts to reinforce the trivial status of Native people within the broader narrative of the settlement of North America.

Such statements are evocative of Molly Farrell's analysis of modes of enumeration employed in *The Soveraignty and Goodness of God.* But where Farrell claims that Rowlandson's attempt at counting "reveals the inability of numerical categories to serve as a means of separating kin from enemies,"[25] in the case of Bradford's first gaze into the North American wilderness, just the opposite appears to be the case. Likewise, in Increase Mather's *A Brief History of the Warr with the Indians of New-England,* describing the conditions some fifty years later, English soldiers in pursuit of Indian enemies through the wilderness of New England are characterized as lost and "bewildered in the Woods."[26] I maintain that the very perception of the Other as an uncountable and multitudinous horde always already renders them as an enemy to be dreaded, feared, and eventually destroyed. This is certainly the sense conveyed by Mather's *A Brief History.* Organized as a chronicle of Indian attacks and Puritan military engagements, Mather consistently abstains from placing a number on enumerating Native casualties in his descriptions of various battles, stating, for example, "how many *Indians* were killed is unknown."[27] The analogous inability of Bradford and other Puritans to see anything more than "a vast and desolate wilderness" when looking out from their ships' decks and, later, vantage points within the confines of fortified settlements onto the North American coast and the darkening forests of the interior, condemns them to a precarious future of conflict and war.[28]

For the English settlers of the Massachusetts colonies, the culmination of this conflict would come with the eruption of King Philip's War in 1675, which forms the historical context for the Indian attack on the settlement of Lancaster and Rowlandson's captivity.

The well-traveled conception of wilderness as desolate waste is a prominent motif throughout *The Soveraignty and Goodness of God*, where it is practically elevated to the status of accomplice to Rowlandson's captors. Having survived the attack and the first night of captivity, Rowlandson hopelessly states, "But now, the next morning, I must turn my back upon the Town, and travel with them into the vast and desolate Wilderness, I knew not whither."[29] We note in this expression a similar bewilderment in the face of Native North America as expressed by Bradford, with neither figure knowing what to make of these yet-to-be-claimed places.

The representation of the wilderness as a physical and spiritual void becomes most evident in the scene involving the death of Rowlandson's six-year-old daughter, Sarah. In the Third Remove,[30] dated February 18, eight days after the raid on Lancaster, the circumstances of Sarah's death are solemnly related. The next morning, Rowlandson is forced to leave her daughter's body when called to her captor Quinnapin's wigwam, and while there, the child is taken and buried by some of the other Natives in the group. After being led to the grave and taking a last look at Sarah's resting place, Rowlandson laments: "*There I left that Child in the wilderness, and must commit it, and my self also in this Wilderness-condition, to him who is above all.*"[31] It is as if Rowlandson and her children are being swallowed up by the vastness of a menacingly incomprehensible landscape, and in this moment her desperation is palpable: "I had one Child dead, another in the Wilderness, I knew not where."[32] Following her redemption from captivity and return to Boston in the Twentieth Remove, Sarah's death becomes a source of renewed anguish for Rowlandson as she explains: "that which was dead lay heavier upon my spirit, than those which were alive amongst the Heathen: thinking how it suffered with its wounds, and I was in no way able to relieve it; and how it was buried by the Heathen in the *Wilderness* from among all Christians."[33] Although Rowlandson is now free of "the merciless and cruel Heathen" and restored to the company of "compassionate Christians," the traumatic memories born of her captivity among the Indians from *within* "the vast and howling *Wilderness*," retain the capacity to haunt.[34]

The desire to reconcile the providential settlement of New England through the alibis of unclaimed or vacant land also forms an

Figure 8. Mary Rowlandson with her daughter, Sarah, c. 1880s, from the author's private collection.

essential narrative element of William Bradford and Edward Winslow's history of Plymouth, known commonly as *Mourt's Relation* (1622). The account of the initial survey of Cape Cod that was completed in November 1620 by passengers of the *Mayflower* under the leadership of Miles Standish is amenable to this purpose. Although Standish and his men catch sight of five or six Native people upon making landfall, after tracking them through the night and into the next day these "savages" disappear into the surrounding wilderness.[35] Following this brief encounter, the English come upon a series of graves, deserted food stores, and other provisions, eventually leading to the discovery of two abandoned houses.[36] The conduct of Standish and his men in their initial decision to leave the first of the graves "untouched, because we thought it would be odious unto them to ransack their sepulchres," soon gives way to looting a buried store of corn and a kettle, preceded by the violation of a burial mound, from which "we brought sundry of the prettiest things away with us and covered up the corpse again."[37] Reading this account with a responsiveness to Native experiences and subjectivities, one cannot help but suffer an unsettling dread informed by the knowledge of the magnitude of the disaster that lay in store for the Native people of the region as a result of the English arrival at Plymouth.

Cotton, in his sermon—anticipating John Locke's treatise on property—grounds the land claims of the English on the premises of use-value and improvement. He cites the Biblical story of Abraham and Isaac's experiences among the Philistines as an example, insisting that "a Principle in Nature, That in a vacant soyle, hee that taketh possession of it, and bestoweth culture and husbandry upon it, his Right it is."[38] In Mather's *Brief History,* a similar sentiment forms the basis for God's displeasure, as he states, "nor were our sins ripe for so dreadful a judgment, until *the Body of the first Generation* was removed, and another Generation risen up, which hath not so pursued, as ought to have been, the blessed design of their Fathers, in following the Lord into this Wilderness, whilst it was a land not sown."[39] In Mather's example, the status of the wilderness as an uncultivated space is used as an implicit indictment of Native peoples, while also serving to condemn his fellow Puritan settlers for being negligent in their responsibilities to bring these places under their proper dominion. One of the primary functions of statements such as these was to reinforce the classification of Native cultures as inherently degraded and uncivilized by defining them in negative contrast to European peoples, who had achieved and maintained their elevated status through establishment of permanent settlements made feasible by agriculture and the domestication of livestock.

Although the themes of savagism, divine providence, and spiritual redemption are ubiquitous elements in Puritan writing, what ties Cotton's sermon to the Rowlandson narrative is the theological meaning packed into the concepts of settlement and removal. Due to the salience of Cotton's support for "the establishment of the True Church in the New World,"[40] he also supplies an expedient theological justification for the expansion of the original providential settlements in New England and the rhizomatic planting of new ones, as was the case with Rowlandson's village of Lancaster. The fact that Cotton's sermon seems to anticipate the eventuality of expansionism as early as 1630 is as provocative and revealing as the justification for English settlement itself. With the need for additional land seemingly already in mind, Cotton introduces five conditions, with multiple subcategories divided between "good" and "evill things," as well as "some special providence of God," that he claims "may warrant" settlers' "removeall" from places appointed by God to other locations.[41] Reading *The Soveraignty and Goodness of God* through the lens of Cotton's sermon offers significant insights into the structural framework and theological basis for the demarcation of the twenty removes that contain the account of Rowlandson's captivity. If we accept the ideas Cotton advocates at face value, as Puritan settlers would have been inclined to do at the time, one can imagine the reluctance that many would have felt when making the decision to remove from settlements that were, according to their most fundamental beliefs, granted to them by God himself.

For contemporary readers, one of the distinctive features of the account of Rowlandson's captivity is the structure of the narrative itself. Rather than using chapters or descriptive section headings, following the initial description of the attack on Lancaster, *The Soveraignty and Goodness of God* is organized into twenty episodic sections, titled "Removes," that trace Rowlandson's movements from her Puritan community into the wilderness and back again. Harkening to the Biblical diaspora of the Children of Israel and the Puritans' identification with them as the "English Israel,"[42] these headings orient readers to an involuntary "errand into the wilderness," while preventing the typological subtext from becoming too stifling. According to Marilyn Wesley, this narrative structure had the purpose of differentiating Rowlandson's account from the Puritan "diary" or "chronicle," common to the expression of "private and public experience."[43] Referring to Slotkin's work, Wesley goes on to suggest that in so doing Rowlandson had "invented" a "structure dependent on geographical rather than chronological arrangement."[44] Similarly, Derounian-Stodola and Levernier express the view that this organizing structure is "virtually unique to Rowlandson," stating that "each remove 'removed' her further from all she knew, so even though progressive marches eventually brought her physically closer to home, she remained distant from it psychologically and spiritually."[45] Although each of these statements offer valuable insights regarding *The Soveraignty and Goodness of God*, they also seem to overlook the broader significance of the narrative structure as a function of Puritan epistemology.

Hayden White has argued that "there are at least two levels of interpretation in every historical work: one . . . the chronicle of events and another in which, by a more fundamental narrative technique, [the author] progressively identifies the *kind of story* he [or she] is telling."[46] If we examine this statement as it relates to *The Soveraignty and Goodness of God*, we can begin to more fully engage the underlying structural framework of the text. While it seems clear that the organization of Rowlandson's "removes" allows readers to gain a better sense of the Puritan psyche and offers insight into the sense of desperation induced by the enveloping wilderness, it can also be profitably read in the context of its interplay with Cotton's theological meaning of removal. "Among the foure or five good things, for procurement of any of which I may remove," Cotton includes the necessity "for the gaining of knowledge . . . for merchandize and gaine-sake . . . to plant a Colony . . . when he may employ his Talents and gifts better elsewhere," and "for the liberty of the Ordinances."[47] While the activity of colony-planting provides an obvious connection to the founding of Lancaster, Cotton's reasons act as the primary rationalization for the Puritans' immigration to North America. In contrast to these positive reasons, Cotton's homily on the removal of settlers, prompted by certain evils to be avoided, seems of particular significance to *The Soveraignty and Goodness of God*.

The first among these is met, according to Cotton, "when some grievous sinnes overspread a Country that threaten desolation."[48] In the first-person description of the attack on Lancaster, Rowlandson is immediately thrust into the role of penitent and offers an explanation of the attack, stating, "the Lord hereby would make us the more to acknowledge his hand."[49] Emphasizing God's manifest presence in these events, she goes on to describe the gruesome deaths of her brother-in-law, sister, and their young son, in addition to the fatal wounding of her own youngest daughter, quoting Psalms 46:8, "behold the works of the Lord, *what desolations* he has made in the Earth."[50] It is as if, in this statement, Rowlandson is answering Mather's call in "declaring the works of God."[51] Operating both as a literary device and as a typological key to the interpretation of her captivity, we can also observe in this passage an implicit reference to Cotton's sermon.

Given the similarity between the language used by Cotton and that employed throughout Rowlandson's narrative, written some sixty years later, it seems apparent that a shared system of reference exists between the two texts. The fact that the term "desolation" is employed to describe the state of Puritan society in peril in both Cotton and Rowlandson's texts links them to a common ecclesiastical heritage. This heritage is carried forward by Increase Mather, who, in his *A Brief History*, describes an observation of a humiliation day of fasting and prayer that occurred at the same time as the Indian attack on Deerfield as, "that which addeth solemnity and awfulness to that Desolation."[52] Within these contexts, the use of such terminology, coupled with the notion of "removal" to signify an escape from the evils that had befallen Puritan society, seems more than tangential. Reading *God's Promise* and *The Soveraignty and Goodness of God* together, it seems as though Cotton's sermon not only established the intellectual framework that Puritan settlers were to follow, but also provided an overarching theological explanation for war with the Indians and the trials of captivity that many settlers were to experience. For, as Cotton warns, "if you rebel against God, the same God that planted you will also roote you out againe, for all the evill which you shall doe against your selves."[53]

The repeated reference to the Sabbath in *The Soveraignty and Goodness of God* draws attention to one of the forms of "grievous sinnes" that Puritan settlers are guilty of and serves as a reminder of their ongoing spiritual responsibilities and the importance of practiced faith. Rowlandson's past deficiencies in properly observing this ordinance represents a distinct example of sin, thus verifying the necessity of providential judgment to bring about her removal. In addition to providing a justification for providential retribution, the identification of Sabbath days also allows readers to plot the duration of Rowlandson's stays at various camps in the New England wilderness. These references emphasize the sequential quality of the narrative, which is anchored by the opening sentence of *The Soveraignty and Goodness of God,* in which the exact date of the attack is provided.[54] Taken together with Rowlandson's statement in the twentieth remove that "I was with the Enemy eleven weeks and five dayes, and not one Week passed without the fury of the Enemy, and some desolation by fire and sword upon one place or another," the accounting of time and duration works to quantify the magnitude of God's judgment.

Within the precise chronology created by these temporal narrative elements, emphasis is placed on the significance of the Sabbath, which operates as a reminder of Rowlandson's past spiritual failures and serves as an opportunity for her restoration to the community of the redeemed. When Rowlandson's Native captors are described as taking part in attacks and other activities on the Sabbath, these references become yet another emblem of Native savagery and heathenism.[55] Furthermore, these details help to characterize Native people as recalcitrant in their resistance to the efforts of Puritan missionaries such as John Eliot to promote religious conversion and deculturation. Following Rowlandson's brief description of her visit to the Nipmuc town of Wenimesset, occurring in the Third Remove, she states, "the next day was the Sabbath: I then remembered how careless I had been of Gods holy time: how many

Sabbaths I had lost and misspent, and how evilly I had walked in God's sight . . . that it was easie for me to see how righteous it was with God to cut off the thread of my life, and cast me out of his presence forever."[56] This statement serves as an acknowledgement of sin, functioning to further distinguish her from the Native people and sets the stage for her eventual redemption. For the Native people involved in the war, however, Puritan typology allows no possibility of penitence and certain punishment awaits.

The last sermon of Mary Rowlandson's husband, the Reverend Joseph Rowlandson, published as an epilogue to the other 1682 editions of *The Soveraignty and Goodness of God*, addresses the nature of providential guardianship over the settlers and warns of the consequences of forsaking one's spiritual responsibility in a rhetoric similar to Cotton's, stating, "and God may in just judgment retaliate, and thereupon forsake them."[57] Although Mary Rowlandson interprets her captivity as a manifestation of divine retribution resulting from her own sins and those of her neighbors, the negative dialectic formed by the matrix of sin and punishment also reinforces the Puritan belief system—and Rowlandson's role as humble penitent—through her frequent expressions of gratitude to God for keeping her safe throughout the ordeal. As readers are reminded in Rowlandson's description of the attack on Lancaster, "but God was with me."[58]

The theological concept of divine punishment and the necessity for personal repentance is a pervasive theme throughout the narrative. The acute sense of guilt Rowlandson expresses fixes the assignment of transcendental meaning to the senseless and traumatic events she experiences, while also foreshadowing her eventual restoration to Puritan society. Consequently, the thetic and metaphorical significance of the organizing structure of Rowlandson's "removes" acts as a persistent reminder of God's providential judgment and Rowlandson's unquestioned acceptance of her penance. In another sense, the stilted internal structure created by these narrative breaks, along with the integration of scriptural citation, serves to weaken its appeal as an unmediated expression of Rowlandson's experiences as a Puritan woman and as a captive.

Despite the emphasis on geography discussed in the scholarship of critics formerly mentioned, Rowlandson's frequent specification of the days that events took place, often found in the initial sentences of each "remove," has the effect of grounding the narrative of her captivity within a precise temporal framework. As with Derounian-Stodola and Levernier, however, Michelle Burnham further emphasizes the relation to geography by concentrating on opposing ideas of physical and psychological dislocation and isolation. She insists that "the division of her narrative into 'removes' enhances the sense that with each successive departure the captive becomes increasingly distant from her own culture and moves further and further into the wilderness where she has contact solely with an alien Algonquian culture."[59] The overstated implication of Rowlandson's geographic and psychological alienation found in Burnham's analysis results in a neglect of the carefully constructed temporal order of Rowlandson's experiences and a misconception of the way that the events described express the broader ideologies of Puritan historiography. What these critics seem to overlook is the way that Rowlandson's travel into the wilderness acts as an implicit anchor of geographical claiming that is paid for by Puritan suffering. Because of her experience the English can claim exclusive rights to the land; it is as if each step extends the boundaries of deterritorialization, while the written descriptions of these travels plant the seeds of reterritorialization through which Puritan settlements continue their rhizomatic penetration into the wilderness. While I have endeavored to show the importance of geographical and chronological frames of reference in regard to Rowlandson's movements during her captivity, the intertextual dialogic between *The Soveraignty and Goodness of God* and a mode of Puritan discourse traced back to John Cotton is what gives the narrative structure its most compelling presence.

As a counterbalance to the harrowing portrait formed from Rowlandson's experience, it is ultimately through God's benevolence that she will eventually gain her freedom from captivity. The predominant selection of the cited Scriptures embedded in *The Soveraignty and Goodness of God* functions to reinforce this interpretation of the events.[60] For example, after "mourning and lamenting" after her "poor children," Rowlandson turns to the Bible for direction and solace, opening to Psalms 55:22: "Cast thy burden upon the Lord, and He shall sustain thee."[61] A closer review of the verse in question, however, reveals that the quote is only a partial one; the verse concludes, "he shall never suffer the righteous to be moved."[62] Read in its entirety, this passage seems much less obliging to the Puritan cause. A similar omission comes during the description of events found in the Thirteenth Remove, relating to an incident in which Rowlandson comes to the aid of an ailing fellow captive, John Gilberd, to help him to build a fire.[63] After returning to her Native captor, she explains: "now had I need to pray *Pauls* prayer, 2 Thessalonians 3.2. *That we may be delivered from unreasonable and wicked men*."[64] In this instance the omitted passage reads: "for all men have not faith."[65] Clearly, the inclusion of these verses in their entirety would have contributed ambiguity to the distinction being drawn between Puritan settlers and Native "heathens," which may help to explain omission.

If this manner of scriptural citation was an isolated practice in *The Soveraignty and Goodness of God*, its significance could be dismissed as an innocuous matter of authorial oversight or creative prerogative. However, the fact that Biblical verse that is *contradictory* to the text's internal religious message is repeatedly omitted suggests a pattern of decontextualization, with the implicit ideological intention of influencing a reader's perceptions of the events of the narrative. Instead of utilizing Biblical scripture as a means of self-abasement and a path to repentance in the account of Rowlandson's captivity, as it has often been presented,[66] the choice of scriptural examples and their strategic abridgements seems to convey an incontrovertible Biblical justification for the dispossession of Native people throughout the New England colonies.

Much like the rhizomatic connections linking North America and Europe in the motif of transatlantic literary exchange, the Puritan conception of the New England landscape was organized along a similarly structured network of interconnected ideas and texts. This leads us to the observation that Rowlandson's removes unfold according to the theological guidelines originally established in Cotton's sermon. Thus, for Rowlandson to achieve her eventual salvation from captivity, as well as from the affliction of sin, her removes must unfold in intertextual harmony with Cotton's theological order. When examining Rowlandson's movements within the intellectual framework articulated by Cotton, one cannot help but notice a dynamic symmetry between the texts. The efficacious combination of divinely sanctioned reasons for the removal of Puritan settlers from their plantations establishes *The Soveraignty and Goodness of God* as a remarkably accommodating text that reinforces Puritan claims to the land, while providing a rationalization for colonial expansionism through the alibis of Puritan suffering and providential retribution.

Following his exegesis on the conditions of God's providential influence in Puritan migration to North America, Cotton then takes up the question of practicality: "what is it for God to plant a people?"[67] In the concluding section of the sermon, this rhetorical query is utilized to summon "a Metaphor," offered to account for God's intention to cultivate and protect his chosen people and "make them to take roote there."[68] In this example, Cotton's sermon offers a particularly cohesive understanding of the agronomical imagery in *God's Promise*, in which the English settlers of New England are represented as trees that are divinely planted so as to "dwell in their own place."[69] Increase Mather, also one to exploit this metaphor, describes an assault on the home of the Clark family in Plymouth, in which "the *Indians* destroyed them all, root and branch, the Father, and Mother, and all the Children."[70] References such as these act to reinscribe the relation of God to the Puritan settlers, and of the Puritan settlers to the land, as one that is both organic and rhizomatic in nature. The means by which this knowledge is deployed, once it is accepted, has the additional effect of negating the very historical presence and claims of the Native people who inhabited these contested spaces.

More specifically, the conditions for removal set forth by Cotton allow for the reconciliation of Rowlandson's passage into the wilderness with the metaphor of settlers as the harvest of the providential divine. Rowlandson's captivity thus becomes a vehicle by which new land can be claimed as a consequence of just war, and as a means of national redemption through communal repentance and the act of rooting out the evil exemplified by Native cultural presence. Out of the complex archive formed by these texts, military and ideological means of dispossession are enacted. The cartographical impulse that drives such activity is precisely what Edward Said identifies as being at the heart of the colonial project, in his insistence that "everything about human history is rooted in the earth, which has meant that we must think about habitation, but it has also meant that people have planned to *have* more territory and therefore must do something about its indigenous residents. At some very basic level, imperialism means thinking about, settling on, controlling land that you do not possess, that is distant, that is lived on and owned by others."[71] Indeed, the lands that the English invaded along the mid-Atlantic coast throughout the seventeenth century were owned by Native people, and the settlers' failure or refusal to acknowledge this fact is not sufficient to extinguish such claims.

At the beginning of the Twentieth Remove, Rowlandson furthers this agenda by providing explicit support for Cotton's thesis, noting that for Native people "it was their usual manner to remove, when they had done any mischief, lest they should be found out."[72] Although this statement is provided in the context of the military activities of the unified Native forces during King Philip's War, it still works to reinforce the conception of Native societies as rootless and nomadic in their relation to the land. The stark dissimilarity between English and Native culture that Rowlandson's statement implies offers additional support for colonial claims to land based upon the generative idea of providential design expressed through agricultural metaphors that pervade the writings of Cotton, Winthrop, Bradford, and Mather. Although the Puritans were largely successful in promoting a conception of Native culture as bereft of private property and valid claims to the land, the exhaustive work of Ives Goddard and Kathleen Bragdon in collecting all the surviving examples of Massachusett (Pokanoket, Natick, Nantucket, Mashpee, and Nauset) writing demonstrates just the opposite, as "most common among the manuscripts that have survived are records of land transactions between Indians and other Indians."[73] Existing on the threshold between oral and written culture, the surviving—but no doubt mediated—speeches of Metacomet certainly seem to bolster such a reading.

Given the obvious benefits resulting from conflict over territory, it is understandable that writers such as Cotton, Winthrop, and Mather would endeavor to portray frontier expansionism in a way most advantageous to their societal goals and interests. Be that as it may, it is unclear why modern scholars would be so inclined to minimize the serious historical ramifications that such a reality implies. Attempting to counter this particular strain of revisionism, Francis Jennings, in his work *The Invasion of America*, points out that while "in the words of Alden T. Vaughn, the Puritans 'had no reason to conceal their attitudes or actions towards the Indians,'" he had "found plenty of reason."[74] A similar, if not more subtle form of evasion regarding conflict over land is articulated in Jill Lepore's *The Name of War*, in which she states, "the colonists did call what happened 'King Philip's War,' and the very fact that what their enemies called it has not survived ('Metacom's Rebellion' being mere conjecture) is part of what the fighting was about in the first place: it was a contest for meaning—and the colonists won."[75] Although she does mention land as a factor in the conflict, the overwhelming bulk of the story Lepore conceives focuses on the distinction in the use of language—written versus oral, memorized versus inscribed—between Native and English culture. By reinscribing Native efforts to defend their lands and preserve their ways of life in terms of differing linguistic and denotative practices, Native claims are effectively buried beneath a mass of Puritan voices. The works of historians such as Miller, Vaughn, and Lepore, notwithstanding, as early as the nineteenth century doubts were already being raised about the veracity of Puritan historical accounts.

Commenting on Cotton Mather's opus work, *Magnalia Christi Americana* (1702), the prominent nineteenth-century historian and longtime president of the New England Historic Genealogical Society, Samuel Drake, remarked that it "contains no marks of care and pains-taking" and later characterized it as "a stupendous Monument of Learning, Piety, Absurdity, and, I had almost said, Frivolity."[76] If the Hobbesian savages portrayed in Puritan narratives were merely hollow tropes of empire, this was true because in their literary transfiguration the Native people of North America became a monolithic *tabula rasa* onto which the fears and transgressions of English colonists were projected as a means of exorcising the demons of violence and oppression. As Derounian-Stodola observes, "over the course of one hundred and fifty years, as the European-Americans' demand for land increased . . . religion and nationalistic propaganda rejoined forces to demolish anything in the way of territorial expansion."[77] Regrettably, as the bloody toll of the Indian Wars of the nineteenth century—marked by massacres such as those that took place at Sand Creek and Wounded Knee—and the advent of federal policies aimed at cultural genocide through assimilation attest, it appears that, for the Native people of North America, in the over 300 years since the publication of *The Sovereignty and Goodness of God*, little has changed. Perhaps the analysis made by Craig Womack, observing the preference of American readers to avoid work by Native authors that explicitly addresses the appropriation of Native lands, extends to the field of history as well.[78] Regardless, considering the almost unrelenting struggle of the English for territorial control of North America that began in the early seventeenth century, I would be remiss if I failed to address the pervasive influence that such attitudes have exerted on American historical discourse.

As Jennings points out, there existed a perpetual state of low-intensity warfare between Puritan settlers and the Native inhabitants of what was later to become Connecticut and Massachusetts, which continued unabated from 1634 to 1677.[79] Despite what some historians may imply, the pressure exerted by the influx of settlers to colonial New England, and their concomitant need for land, was a major factor behind these hostilities. And yet, to read the accounts that fill the pages of American history textbooks, one would think that English conflict with Native nations was the result of a more ambiguous clash of religious belief and incommensurable cultural practice. Writing about the early colonial period in America's history, Howard Zinn has noted: "behind the English Invasion of North America, behind their massacres of Indians, their deception, their brutality, was that special powerful drive born in civilizations based on private property."[80] What better way to obscure this conception of history than by reinscribing, in a sense, mythologizing, American colonial history itself? It was, of course, through the process of cultural production, driven by figures such as John Cotton and Increase Mather, that the account of Mary Rowlandson's captivity became a central text in articulating the cartographic impulse of Puritan society.

3

"And I Only Am Escaped To Tell The News"

Witnessing History in the True Narrative of Mary Rowlandson's Captivity

ROY HARVEY PEARCE'S 1947 essay, "The Significances of the Captivity Narrative," marks the first significant study of the Indian captivity narrative. Since then, scholars have employed a variety of critical approaches, from gender, cultural studies, and new historicism to more recent studies in the fields of phenomenology, ecocriticism, and even posthumanism.[1] Within this body of scholarship, critics have considered issues such as the tension between the spiritual and secular, notions of gender and sexuality, the social impact of print culture in colonial North America, and the myriad of cultural disruptions caused by English colonialism.

Despite the substantial body of scholarship produced on the Indian captivity genre, scant attention has been devoted to the subjectivities and motivations of the Native people at the center of these literary discourses. Given the nature and function of captivity narratives, written in the context of colonial warfare, it is not difficult to understand why Native subjectivities are absent from such accounts, but why this is the case in scholarly works about captivity is much less clear. One of the reasons for this may be attributed to the scarcity of written sources produced by Native people during the seventeenth and eighteenth centuries, along with the inherent difficulties in accessing and synthesizing the materials that are available. These challenges, however, do not sufficiently account for the tendency of scholars to tacitly accept Indian captivity narratives as valid historical accounts of intercultural colonial conflict. In this chapter, I address this critical issue by first examining the literary status of Indian captivity narratives in contemporary scholarship and the place of Native people within such discourse. Once these issues have been examined through the use of some representative scholarly examples, I offer some suggestions as to how present and future scholars can address Native subjectivities and the historical legacy of colonialism in a more equitable manner.

The Soveraignty and Goodness of God is self-evidently a work of historical, religious, and social significance in the development of American literary history. In some ways, its longstanding literary importance is also the source of its authority and veracity. In both the earliest extant American edition and the subsequent English edition, both published in 1682, it is clear that the narrative is intended as a "true history" of the events relating to Mary Rowlandson's captivity within the wider context of King Philip's War. In the Cambridge second edition, published by Samuel Green, *The Soveraignty and Goodness of God*, the allegorical function of the text is also apparent. This intention is made clear through the use of a Biblical subtext that serves as a typological interpretive key to enhance and reinforce the narrative legitimacy of the work. The effective melding of ecclesiastical and personal observation is conveyed through Rowlandson's status as an eyewitness and active participant in the events described. The privileged narrative position Rowlandson occupies due to these attributes is brought to the readers' attention before her narrative even begins in the subtitle, which identifies the narrative as, "*Written by her own hand for her private use . . . for the benefit of the afflicted.*" The title of the London edition, published later in 1682, similarly presents Rowlandson's narrative to English readers as *A True History of the Captivity & Restoration of Mrs. Mary Rowlandson, A Minister's Wife in New-England*. Rather than serving the immediate needs of colonists, the London edition provides a window into colonial experience for the edification of transatlantic readers whose knowledge of Native cultures would have been informed by the modes of literary and artistic representation found in travel and exploration narratives, as well as colonial promotional literature, rather than from firsthand experience.[2] The overt claim to narrative veracity found on these title pages, along with Rowlandson's identification as a "minister's wife" operating as another signifier of narrative reliability, is reinforced by the compelling articulation of historical witnessing indicated by the phrase: *Written by her own hand, for her private use.*[3] In the 1682 and later editions, the title pages of Rowlandson's captivity narrative operate not simply as promotional features but, more notably, as metalinguistic signifiers of narrative truth that not only (re)presents but stands in for the testimony of the eyewitness in Rowlandson's absence.

Likewise, in *A Brief History of the Warr With the Indians of New England*, Increase Mather also seeks to deemphasize the intentionality of his authorship as a means of bolstering his credibility in contrast to accounts previously published by William Hubbard and John Easton, the later of which he describes as "a Quaker in Road-Island, who pretends to know the truth of things."[4] He begins his own historical account by stating, "although I was not altogether negligent, in Noting down such Occurrences, respecting the present *War* with the Heathen in *New-England*, as came to my knowledge . . . yet what I did that way, was merely for my own private use; nor had I any thought of publishing any of my *Observations.*"[5] This statement serves a similar promotional function to that appearing in *The Soveraignty and Goodness of God* just six years later. Jill Lepore, writing in *The Name of War*, however, seems to take Mather at his word as it regards the production of his *A Brief History*, stating, "although Mather never intended to write a history of the war, he kept careful track of it."[6] Just how she comes to this conclusion is perhaps the most interesting aspect of her argument as she inexplicably cites Mather's own statement as the evidence to support her view.

The reiteration of explicit claims of single authorship became a common feature of Indian captivity narratives produced in the years following the publication of the Rowlandson narrative. The captivity narrative of John Gyles, for instance, published at Boston in 1736, relating his experiences amongst the Wolastoqiyik (Maliseet) is titled *Memoirs of Odd Adventures, Strange Deliverances, etc., in the Captivity of John Gyles, Esq., Commander of the Garrison on St. George*

River, in the District of Maine. Written by Himself.[7] Similarly, Increase Mather exploits this function in several of his texts as well, including the introduction of his *A Relation of the Troubles which have hapned in New-England*, in which he invokes the qualifier, "written by his own hand," in reference to "a large manuscript of Governor *Bradfords*.[8] Yael Ben-Zvi, following the suggestion of Alden Vaughn and Edward Clark, voiced skepticism concerning the veracity of such declarations, asserting that statements of authorship "may not be entirely true."[9] He goes on to reject the claim altogether in regard to the captivity narrative of Susanna Johnson, expressing the general consensus that her "text was composed by the lawyer John C. Chamberlain."[10]

The significance of Rowlandson's self-constituting and self-fashioning role of witness-as-author is further illustrated by the fact that "the particular circumstances of the Captivity, and Redemption of Mrs. Mary Rowlandson; and of her children," had been advertised a year before its publication in the first American edition of John Bunyan's *The Pilgrim's Progress (1681)*, as "being pathetically written, with her own hand."[11] In his analysis of the distinctive authority of witness literature, Horace Engdahl has observed, "One does not become a witness only by observing an event with one's own eyes. A witness is a person who speaks out and says, "'I was there, I saw it, I can tell people!' As an act of speech, testimony is inseparable from this kind of self-reference and from the accompanying claim to immediate credence."[12] The putative composition of the account of Rowlandson's experience by the captive, herself, allows *The Soveraignty and Goodness of God* to assert an unassailable claim to authenticity, while simultaneously appropriating the role of colonial historian. Despite the anonymous claim in "The Preface to the Reader" that "this narrative was penned by the Gentlewoman her self,"[13] along with the prevalent use of a first-person narrative voice, the polemical and ecclesiastical character of the narrative is suggestive of an artfully emplotted simulation of historical writing, rather than a demonstration of historiography, from which it is estranged.

The explicit appeal to historical veracity in *The Soveraignty and Goodness of God*, and the privileging of English subjectivities as normative that enables the dissemination of Rowlandson's testimony in her absence, contributes to the text's vital ideological value and efficacy. Jacques Derrida, commenting on the interconnection between repetition and alterity in linguistic meaning, suggests that the inherent power of the written word lies in its capacity to be endlessly repeated, "despite the absolute disappearance of every determined addressee."[14] The titular claim of Rowlandson's authorship and the promotion of narrative truth claims function as axiomatic statements of fact that self-reflexively corroborate the testimony of the witness-as-author. Consequently, this literary device also operates as an interpretive supplement to and reiteration of the text itself.

Despite its culturally insensitive portrayal of Native people, historians and critics alike have long displayed a willingness to accept *The Soveraignty and Goodness of God* as a reliable account of the events relating to King Philip's War. As we have seen, Puritan authors employed a variety of meta-textual strategies to reinforce the legitimacy of their own accounts, and as the work of subsequent scholars show, these were often effective. Frederick Lewis Weis' preface to the 1903 edition, reprinted again in 1930, characterizes the work as "an authentic and graphic delineation of the manners and customs of the primitive children of the soil from whom our ancestors relentlessly wrested their beautiful and beloved heritage in order to enrich us and our posterity."[15] Likewise, in an edition published in 1990, Mark Ludwig introduces the Rowlandson narrative as "the true story of her capture by the Indians in a bloody massacre and of her service as their slave for three months."[16] As these examples illustrate, the influence of Puritan historiography and the stereotypes about Native people that they promote have persisted to the present day.

In the introductory essay on the historical relevance of captivity narratives that opens Frederick Drimmer's anthology of captivity narratives, he claims, "as true stories of strange adventure and perilous escape, also, they do not have many rivals."[17] Drawing a comparison between Indian captivity narratives and works in other literary genres, Drimmer states, "these stories were *real*," and reinforces the claim by insisting that "each of the captives in this book tells of things that he saw with his own eyes."[18] Implicit in Drimmer's appeal to the power of witnessing is the contention that captivity narratives represent much more than sensationalized tales of frontier conflict: "by and large they bear the stamp of truth," and "have been accepted as authentic since their earliest publication, and have frequently been used as sources by historians and anthropologists."[19] Aside from their continued literary significance, the fact that captivity narratives were "frequently" cited as valid source materials to describe Native culture and society reveals just how influential such texts could be. The similar tendency of accepting captivity narratives as historically accurate accounts of intercultural contact is problematic, to say the least, and highlights the epistemological predicament that attends the reception of narratives outside of their original contexts. The reading practices noted above demonstrate the acute peril inherent in Derrida's claim that "every sign, linguistic or nonlinguistic, spoken or written . . . can be *cited*, put between quotation marks," and, in a sense, extends the capacity of texts to "break with every given context, and engender infinitely new contexts in an absolutely nonsaturable fashion."[20]

Kathryn Derounian-Stodola and James Levernier assert that "despite the publication of thousands of captivities since Rowlandson's, readers have singled out particular text as a great work of narrative nonfiction, eloquent and dramatic in its timeless appeal."[21] Other scholars, such as Richard VanDerBeets, seems to conflate the Indian captivity narratives with modern ethnohistory, claiming that accounts such as Rowlandson's "constitute valuable specimens of ethnological reportage," and that "many of the narratives of Indian captivity are repositories of eyewitness information relating to the major Indian-white conflicts throughout the course of American history."[22] To support his reading of the genre, VanDerBeets cites *The Soveraignty and Goodness of God*, characterizing it as a source of "additional insight into King Philip's War and even King Philip himself, whom Rowlandson met and spoke with during her captivity."[23] As these examples indicate, few scholars seem interested in challenging the elevated status of *The Soveraignty and Goodness of God*, while fewer still deviate from this approach to address the marginalized voices of the Native people within captivity texts, who are often sublimated as little more than features of the landscape.

While the examples just cited are characteristic of much of the recent scholarship on the Indian captivity genre, earlier scholars such as Roy Harvey Pearce and Phillips Carleton were much less deferential to Puritan historiography in their assessments. On the contrary, Pearce and Carleton consistently questioned the basic mimetic assumption that Indian captivity narratives represent reliable accounts of cultural interactions between Native people and Euro-American settlers. Pearce contends that, in published accounts of captivity, "matters of pure historical fact . . . and ethnological data—that is, of content abstracted from treatment—are beside the point; what is important is what the narrative was for readers for whom it was written."[24] Given the opposing tendencies found in subsequent criticism, it seems that scholars have not found Pearce's view compelling. Consequently, the proliferation of meaning attributed to Indian captivity narratives, and their capacity to break from "any center of absolute anchoring,"[25] whereby the connections between experience, context, and narrative are effaced, can be better understood as both a function and a symptom of the iterability of such texts. One of the primary ways the discursive capacity of *The Soveraignty and Goodness of God* finds expression is in the willingness of its readers to accept the narrative as a reliable eyewitness account of the events described, which necessitates a corresponding ambivalence to the subjectivities of Native people.

A common motif of early captivity narratives is an initial description of a ruthless and seemingly indiscriminate assault by a Native war party upon an unsuspecting, usually sleeping, village. As a harbinger of what was to become a recurring feature of Indian captivity narratives, *The Soveraignty and Goodness of God* dramatically begins: "On the tenth of February, 1675,[26] came the Indians with great numbers upon Lancaster: Their first coming was about Sunrising; hearing the noise of some Guns, we looked out; several Houses were burning, and the Smoke ascending to Heaven."[27] For Carleton, such openings function to set the stage for a dramatic "escape or return," and provide narrative "coherence."[28]

Hayden White explores the problematic nature of the "epistemological status of historical *explanations*" in his widely influential work, *Tropics of Discourse*.[29] Informed by an anti-causal analysis of historical discourse, White holds that "descriptions of events *already* constitute interpretations of their nature."[30] Observations such as these emphasize the view that an author's subjectivity, as well as the means by which a narrative is constructed, is as important as the actual content in assessing the significance of historical accounts. The way an author of any historical text chooses to order the elements of a narrative, such as the date, time, and location that an event took place, in addition to the range of specific actions and relations of the persons involved, are all essential elements of storytelling. By directing his critical attention to the motivations of the historian, rather than just on the various agents of a narrative, White is able to isolate "components of specific *kinds* of plot structures" and assess the ways these "components" are ordered into different types of narrative.[31] The process as a whole, along with its narrative results, combine to form what White defines as "emplotment."[32] Examining Indian captivity narratives in light of White's critical historiography can be helpful in attaining a better understanding of the textual strategies involved, while also revealing some of the implicit motivations behind their deployment.

All the reader can truly gather from the opening to *The Soveraignty and Goodness of God* is that the town of Lancaster was, indeed, attacked by a group of Native warriors in February of 1676. The emphasis on Rowlandson's exclusive subjectivity operates as an intentional strategy that firmly grounds *The Soveraignty and Goodness of God* in the tradition of witness literature. The testimony offered by Rowlandson is made all the more persuasive by the assertion of narrative authority and her implied positioning as the sole literate witness to the attack on Lancaster, which she singles out as "the dolefullest day that ever mine eyes saw."[33] This powerfully affective sentiment is emphasized a few lines later by the statement, "Now is that dreadfull hour come, that I have often heard of . . . but now mine eyes see it."[34] The articulation of colonial anxiety and terror that pervades statements such as these operates as a private and exclusive claim to the information conveyed to readers, while at the same time establishing Rowlandson as the only reliable informant.

The latter of the two above-cited expressions of terror also represents a moment when the text falls back upon itself, implying two distinct yet mutually exclusive meanings. Less than a page after the initial description Rowlandson acknowledges that the fear of Indian attack was something that was openly discussed among English settlers, and embodied more than just a passing concern: "I had often before this said, that if the Indians should come, I should chuse rather to be killed by them than be taken alive."[35] The impasse created by the disclosure that the attack on Lancaster was viewed as provoking the contemplation of one's mortality lies in the irreducibility between the way the narrative is framed and the implications of statements such as the one just cited.

The deployment of a personal yet simultaneously detached narrative position represents an effort to fix meaning in accordance with what Michel Foucault terms a "regime of truth,"[36] which "is linked in a circular relation with systems of power which produce and sustain it."[37] The effect of this process is that the corresponding regime of truth established in *The Soveraignty and Goodness of God* necessarily preempts the possibility of considering the attack on Lancaster and Rowlandson's captivity from alternate perspectives, especially those aimed at inverting the ensconced privilege of the narrator's position. As a result, questions aimed at determining the identity of the Native attackers, where they came from, and why they carried out the raid are reduced to matters of subordinate, or even trivial, importance. The primary function of the account of Rowlandson's captivity is to encourage readers to identify with her perspective, while also serving to alienate, dehumanize, and ultimately negate the presence of Native peoples. *The Soveraignty and Goodness of God* is so bereft of contextual information that readers are not even provided with the cultural identities of the Native American forces responsible for the attack.[38] Instead they are reduced to an indistinguishable horde of "murtherous wretches"[39] and "bloody heathen,"[40] whereby the issue of historical detail is sublimated in deference to the broader narrative trajectory. As Molly Farrell has noted, in the case of this text, "innumerability leads to terror."[41]

Homi Bhabha, addressing the ideological dimension of literary texts, has characterized descriptions of events that rely upon "terrifying stereotypes of savagery, cannibalism, lust and anarchy" as "signal points of identification and alienation, scenes of fear and desire in colonial texts."[42] In the discussion of the opening of the Rowlandson narrative included in her book, *White Captives*, June Namias asserts that the dramatic description was intended to focus the "reader's attention on a catastrophic scene of a small community in mayhem."[43] As compelling as Namias's interpretation may be, it also seems that beginning the narrative in such fashion works to obscure the narrative's broader historical context, while reinforcing its efficacy as a "signal point of identification and alienation."

Figure 9. Indian attack on a Puritan settlement during King Philip's War, c. 1880s, from the author's private collection.

Within the account of Rowlandson's captivity, the attack on Lancaster and its aftermath seems of secondary concern to the overarching metanarrative inherent in Puritan historiography and theology. This intention is made clear in the subtle yet evocative image of "Smoke ascending to Heaven" in the midst of the attack.[44] In addition to producing a historically detached narrative, *The Sovereignty and Goodness of God* actively contributes to a mode of intertextual, typological writing, in which historical events are represented in concurrence with a preexisting ideological and religious framework. By strengthening conceptions of Puritan self-identification and community, through the reiteration of Calvinist values and beliefs, the narrative of Rowlandson's captivity operates as a particularly effective tool for the deterritorialization and dispossession of Native land.

Increase Mather's *A Brief History of the Warr with the Indians in New-England* (1676) includes a description of the attack upon Lancaster anticipating the stylistic reiterated in *The Soveraignty and Goodness of God.* In a passage remarkably similar to the one that opens the Rowlandson narrative, Mather writes, "for upon the 10th. day of *February* some hundreds of the *Indians* fell upon *Lancaster*, burnt many of the Houses, kill'd and took Captive above forty persons."[45] The resemblance between the two accounts is strikingly suggestive of the influence that Mather is believed to have exercised in the production of the later text. In addition to publicizing Rowlandson's experiences among her Native captors, Mather was also instrumental in bringing the stories of other captives to public attention. In *An Essay for the Recording of Illustrious Providences* (1684), for instance, Mather offers several accounts of captivity, including that of Quintin Stockwell. While purporting to record the details of Stockwell's ordeal after being taken captive during a raid on the town of Deerfield Mather invokes another statement of independent production, stating that this account was composed "in the Words by himself expressed." In addition, Mather also begins this narrative in a similar fashion to that found in the two versions of the attack on Lancaster described above, as it similarly begins, "In the year 1677. September 19. between Sun-set and dark, the *Indians* came upon us."[46]

Carrying on the family tradition of demonizing Native people, Cotton Mather, who in the words of the historian Samuel Drake "could hardly be confined to the drudgery necessary for the collection and nice arrangement of facts,"[47] begins his account, included in *Magnalia Christi Americana*, of a raid on the then Dutch town of Schenectady by a force of allied French, Mohawk, Sault, and Algonquin warriors, using nearly identical language: "On March 18. [1690] the *French with Indians* . . . fell suddenly upon *Salmon Falls*, destroying the best part of the Town with Fire and Sword. Near *Thirty* Persons were Slain, and more than *Fifty* were led into what the Reader will by and by call, *The worst Captivity in the World*."[48] Among the numerous accounts detailed in this work, Cotton Mather employs this formulaic opening in his account of Hannah Dustan's captivity, which Pearce characterized as little more than "a vehicle of Indian-hatred."[49] Dustan's captivity narrative opens with the statement, "On March 15, 1697, the *Salvages* made a Descent upon the Skirts of *Haverhil*, Murdering and Captiving about Thirty-nine Persons and Burning about half Dozen Houses."[50] Given the uncanny similarities between these opening descriptions, Derrida's notion of iterability is of particular interest here, as he observed: "this citationality, duplication, or duplicity, this iterability of the mark is not an accident or an anomaly, but is that without which a mark could no longer even have a so-called 'normal' functioning."[51] As the examples from the work of Increase and Cotton Mather attest, by the end of the seventeenth century the reiteration of the motif of a sudden and brutal attack perpetrated by unidentified Native people against unsuspecting English colonists had become an integral part of the normal functioning of both Puritan historiography and the Indian captivity genre.

The "unexpected" initiation of bloody conflict portrayed in these early accounts seems implicitly designed to characterize or emplot the Puritan settlers into the roles of victims, pounced upon, as they were, by the "merciless heathen" lurking in the "vast and desolate wilderness." Considering the far-reaching influence that the Mathers wielded in Puritan society, the close interplay apparent between the texts discussed appears attributable not simply to coincidence, but as the product of the implicit intertextual dynamic that attended much of Puritan textual production. The fact that publishing in the Massachusetts Bay Colony was strictly regulated by the General Court offers insight into the reproduction of these stylistic elements, while helping to explain why such patterns persisted as long as they did.

For Puritan historiographers, the vivid descriptions of "the troubles which have happened by the *Heathen* in this land" provided a kind of retroactive justification for the policies of military aggression launched against Native people.[52] Francis Jennings has argued that recurrent descriptions of "savage war" was one of the most effective means by which Euro-American writers demonized Native peoples: "myth contrasts civilized war with savage war by accepting the former as a rational, honorable, and often progressive activity while attributing to the latter the qualities of irrationality, ferocity, and unredeemed retrogression. Savagery implies unchecked and perpetual violence."[53] Of course, conflict with Native peoples was an all-too-common occurrence in early colonial society, as William S. Simmons has noted,[54] and an occupation English settlers had been almost continuously engaged in since their arrival in North America.

Examining Puritan historiography in dialogue with the broader philosophical notions championed by scholars such as Said, Bhabha, and Derrida allows us to more fully understand how the power of the written word was utilized by Puritan writers to advance their social and political aims. One of the main concerns of leaders such as Increase and Cotton Mather was to extend the reach and influence of a social and religious order founded on the framework of Calvinist doctrine. The conception of New Jerusalem as the materialization of the city upon the hill stood in stark contrast to the abject barbarism of Native cultures, whose members were viewed as savages "lurking" in the "woods and swamps and dark corners of the earth."[55] In colonial texts produced in seventeenth-century North America, Calvinist epistemology played a central role in promoting the desired religious and political objectives of Puritan society.

As with many of the texts produced in the Puritan colonies, *The Sovereignty and Goodness of God* displays distinct similarities with the Christian allegory, best exemplified by *Paradise Lost* (1667) and *The Pilgrim's Progress* (1678). One of the common features of Christian allegories and captivity narratives is the guiding presence of a structurally coherent array of binary oppositions. The binary circuit of the Euro-American Christian settler and Native "savage" was invoked in colonial literature to reinforce distinctions of civilization and wilderness, while serving as an expedient rationale for armed conflict. Through the deployment of this system of differentiation, the Native inhabitants of North America were inextricably linked to the physical landscape of the "New World." Thus, Native people represented not only the antithesis of proper human behavior, but also the very emblem of postlapsarian exile and spiritual decay, bound up in the notion of original sin. Citing the Puritan minister Thomas Shepard, who starkly described the bodies of Puritans as "living coffins to carry a dead soul up and down," Michael Hall writes that "the corollary was that human ability had no role at all in a person's spiritual growth, all of which depended on the gift of God's grace, totally free, unconditioned, and unmerited."[56] In light of the pervasiveness and intensity of such beliefs, the resulting mitigation of human agency becomes a dominant trope in Puritan literary discourse and forms a central theme in *The Soveraignty and Goodness of God*.

The typological structure imposed on the description of the attack on Lancaster and Rowlandson's subsequent captivity naturalizes divine providence, while supplying an interpretive framework for Rowlandson's experiences among the Indians. Far from representing an impartial account of historical events, *The Soveraignty and Goodness of God* achieves its most potent actuality as an allegory of transgression and redemption masquerading as historical mimesis. The frequent narrative fissures created by the interpolation of Biblical scripture supply the primary means by which this text coalesces into an allegorical struggle between Christianity and paganism, culture and savagery, civilization and wilderness. The Biblical citations allow the significance of the events portrayed to transcend their historical meanings and become an object lesson for Puritan readers that reveals God's inscrutable judgment, as well as his everlasting love and protection. Following the description of the opening assault, the divine nature of the events is emphasized by reference to the systematizing exhortation in Psalms 46:8: "Come, behold the works of the Lord, what desolations he has made in the Earth."[57] This invocation of divine providence marks the establishment of a narrative strategy that will be exploited time and time again throughout the narrative.

Subsumed within this ecclesiastical hermeneutic, however, is yet another layer of signification, where the inward gaze of religious contemplation is directed outward to obscure the bleak realities of colonial history. Through the careful mediation of Rowlandson's experiences, the narrative functions to disidentify the struggle of individual settlers from their immediate historical circumstances and reinscribe them within the confines of Puritan metaphysics. As White reminds us, "events are *made* into a story by the suppression or subordination of certain of them and the highlighting of others, by characterization, motific repetition, variation of tone and point of view, alternative descriptive strategies and the like."[58] In the case of *The Soveraignty and Goodness of God*, the suppression of vital events, such as the fact that the attack described was just one of many that occurred during the course of King Philip's War,[59] allows the Native offensive at Lancaster to be emplotted as a barbarous act of unprovoked aggression. White further notes, however, that "it is a fiction of the historian that the various states of affairs which he [or she] constitutes as the beginning, the middle, and the end of a course of development are all 'actual' or 'real' and that he has merely recorded 'what happened' in the transition from the inaugural to the terminal phase."[60] The construction of such a selectively ahistorical narrative in *The Soveraignty and Goodness of God*, enhanced by the steady repetition, frequently exploited in references to the Indians, of demonizing motifs and language—as "merciless heathen," "barbarous savages," and "bloody Devils"—combines to ensure the ready acceptance of a binary that casts English settlers in the role of victims and the Indigenous people as merciless villains.

In fact, throughout the course of the whole narrative, there is barely any mention of the events of King Philip's War itself. Details of recent or past conflicts are referred to only in passing, as in the First Remove when Rowlandson recalls, "seven were killed at Lancaster the summer before upon a Sabbath day."[61] Even this seemingly straightforward statement, however, is not presented to contextualize past events, since no further details of this incident are supplied. Instead, this abbreviated historical reference is offered as yet another instance of Native savagery to further incite the ire of Puritan readers. The emphasis on the circumstance that the previous attack occurred on the Sabbath conveys a clear indication of

Native paganism. While the significance of such a detail may escape the attention of modern readers, the importance of the Sabbath would not have been lost on Puritan readers of the time. Aside from its referential meaning as past event, the reference to the Sabbath serves as a reminder of the grim threat that Native people posed to the ecclesiastical framework of Puritan society, in which the observation of the Sabbath had been legally codified. According to the laws of the Massachusetts Bay Colony, those found guilty of "profaning the Lord's day" were subject to fines as well as harsh punishments, such as being "set in the stocks, whipped, caged and pilloried."[62] Moreover, as Paul Virilio contends, prohibitions regarding the Sabbath were instituted "because religious politics were defined with respect to death, to the great interruption, to the 'last judgement,' as they say in the Scriptures ('Apocalypse')."[63] Although the efforts of missionaries such as John Eliot had resulted in a significant population of converts, the efforts to assimilate Native people into Puritan society soon came to be seen as largely inadequate, due to the commitment of many Native people to their own distinct spiritual beliefs, as well as the consistent efforts of Native leaders such as Massasoit to oppose conversion among the Pokanoket.

The decontextualization of the attack on Lancaster found in *The Soveraignty and Goodness of God* was put forth despite the fact that open hostilities between the settlers of the English colonies, including those of Massachusetts Bay, Plymouth, and New Haven, Connecticut, and the allied tribes under the leadership of Metacomet had been simmering for years. In his study of English frontier expansionism, William Haller points out that as early as 1630, immigration and natural population growth had prompted the establishment of new settlements and additional appropriations of Native territory.[64] The resulting demographic pressures would eventually force the remaining New England Indians into war in an attempt to stop the relentless English advance.[65] Similarly, as historians Eric Schultz and Michael Tougias show, the "pressure to acquire land and secure new commercial opportunities in the decades before King Philip's War" only exacerbated an already fragile balance between the Puritans and their Indigenous neighbors.[66]

In his sympathetic account of this period, Ebenezer Pierce observed that the English had uncovered evidence that Metacomet was preparing for war as early as the spring of 1671, a claim that was "further confirmed by the reluctance he showed to comply with their request to visit Taunton" in that same year.[67] Coincidently, it was at a hunting lodge near this very same town nine years earlier that Metacomet's brother, Wamsutta, then the head sachem of the Pokanoket, was ordered at gunpoint to travel to Plymouth to answer charges of fomenting resistance to English rule. Mindful of Metacomet's thoughts of this previous situation—and the fact that Wamsutta fell mysteriously ill and died shortly after his departure from Plymouth—one can understand his reluctance to acquiesce to a meeting with Puritan officials. Robert B. Caverly reinforces this point in *The Indian Wars of New England* (1875), stating that in the months leading up to the outbreak of open warfare "everywhere among the planters, as well as among the natives, '*loud rumor*' *spoke;* and it spoke of blood, carnage, and despair."[68] Considering the widespread familiarity that settlers would have had with these events, it seems highly improbable that Mary Rowlandson would have been unaware of the escalating conflict, which had such an indelible effect on New England colonial society.

In the preface to *The Soveraignty and Goodness of God*, Ter Amicam states that Mary Rowlandson's husband, Joseph, was in Boston at the very time of the attack, having "gone down to the Councill of the Massachusets to seek aid for the defence of the place."[69] This detail is further clarified by George Madison Bodge, who says that as a result of suspicions arising from the first Lancaster attack, several "friendly Indians," one of them a Christian convert known as James Quanapohit,[70] "went among the hostile Indians about Brookfield and Waschuset" to gather information for the English and returned with "a full and detailed report of the plan of the hostiles for the destruction of Lancaster."[71] In this meeting, which took place on January 24, 1676, in Boston, Quanapohit informed the Governor and General Council that an allied group of Native warriors were planning to attack the outlying settlement of Lancaster, as well as those at Groton, Marlboro, Sudbury, and Medfield. Quanapohit further warned that the attack would take place "about twenty days from Wednesday last."[72] Inexplicably, according to historian Marion Fuller Safford, after "having sent [Quanapohit] to gather this information . . . the Governor and his Council did nothing whatever to ward off the blow."[73] Upon hearing this "alarming" information, and of Puritan leaders' decision not to act upon it, the people of Lancaster sent representatives led by the Reverend Joseph Rowlandson to urgently appeal to the General Court for assistance, "which was being tardily attended to when the blow fell, just as predicted."[74] Although the specific reasons behind the failure of Puritan officials to act on these concerns remain unclear, the attacks provided the justification needed for the declaration of war issued by the General Court, which was the vehicle by which they gained possession of the remaining Wampanoag lands. An explanation for the General Court's inaction regarding the defense of Lancaster, and other outlying Puritan settlements, lies in the volatility of the situation and the eagerness of some Puritan leaders to pursue a military solution.

As wife of the town's minister and daughter of one of the largest landowners in Lancaster, it would seem that Rowlandson would be much more knowledgeable about contemporary events than she reveals in her narrative. The fact that she was a woman who would have certainly suffered at least some degree of societal repression, which was a common feature of New England colonial society, does not fully explain the conspicuous lapse in detail, either. A letter written to the Rhode Island governor by Mary Pray testifies to the widespread fear and suspicion of Native people that held sway throughout the English colonies during this time. Submitted as an appeal for protection, Pray "humbly" appeals to the Governor "that for the good of the towns upon the main he would clere the Iland [Rhode Island] of those wicked Indians that are with them [the Narragansett] who wil undou[b]tedly Run away in the spring and Ralley in there forces together and destroy us and many others."[75] In this extraordinary historical document, modern readers are given a window into the expression of a female settler's fear and suspicion of Native people in the form of an appeal for preemptive war against the Narragansett, representing an explicit call for their annihilation.

The stark picture formed by these documents seems at odds with Michelle Burnham's contention that "prior to her captivity, the Indian culture did not exist for Mary Rowlandson and her readers other than in the form of a typological symbol."[76] If anything, transforming Native people into "typological" figures is precisely what the authors of colonial histories and captivity narratives worked to accomplish. Support for this assertion can be found in Increase Mather's *A Brief History of the Warr with the Indians in New-England*, in which the previous attack upon Lancaster referred to in *The Soveraignty and Goodness of God* is recounted. Mather states that on "August 22. (1675) being the Lords Day, the Indians about *Lancaster* killed a Man and his Wife, and two children in the afternoon exercise."[77] In addition to the casualties cited by Mather, according to a footnote accompanying this passage, four other men were also killed during the attack on that same day.[78] It is unclear why Mather would be remiss in discussing these additional victims, unless perhaps he sought to focus his readers' attention on the massacre of an entire family presented as a microcosm of the grave threat that Indian aggression represented to Puritan society.

As these descriptions suggest, the threat of Native raiding parties on outlying settlements was a prevalent source of communal anxiety for English settlers living in New England during this time, not just for those outside the secure boundaries of fortified settlements such as Boston or Plymouth. In addition to personal letters, sermons, and jeremiads composed to highlight God's illustrious providences, news of Indian attacks was also widely circulated throughout the New England colonies. Shelia McIntyre observes that before the establishment of New England's first newspaper, the *Boston News-Letter*, in 1704, the exchange of personal letters between New England ministers was among the most common and "effective means of diffusing information."[79] The selective nature of the information found in *The Soveraignty and Goodness of God* is highlighted by the failure to situate Rowlandson's captivity within the broader historical context of the internecine war that was erupting across the frontier. The historical picture that emerges from these details belies the sense of shock and surprise that is evoked in the opening pages of the narrative.

The episode in which Rowlandson describes her meeting with Metacomet, in whose dwelling she stayed for a short time during her captivity, provides another example of narrative dissonance. Here again, the incongruity between the demonizing rhetorical strategies and the implicit claims of historical accuracy invoked throughout the narrative are apparent. In Rowlandson's description of this meeting, there is not the slightest indication of the seething hostilities that were intensifying all around her and her fellow captives:

> *During my abode in this Place,* Philip *spake to me to make a shirt for his boy, which I did, for which he gave me a shilling: I offered the money to my master, but he bade me keep it, and with it I bought a piece of Horse flesh.* Afterwards he asked me to make a Cap for his boy, for which he invited me to Dinner. I went, and he gave me a Pancake, about as big as two fingers; it was made of parched wheat, beaten, and fried in Bears grease, but I thought I never tasted pleasanter meat in my life.[80]

The nature of Rowlandson's extraordinary interaction with Metacomet, a figure widely considered the most feared and hated Native leader of the time, is strikingly mundane. The complete lack of any hint of incivility on Metacomet's part seems to challenge and contradict the negative depiction of Native people that saturates the narrative as a whole.

In *American Puritanism and the Defense of Mourning* (1990), Mitchell Breitwieser insists that this brief meeting between Rowlandson and Metacomet represents an important instance of cross-cultural exchange and marks a shift in the narrative whereby Rowlandson is transformed from a passive captive to one who "begins to participate in an economy."[81] He maintains that the subtle shift in Rowlandson's role during the course of the narrative signals the development of a more attuned sense of cultural understanding, enabling her to discard the "emblem of the diabolical savage," which "dominates only the first few pages of the narrative."[82] In Breitwieser's reading of the communicative and economic context of this meeting, Metacomet is characterized, in contrast to his father, Massasoit, as among "a newer and less cooperative generation of leaders."[83] It is within this broader historical and interpersonal context that Breitwieser defines Rowlandson's new role among her Indian captors: "the Algonquian leader relieves her from having to depend on the whims of gift givers and provides her with social agency, with effective means of securing her own well-being. Her entry into exchange lifts her out of the abjection of being on the dole, and thus creates a measure of equality between herself and the captors, with whom she can now barter, that is, set the terms, rather than only accept. But if she is in this way raised out of abjection, the Indian is also set loose from the emblem: Philip enters the narrative not as archbeast, but instead as trading partner."[84] Breitwieser goes on to suggest that Rowlandson's "restricted economic integration into the life of the tribe would seem to evidence . . . an incipient Indianity, both a forgetting of the captors' true nature and an expression of a woman's pride in her cleverness and autonomy."[85] Equipped with a newly acquired sensitivity, according to this line of reasoning, Rowlandson is driven to reassess her former views and becomes "disaffected with the value system" of Puritan society.[86] The radical Nietzschean transformation that Rowlandson experiences results in her recognition of "Indian society *as a society*, rather than as lawless animality."[87]

Michelle Burnham offers a similar interpretation of this interaction, in which she ostensibly supports Breitwieser's main conclusion but departs from his "brilliant analysis of the phenomenology of grief," asserting that "what Breitwieser calls realism, I would instead call dialogism."[88] Seemingly lost in both Breitwieser and Burnham's analyses of Rowlandson's interaction with Metacomet is any consideration of his distinct subjectivity. Thus, while these interpretations advance unconventional approaches to understanding the Rowlandson narrative, Metacomet's absent presence inevitably consigns both to the status of simulated monologues in what Vizenor would term, "the ruins of tribal representations."[89] In spite of these limitations, Burnham goes on to further distinguish her view from that of Breitwieser, asserting that despite his recognition of the importance of intercultural exchange, he fails to take proper notice of "the significance of Rowlandson's acculturation into Algonquian society."[90] It is precisely this lack of vision, so Burnham claims, that leads Breitwieser to "ignore the effect the captive's culturally liminal position has on her recollective language."[91] It is my contention, however, that in placing so much emphasis on Rowlandson and the economic exchange with her Native captors, rather than on the specific circumstances of it, both Burnham and Breitwieser conflate its significance at the expense of minimizing the extent of the demonizing rhetoric found throughout the narrative, as well as its complicity in the reterritorialization of Indian lands.

This situation is all the more conspicuous when one considers the frequent descriptions of Metacomet as the fearsome, bloodthirsty savage that appear in the writings of Rowlandson's contemporaries, as well as in the work of the succeeding generations of historians. Consider, for instance, the difference between the description of Metacomet cited above and that offered in Benjamin Thompson's epic poem, "New England's Crisis" (1676): "and here methinks I see this greasy lout / With all his pagan slaves coiled round about, / Assuming all the majesty of his throne / Of rotten stump. . . ."[92] In this inflammatory example, Thompson utilizes motifs that evoke the specter of an Indian Satan surrounded by an army of vile demons, inextricably associated with the frontier wilderness. Thompson continues his invective against Metacomet, and Native people in general, throughout the rest of the poem, reiterating the conventional demonizing stylistic of animalistic imagery found in the work of other Puritan writers.

The sense of fear and loathing that the English harbored for Metacomet is laid bare by the manner of his death and the subsequent treatment of his corpse. Pursued back to his home in what is presently Mount Hope, Rhode Island, in August of 1676, Metacomet's death came at the hands of an English company commanded by Benjamin Church. Following a brief skirmish, Metacomet was said to have been shot and killed by "a disenchanted Pocasset" known as Alderman.[93] According to the account of these events found in Mather's *A Brief History*, "an English-man and an Indian endeavoured to fire at him, the English man missed of his aime, but the Indian shot him through the heart, so as that he fell down dead."[94] Following this exchange of gunfire, soldiers under Church's command advanced on Metacomet's position near the swamp and took possession of his body. Metacomet's death doesn't quell the English thirst for retribution, as his corpse is subjected to additional abuses. According to Mather: "And in that very place where he first contrived and began his mischief, was he taken and destroyed, and there was he . . . cut into four quarters, and is now hanged up as a monument of revenge & Justice, his head being cut off and carried away to Plymouth, his Hands were brought to

Boston."[95] Following this brutal treatment, whereby Metacomet was transformed into a horrific emblem of English colonial power, his head was then taken back to Plymouth as a grisly trophy; it was impaled upon a gate post, where, for nearly thirty years, it served as a reminder to Native people and colonists alike of the consequences of insubordination to Puritan authority.

Because Metacomet had been killed and Native resistance effectively neutralized by the time Rowlandson's narrative was published, there was no longer an ideological rationale to demonize him further. Such an explanation seems plausible, especially considering the abundance of material already dedicated to that purpose. Lamentably, the same cannot be said about other Native people who came into contact with Rowlandson throughout the rest of the narrative. In contrast to the interpretations promoted by Breitwieser and Burnham, following the account of Rowlandson's remarkably ordinary dealings with the "archbeast" Metacomet, characterizations of Native people as "heathens" continue to hold sway with their successive and repeated reference as "barbarous," "merciless," and "cruel."[96]

Figure 10. The Death of Metacomet, frontispiece from William Apess's *Eulogy on King Philip*, 1837. Courtesy of the Huntington Library.

Despite the frequent reiteration of demonizing motifs throughout *The Soveraignty and Goodness of God*, Breitwieser seems to disregard the function and significance of such language and instead presents the questionable observation that such rhetoric "dominates only the first few pages of the narrative."[97] The accumulated force of *The Soveraignty and Goodness of God* itself negates this assertion, while there seems little textual evidence to support the kind of epiphany that Breitwieser attributes to Rowlandson. The very publication of Rowlandson's captivity narrative and its place in the overarching context of King Philip's War is clearly at odds with this conclusion. Similarly, Burnham's claim concerning Rowlandson's acculturation into Algonquin culture is highly fraught, especially given the contempt for practically every aspect of Native culture that is articulated throughout the text, most fervently in the judgments leveled against the Christian, or so-called praying Indians, who act as translators and go-betweens during the negotiations for Rowlandson's release.

Rowlandson reaffirms her conviction in the Puritan view of the "true nature" of her captors in the narration of events subsequent to her first meeting with Metacomet, of whom she says, "*there was little more trust to them than to the master they served.*"[98] Once again, we find not only a reiteration of the demonizing language that marks the opening pages of *The Soveraignty and Goodness of God*, but also a reductionist synthesis and creative transformation of Metacomet into the image of Satan himself. Even if the meeting between Rowlandson and Metacomet could be interpreted as the narrative's epiphanal moment, it is unclear how the mere absence of racist language in this one episode could be seen as indicative of an enlightened sensitivity in Rowlandson's character. To assert, as Breitwieser does, that the Indian figure as the "archbeast" had been "raised out of abjection," based solely upon Rowlandson's fleeting interaction with Metacomet, is just not supported by the textual evidence. In a very real way, Breitwieser's critical apparatus has the unintended result of eliding Rowlandson's complicity in colonial English aggression and effectively rendering Native subjectivities silent by transforming Metacomet's actions into a testimonial of Rowlandson's virtue. The discretion displayed in the description of Rowlandson's interaction with Metacomet, coupled with the absence of any substantial information regarding the context of her captivity, raises serious questions concerning the historical reliability of the events portrayed in *The Soveraignty and Goodness of God*. Although Metacomet was not able to provide an explanation for the actions attributed to him in this text, some of his words have survived, passed down through the generations in the spirit of Wampanoag oral tradition and sacred history.[99] In the speech William Apess ascribed to Metacomet in his *Eulogy on King Philip*, whereby neighboring tribal groups are rallied to his confederacy, Metacomet presents a long list of grievances against the settlers of the New England colonies, stating:

> Brothers, you see this vast country before us, which the Great Spirit gave to our fathers and us; you see the buffalo and deer that now are our support. Brothers, you see these little ones, our wives and children, who are looking to us for food and raiment; and you now see the foe before you, that they have grown insolent and bold; that all our ancient customs are disregarded; the treaties made by our fathers and us are broken, and all of us insulted; our council fires disregarded, and all the ancient customs of our fathers; our brothers murdered before our eyes, and their spirits cry to us for revenge. Brothers, these people from the unknown world will cut down our groves, spoil our hunting and planting grounds, and drive us and our children from the graves of our fathers, and our council fires, and enslave our women and children.[100]

While the authenticity of such speeches has long been questioned as rooted in "the idealization of Indian orality," we are left to contemplate the silences in a historical record forged almost exclusively by the English.[101]

The account of John Easton, a Rhode Island official dispatched to negotiate with the inflamed Native people as a last ditch effort to avert war, while not quite confirming the authenticity of Metacomet's speech, nevertheless conveys the spirit of his appeal. According to Easton's testimony, Metacomet leveled a litany of charges against the English, condemning what he perceived to be the anti-Indian prejudice of the General Court, the introduction of alcohol by English traders by which they "cheted them in bargens," and the practice of recognizing illegitimate leaders "that wold give or sell them there land, that now they had no hopes left to keep ani land."[102] Easton expresses his familiarity with the grievances articulated by Metacomet, which suggests that tensions were both long-standing and well-known, while also confirming their legitimacy, stating, "we knew it to be true."[103] Whatever else these examples might represent, the statements conveyed by the divergent perspectives of Easton and Apess are united in detailing Metacomet's strident but rational appeal for justice, which reads more like the thoughtful deliberations of a political leader than the vengeful rantings of a fearsome savage.

To portray the tragic events that led Metacomet to take up arms against the colonists as an effect of his "less cooperative" leadership style, as Breitwieser does, is to disregard the complex series of events that led to war in the first place. In a 1671 meeting before the Massachusetts Commissioners, convened in the aforementioned town of Taunton, the records show that Metacomet had previously brought forth many of the same complaints he would later express to Easton in regard to the behavior of the Massachusetts colonists. In this earlier meeting, Metacomet alleged "that the English injured the planted lands of his people" by failing to fence their livestock, which allowed them to roam freely onto Native territory, damaging and destroying crops and spoiling the fields in the process.[104] In the face of an array of Puritan documents condemning the character and behavior of Metacomet, the account of the meeting before Massachusetts Commissioners and the testimony of John Easton provides modern readers with a poignant depiction of Metacomet and the events leading up to the outbreak of war.[105] In his final judgment of these events, Easton lays the responsibility for the war directly at the feet of the English, and specifically condemns Puritan ministers for inciting war, "I am so perswaided of new England pri[e]sts thay ar so blinded by the spiret of persecution and to maintaine to have hyer, and to have rume to be mere hyerling that for his managing what he Caleth the gospel, by violenc[e] to have it Chargabell for his gaine from his quarters and if ani in magestrasy be not so as ther pack horses thay will be trumpeting for inovation or war."[106]

Russell Bourne has estimated that by the 1670s, due to the effects of war and disease, the Native population in southern New England had been reduced to twenty thousand, while the English colonists had increased to as many as fifty thousand.[107] Given the increasing strain on the land and natural resources brought on by relentless immigration and settlement of the mid-Atlantic coastal region by English, Dutch, and French colonists, coupled with the settler's expansionist ambitions and persistent refusal to recognize the validity of Native claims to the land, the outbreak of open warfare was inevitable.

As a result of these factors, the Native peoples inhabiting coastal New England found themselves in an increasingly tenuous position throughout the seventeenth century. And while the territories of the Narragansett, Wampanoag, Pocumtuck, and Nipmuc were being virtually overrun by European colonists in search of freedom and opportunity, these marginalized tribal groups were also being pressured by the Mohawk and the allied Iroquois tribes to the north and the west. Even before the arrival of the English, there was already a long history of intertribal conflict relating to raiding activities and territorial rivalries that led to the abandonment of Algonquin villages in the Connecticut River valley, and the relocation of affected Algonquin beyond the reach of their Mohawk enemies along the eastern Atlantic coast.[108] Given the complexity of intertribal relations and the serious threat that the English, along with their Mohawk and Iroquois allies, represented to their ways of life, the situation of the Pequot, Narragansett, and Wampanoag was clearly intolerable. It is also worth noting that far from being merely reactive to the situation, the Mohawk had sought to prevent incursions into their own tribal lands, and had used the Algonquins as a buffer against English advances. Consequently, the Native nations of coastal New England were left with little choice but to try to coexist among ever-increasing numbers of English settlers.

In their efforts to come to terms with Puritan representations of Native people, critics such as Breitwieser and Burnham tend to overlook the grievances that Metacomet expressed on behalf of New England Indian people. As we have seen, however, the array of evidence gleaned from contemporaneous Puritan writings paint a much more complex and, for Native people, devastating portrait of King Philip's War. Recent efforts to explain and justify the many problematic attributes of *The Soveraignty and Goodness of God*, and to again redeem Rowlandson's character, have led some scholars to obscure rather than illuminate the historical record of colonial New England as it relates to Native people. This has most often been manifested through the development of complex critical interpretations that serve the functions of particular theoretical paradigms and ultimately reinforce conventional representations of Native Otherness. At the same time, such criticism, intentionally or not, has the very real effect of depriving Native subjectivities of historical agency and an essential lived humanity as they seem to only exist in the context of their interactions with the English. We must not forget that *The Soveraignty and Goodness of God* is much more than it purports to be. The fact that its narrative is told through the perspective of a minister's wife, or that it contains a narrative of repentance and redemption, does not invalidate its simultaneous status as a war machine. Perhaps, these very qualities are what make it so effective, and judging from its treatment by contemporary scholars, so convincing in the end. It is a regrettable state of affairs indeed when, even after more than three hundred years, in the words of William Apess, the figure of Metacomet and what he fought and died for continues to "lie buried in the shades of night."[109]

4

Fractured Histories, Captive Subjects

The Masque of Textual Effacement

In writing, the point is not to manifest or exalt the act of writing, nor is it to pin a subject within language; it is, rather, a question of creating a space into which the writing subject constantly disappears.
–Michel Foucault

THE TRAUMATIC EVENTS OF King Philip's War and its aftermath left an indelible impression on the Puritan body politic and nationalist colonial identity. As the proliferation of captivity narratives and historical texts in the years that followed illustrates, English conflict with Native nations and the French was widely seen as a sensational and devastating confirmation of God's illustrious providence. During this same period, Puritan leaders were also struggling to preserve their political autonomy from England, which culminated in the revocation of the Puritan charter in 1689. Despite this development, Puritan leaders were intent on maintaining the social and political order established in the preceding generation by leaders such as William Bradford and John Winthrop. The sense of political disorder arising from the growing rift with the English Crown was exacerbated by a restless and fragmenting population that had grown, with the expansion of frontier settlements ever farther from Boston and Plymouth, increasingly detached from Puritan authority.

For ministers such as Increase Mather and William Hubbard, the impulse to reassert ecclesiastical control and restore order found expression in a two-pronged ideological approach intended to strengthen Puritan community. It was hoped that the improvement of social cohesion could be accomplished through the instruction offered in sermons and jeremiads, as a supplement to the sponsorship and production of historical and literary texts. In his work on the history of printing in colonial New England, George Selement has documented the prodigious output of Puritan ministers during this period. As a case in point, Selement cites Cotton Mather's *Magnalia Christi Americana*, which affirms the responsibilities of Puritan clergy to not only exhort and admonish but also "Administer the Sacraments, Visit the Afflicted, and manage all parts of Church-Discipline; and if any Books for the service of Religion, be written, Persons thus extreamly incumbred must be the Writers."[1] Corroborating Mather's exposition of ministerial duties, Selement cites data indicating that between 1561 and 1703 Puritan ministers published 1,567 separate imprints.[2] Of these, there were 1,360 imprints published after 1620, with John Cotton, Richard Mather, Increase Mather, and Cotton Mather accounting for an astounding 532 works.[3] Given these figures, it would be difficult to underestimate the profound and enduring influence these four writers wielded in colonial New England society.

The inclination of clergy to produce written texts was also supplemented by the promotion of works composed by other learned settlers that reinforced Puritan ideology. The frequent appearance of introductory and prefatory materials by Puritan ministers in the works of non-clergy became a primary method of promotion and endorsement for the work of lay writers. Although "The Preface To The Reader" that introduces *The Soveraignty and Goodness of God* is credited to the pseudonymous Ter Amicam, the author's decision to conceal his identity has fueled much speculation, with most scholars attributing the text to Increase Mather. Before the issue of the preface is addressed, however, it is essential that we consider the conditions surrounding the production of *The Soveraignty and Goodness of God.*

The original manuscript on which *The Soveraignty and Goodness of God* is based is not extant; also, only a few leafs—used in the binding in a copy of Samuel Willard's *Covenant-Keeping* (1682)—are all that is known to exist of the first edition that was printed at Boston earlier in the same year.[4] The indeterminacy created by this situation has provided the impetus to scrutinize the historical integrity and authorship of the text. Within months of the publication of this lost first edition, two successive reprints were issued in Cambridge, Massachusetts, on the press of Samuel Green, with another printed in London, England, by Joseph Poole. It seems reasonable to assume that the lost first edition would have been used as the copy-text for the first of the two Cambridge editions, as well as for the London edition.[5] Citing the unpublished scholarship of Robert Diebold, Kathryn Derounian-Stodola also expresses this view, "but because of the many variants in the two Cambridge editions," she takes the additional step of identifying the "forth edition," printed in London, as "probably the most reliable."[6] Just how or why the "variants" alluded to cause her to privilege the last of the editions to be published in 1682 over either Cambridge edition, in the absence of both the original Rowlandson manuscript and the Boston first edition, is unclear.

Without being able to account for the lack of consistency between the subsequent editions, such a postulation seems at odds with practices used in the field of textual criticism. Noted bibliographers such as Ronald B. McKerrow and W. W. Greg take the position that "it is normally the first edition alone that can claim authority."[7] As such, Derounian-Stodola's preference for what is in essence the fourth edition, printed in London by Joseph Poole as *A True History of the Captivity & Restoration of Mrs. Mary Rowlandson*, recedes "at least one step further from the author's original in so far as the general form of the text is concerned."[8] Based on the critical standards denominated by McKerrow and Greg, the privileging of the London edition as the most reliable edition, regardless of any information that can be gleaned from the collation of the subsequent editions, is simply untenable. According to McKerrow, "to take a reprint, even a revised reprint, as a copy-text," is

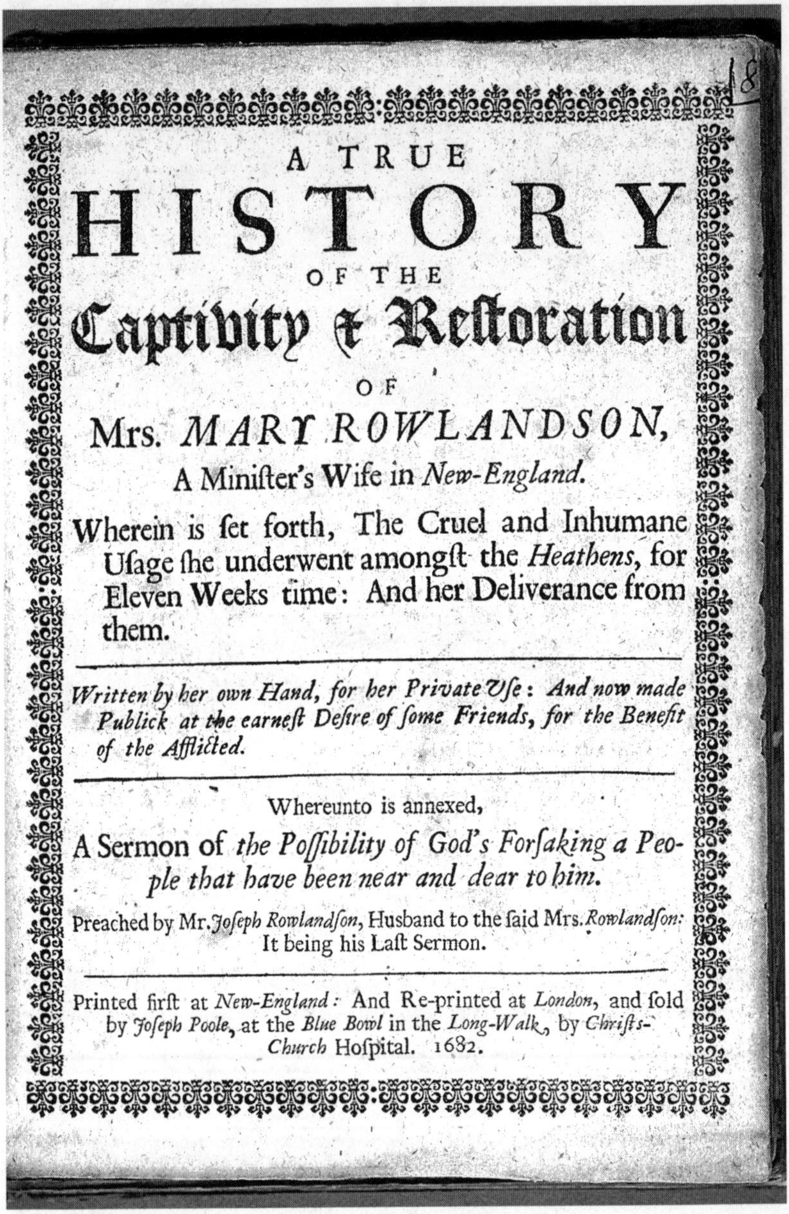

A TRUE
HISTORY
OF THE
Captivity & Reſtoration
OF
Mrs. *MARY ROWLANDSON*,
A Miniſter's Wife in *New-England.*

Wherein is ſet forth, The Cruel and Inhumane Uſage ſhe underwent amongſt the *Heathens*, for Eleven Weeks time: And her Deliverance from them.

Written by her own Hand, for her Private Uſe: And now made Publick at the earneſt Deſire of ſome Friends, for the Benefit of the Afflicted.

Whereunto is annexed,
A Sermon of *the Poſſibility of God's Forſaking a People that have been near and dear to him.*

Preached by Mr. *Joſeph Rowlandſon*, Husband to the ſaid Mrs. *Rowlandſon*: It being his Laſt Sermon.

Printed firſt at *New-England*: And Re-printed at *London*, and ſold by *Joſeph Poole*, at the *Blue Bowl* in the *Long-Walk*, by *Chriſts-Church* Hoſpital. 1682.

Figure 11. Title page of *A True History of the Captivity & Restoration of Mrs. Mary Rowlandson*, printed in London by Joseph Poole, 1682. Courtesy of the Huntington Library.

"indefensible."[9] Thus, without either the original manuscript or the Boston first edition, there can be no authoritative edition of the captivity narrative of Mary Rowlandson.

The standing of the three subsequent 1682 Rowlandson editions is further complicated by the statement found on the title page of the Cambridge second edition, printed by Samuel Green, indicating that it had been "Corrected and amended." While Gary Ebersole has been quick to discount the imposition of a "ministerial hand" as the source of any such corrections, or that anyone else had a significant role in the production of the narrative,[10] David Minter and David A. Richards assert, "Increase Mather encouraged Rowlandson to write the narrative, sponsored its publication, and supplied its preface."[11] Despite the serious bibliographic challenges created by this situation, the explanations offered by these critics have failed to settle the controversy. In fact, the inability of critics to either confirm or refute Mather's alleged editorial and/or authorial role in the creation of *The Soveraignty and Goodness of God*, or expressly identify any textual emendations, has continued to fuel speculation. Even scholars seemingly convinced of Rowlandson's autonomous authorship admit that the specific chain of events that culminated in the production of the text itself remains a mystery. In the absence of verifiable contextual information, Derounian-Stodola acknowledges that "where or when Mary Rowlandson wrote her narrative" cannot be determined.[12] The inability to establish even these most basic yet elusive facts leaves scholars in the compromised position of analyzing a text without access to the fundamental details regarding the circumstances of its original production, how it came to be published, who may have sponsored the work and why, and what, if any, changes took place as it underwent the transformation from spoken story to manuscript to printed book. All that is known for certain is that the first edition of *The Soveraignty and Goodness of God* was printed in Boston during the year 1682, some six years after the attack on Lancaster.

In a more recent essay, in which Derounian-Stodola revisits the likelihood of an outside influence in the production of the Rowlandson text, she reasons, "it would be naïve to assume that her husband or her senior spiritual advisor [Increase] Mather would not at least have read her manuscript and given her suggestions for improvement. Quite possibly their intervention extended to editorial additions and revisions."[13] After this intriguing statement, however, Derounian-Stodola leaves her readers guessing as to what the nature of the improvements and the probable "additions and revisions" might have been, since she doesn't offer any specific examples to substantiate her conjectures. Bryce Traister, in an essay in which he conceives Rowlandson as a harbinger of modernity, offers a refreshingly straightforward answer to why critics have been remiss in addressing such issues: "lacking any textual archive by which editorial emendations and collations might indicate either singular or plural authorship, and assuming the biblical literacy and intelligence of Mary Rowlandson (to say nothing of not wanting to diminish her achievement or gender by questioning her text's composition), we have stayed away from precisely this sort of speculative skepticism."[14] Plagued by an array of seemingly unanswerable and controversial questions, many critics writing on *The Soveraignty and Goodness of God* express their ambivalence, as Traister observes, by simply moving on to other topics. The relationship between critic and text that Traister diagnoses is not a new development, however, while his use of the term speculative skepticism seems ironic given the ramifications of his reasoning.

As Michel Foucault pointed out in his seminal essay "What is an Author?," "it is a very familiar thesis that the task of criticism is not to bring out the work's relationships with the author, nor to reconstruct through the text a thought or experience, but rather to analyze the work through its structure, its architecture, its intrinsic form, and the play of its internal relationships."[15] For Foucault, attempts at recovering the ephemeral emotions, feelings, and unstated ideas distract us from the physicality of the text. Brian McGinty is one scholar who takes a straightforward approach to the issue of authorship in his assessment of the Indian captivity genre, stating, "Although typically attributed to the captives themselves, the narratives were almost always shaped, if not entirely composed, by other writers. Many of the writers were clergymen, in part because the Indian-white struggle for control of North America was seen largely in religious terms, in part because clergymen were . . . the most literate members of white communities and, as such, best prepared to help less educated men and women complete a difficult literary undertaking."[16] Despite such declarations of widespread fabrication in the Indian captivity genre, only a few detailed studies of this practice have been undertaken. Similarly, Lorrayne Carroll, who addresses Cotton Mather's composition of the captivity narrative of Hannah Swarton, as well as John C. Chamberlain's authorship of the captivity narrative attributed to Susannah Johnson, in her work, *Rhetorical Drag*, and asserts in an earlier essay that "indeterminate authorship is a hallmark of earlier women's captivity narratives."[17] Despite such conclusions, or because of them, Carroll displays a hesitancy in making these claims. Carroll's unwillingness to fully substantiate this assertion is most evident in her evaluation of the current state of captivity scholarship, about which she states: "foregoing an often futile antiquarian and essentialist quest for the 'real' person who is the actual author of the text, most scholars reasonably and correctly move on to significant questions about the narrative's cultural work."[18] Although taking a stand for one's ideas and questioning the conclusions of fellow scholars may not be pleasant, it is nonetheless an indispensable charge of all critical inquiry. Given the cultural, aesthetic, and historical stakes involved in writing about Indian captivity, to characterize as both reasonable and correct captivity scholarship that sidesteps the issue of authorship—at least in the context of Carroll's broader claims—runs the risk of sanctioning the very negation that she seeks to remedy. Furthermore, the notion that the "cultural work" of any narrative can be ascertained in any real sense without regard to the establishment of authorship is highly suspect.

In the case of *The Soveraignty and Goodness of God,* the inability to conclusively establish the identities, motivations, and interactions between the individuals involved in its production precludes readers from fully understanding the significance of the events described therein. Likewise, the place that this text holds within the broader context of colonial American literature, Puritan historiography, and King Philip's War, as well as Native American history, is further obscured. The unsettling ambiguities and uncertainties that have resulted from this situation are inseparably linked to the unanswered questions of authorship and authorial intention. In order to understand the complex dimensions of thought, experience, and literary synthesis that combined to produce *The Soveraignty and Goodness of God*, the deeply fraught issues relating to the text's production and authorship must be explicitly addressed.

One possible influence on the text's production can be found in the internal ideological conflicts that had long been simmering between Puritan leaders who adhered to dogmatic and conservative conceptions of Puritan order and those typified by a more moderate and tolerant tone. In the last quarter of the seventeenth century, this tension was perhaps best exemplified by the quarrel carried on between Increase Mather and William Hubbard. The confluence of events that culminated in King Philip's War, and the incongruous ways that this event was variously represented in the context of colonial historiography, exposed a rift that had the potential to further destabilize the already deeply divided Puritan colonies.

Anne Kusener Nelsen has observed that the two texts that best epitomize the conflicting attitudes of these "two defenders of the Puritan regime" were Mather's *A Brief History of the Warr with the Indians of New-England* and Hubbard's *A Narrative of the Troubles with the Indians of New-England*, published in 1676 and 1677 respectively. According to Nelsen, these texts represent competing "attempts at full-scale narrative evaluations of the war,"[19] which typify the deep-seated ideological differences inherent in Hubbard and Mather's contrasting conceptions of Puritan society. The respective titles of these narratives are indicative of the philosophical differences at the core of their ideological struggles. Mather, seemingly drawing upon the concept of *bellum justum*, uses the unequivocal term "Warr" to describe the recent conflict, while Hubbard employs the more subdued and ambiguous term "Troubles." A further point of distinction is found in Hubbard's description of the attack on Lancaster. As we have already seen, the account Mather provides in *A Brief History* bears a distinct similarity to the opening of the Rowlandson narrative. Hubbard's description, by contrast, is distinguished for its measured tone: "Lancaster, or Nashaway. a small town of about 50 familyes, was assaulted *Febru.* 10 1675 by 500 Indians in five severall companies, yet they took but one garrison house, wherein were forty two persons, but eight or nine souldiers, whereof but one escaped, the rest were women and children, who were most of them returned after some months of Captivity."[20] After detailing the killing of one woman, Hubbard, taking a more measured approach, goes on to state, "And to prevent mistakes, let it here be observed, that none of the women were abused, or murthered, but one that was big with child, and unable to travel . . . No credit is to be given to any other reports of Cruelty towards any English Woman in that part of the Country."[21] The differences between the ascriptions of meaning regarding King Philip's War, as well as the competing historical accounts of the attack on Lancaster, are reflective of the fissures within Puritan society at the time. These contrasting views also mirror the clerical rift between those who tended to prefer the ritual observance of celebratory days of thanksgiving and others who favored self-rebuking days of humiliation and fasting.

As the historian Perry Miller has noted, the choice between these divergent religious outlooks can be traced to the Antinomian controversy, which dates to the Massachusetts General Court's decision to exercise its sovereign political authority, acting independently of the New England churches and "voting for a fast for January 19, 1637."[22] In her analysis of these events, Michelle Burnham has characterized the religious disagreement as "the earliest large-scale social, political, and theological crisis in the Massachusetts Bay Colony."[23] In the context of ministerial responses to the rising tide of armed conflict with Native peoples, this internal social struggle—between adherents to what Miller has characterized as opposing "ritualistic responses"—was most commonly expressed in efforts to concretely link their efficacy to the unfolding events of King Philip's War.[24] Even when days of humiliations and fasting failed to bring a reprieve from Native offensives or to anticipate significant military gains in the prosecution of the war, "the clergy had a ready explanation: the people had not sufficiently humbled themselves."[25]

The causative association between ritual and result that Mather plots throughout his A *Brief History of the Warr with the Indians of New-England* certainly supports Miller's observation. Throughout the rather austere chronicle of King Philip's War, in which Mather makes numerous references to the observance of humiliation days, his descriptions are frequently accompanied with news of military setbacks that "seems to argue something of a divine forsaking, and displeasure in heaven against us."[26] After enduring a number of humiliation rituals, English settlers grew weary of the ineffectiveness of these self-abasing ordeals, which in due course, as David Levin notes, "lead authorities to try a Day of Thanksgiving, which was immediately rewarded by news of King Philip's death."[27] It is intriguing that this theological dispute is also reflected in the sermon of Joseph Rowlandson that accompanied the original Boston edition of Rowlandson's narrative and is glossed in its subtitle as being "a Sermon preached at Weathersfield, Nov. 21. 1678. Being a Day of Fast and Humiliation."[28] Reverend Rowlandson's preference for self-rebuke over celebration seems to align him on the side of Mather, at least on this point.

At the most fundamental level, the clearest distinction between these two competing religious perspectives was one of intensity. Those who, like Hubbard, sought a more reflective explanation for historical events tended to favor days of thanksgiving, while adherents of humiliation, such as Mather and his authoritarian followers, tended to explain historical events almost exclusively in the context of divine providence, predicated on the maintenance of a dogmatic system of spiritual reward and retribution. As Nelsen observes, Hubbard, in his sermons and writings, often "stressed the danger of leaning too far in favor of religious intolerance" and frequently issued warnings against falling under the influence of men such as Mather, who "had set themselves up as unapproachable paragons of religious virtue."[29] Mather's *Heavens Alarm to the World*, a sermon published in 1681, provides another exemplary demonstration of providential historiography. As in his previously published A *Brief History*, Mather sublimates the events of King Philip's War within the hermeneutical context of God's providential retribution throughout this work, warning, "the sins which are amongst us, are surer and blacker signs of judgement then any signs in heaven, that we may think of."[30] While the historiographic model advocated in both his A *Brief History* and *Heavens Alarm* functioned as a pervasive reminder of God's active involvement in the lives of his chosen people, it could also be viewed as a means of absolving Puritan settlers of the moral and ethical responsibilities of their actions toward Native peoples. Mather seems to suggest just such a function at the end of his more comprehensive account of the Puritan settlements, *A Relation of the Troubles which have hapned in New-England*

(1677), which ends with the statement, "This is the Lords Doing, and it is marvelous in our eyes."[31] In many respects, the implicit purpose of Mather's *Heaven's Alarm,* as well as other works such as *Illustrious Providences, The Wicked Mans Portion,* and many of his other sermons and writings, as with Rowlandson's *The Soveraignty and Goodness of God,* is to reinscribe the meaning and significance of historical events within the context of Puritan doctrine.

The anonymous author of "The Preface to the Reader" and purported friend of Rowlandson, Ter Amicam, makes the merging of individual experience and providential design explicit in this description of *The Soveraignty and Goodness of God*: "here you may see an instance of the faith and patience of the Saints, under the most heart-sinking tryals; here you may see, the promises are breasts full of consolation, when all the world besides is empty, and gives nothing but sorrow."[32] This passage, which according to Derounian-Stodola[33] "was probably written by Increase Mather,"[34] emphasizes Rowlandson's status as a devoted partisan of the Puritan cause. Carroll takes an even stronger view, as she lists Ter Amicam *as* Increase Mather in the index of her book, *Rhetorical Drag.*[35] It also bears noting that the Willard text, containing the recycled leafs of the lost first edition of *The Soveraignty and Goodness of God* as binding material, also bears a prefatory "To the Reader" provided by none other than Increase Mather.[36] The courageous actions attributed to Rowlandson in the face of her captivity are presented as exemplars to be admired and emulated, while simultaneously depicting the broader context of events as manifestations of God's providential judgment. Just such a means of historical understanding was advanced by a declaration of the Massachusetts Bay Council at a meeting held at Boston on September 17, 1675. In the statement issued by the council—which details the "sins, whereby [God] hath been provoked" and is included in Mather's *A Brief History*—blame for Indian attacks is placed squarely on the backs of the settlers: "we have greatly incensed him to stir up many Adversaries against us, not only abroad, but also at our own Doors (causing the Heathen in this Wilderness to be as Thorns in our sides, who have formerly been, and might still be a wall unto us therein; and others also to be a Scourge unto us)."[37] As it happens, the actions perpetrated by the Indians against Rowlandson throughout

The Soveraignty and Goodness of God are also referred to as a scourge, such as when describing their precarious situation in the Twentieth Remove, "though many times they would eat that, that a Hog or a Dog would hardly touch; yet by that God strengthened them to be a scourge to His People."[38]

The significance of Rowlandson's affective testimony in the face of such challenges, in terms of both the social value and persuasiveness her narrative carried in Puritan society, was predicated on the nature and intensity of the suffering she endured, as well as the sense of piety displayed in her acquiescence to her role as penitent. For New England audiences, Rowlandson's account offered the powerful illusion of a narrative voice that was independent of clerical authority and control. In contrast to the writings of Mather and Hubbard, Rowlandson could be perceived as speaking from her own harrowing experience, which was, at the same time, offered as the shared experience of her fellow settlers. Just as the account of Rowlandson's captivity acted to reinforce and strengthen notions of purpose and order in the Puritan community, through its function as a war machine and as a vehicle of deterritorialization, it also had a devastating impact on the Native peoples beyond the walls of the plantation garrisons, who were defined as little more than demonic instruments of God's divine punishment.

In a theological endorsement of Rowlandson's text, Ter Amicam reminds readers of the purpose of the narrative, stating that "once and again you have heard, but here you may see, *that power belongeth unto God*; that our God is the God of Salvation, and to him belong the issues from Death. That our God is in the Heavens, and doth whatever pleases him."[39] In an artfully composed deployment of metatextual referentiality, Ter Amicam testifies to the veracity of Rowlandson's account, to create a circuit in which it both confirms and is confirmed by Mather's historical and ecclesiastical texts. While God's judgment took the form of Indian depredations and lamentable captivity for unfortunate Puritans who strayed from the flock, it resulted in dispossession, enslavement, and death for untold Native people struggling to maintain their sovereignty and persist as distinct societies. Defined by Puritan writers as little more than instruments of divine retribution, Native subjects were stripped of their individual and collective agency, notwithstanding the assessments of scholars such as David Levin who read Puritan historiography as "a genuine effort to achieve what Mather called an impartial record."[40] The lack of agency and historical voice granted Native people is evident when examining Puritan histories such as those produced by Increase and Cotton Mather, as well as the work of contemporary Americanist scholars. In Levin's essay, for example, Native people appear as little more than ghostly specters, all but written out of the narrative of early New England history. The failure to acknowledge the historical significance of Native subjectivities is apparent in Levin's description of the challenges faced by the newly arriving settlers into North America, whom are described as "a small band oppressed by English authorities, and later overwhelmed by the impossible demands of their financial backers in Old England and the great dangers in the New England wilderness."[41] Although one could argue that Levin's statement contains an oblique acknowledgement of the Native presence as a tacit element of the "great dangers" settlers confronted "in the New England wilderness," by sublimating Native people within the domain of wilderness in the manner of Puritan historians, the active presence of Native people as discrete agents within the historical context of colonial New England is appreciably diminished.

Having now examined the historical and cultural context out of which Puritan writing about King Philip's War arose, we can now return to a discussion of the Rowlandson text more specifically. Richard Slotkin and James Folsom, commenting on the scarcity of available biographical information on Rowlandson, admit, "we know little more of Mary Rowlandson than what she tells us in her *Narrative*, and what we do know is strangely unrevealing."[42] As far as can be determined, Rowlandson left behind no other writings, diaries, or letters that could offer any deeper insight into her experiences as a captive, or as a woman in seventeenth-century Puritan society. Add to this observation the fact that since the original manuscript of Rowlandson's narrative is not extant, it is impossible to say that the surviving versions of the text and the original manuscript that she is believed to have composed are commensurate. Almost everything we know of Mary Rowlandson that is contemporaneous to her life, outside of the minute amount of administrative and genealogical data more recently uncovered,[43] is embedded in the narrative of her captivity and in the histories written by Increase Mather. This alone warrants that a closer examination of the question of authorship be undertaken.

In an effort to reconcile the destabilizing effects that the dubious production and publication of *The Soveraignty and Goodness of God* have had in relation to the text's historical and literary standing, Derounian-Stodola has sought to clarify some of the more obtrusive textual inconsistencies between the three 1682 editions. Regarding the statement found on the title page that the text had been "Corrected and amended," which explicitly asserts the presence of an outside editor, she asserts, following Ebersole's lead,[44] "statements on title pages that a text has been 'amended, digested, revised,' must be taken very cautiously since such claims were often merely promotional."[45] As noted in the last chapter, the use of title statements to support the veracity or otherwise clarify ambiguities in a text marked by phrases such as "A True History" and "Written by her own hand for her private use," following the common practice of the time, served similar promotional and informational functions. After making an analogous claim concerning the use of the terms "amended, digested, revised," however, Derounian-Stodola is unable to marshal any compelling evidence that this was indeed the case in *The Soveraignty and Goodness of God*. What we are left with in the absence of corroborating evidence is the assertion of a distinct and specific condition deduced from an allegedly general practice, which is insufficient to account for the peculiarities of colonial printing.

In an attempt to explain the existence of "numerous examples of phonetic misspellings found throughout the first Cambridge edition," Derounian-Stodola cites a book by George Parker Winship published in 1945, as well as Robert K. Diebold's unpublished 1972 "Yale dissertation."[46] According to Derounian-Stodola, both Winship and Diebold attribute the supposed "misspellings" to the presence of a Native person known as James the Printer, who was known to have worked for a time at the print shop of Samuel Green. More recently, Jill Lepore has taken up this line of thought, constituting Printer as "intricately linked" to Rowlandson due to his alleged participation in the setting of the type.[47] Relying on the work of Samuel Drake and Hugh Amory, Lepore somewhat vaguely asserts, "in 1659 Printer was apprenticed to Samuel Green, Sr., and probably worked with him at the Cambridge Press until sometime in 1675."[48]

Moreover, Derounian-Stodola reveals that Winship arrived at his presumption by attributing the textual "errors" to the work of a typesetter who "had an undeveloped phonetic sense that governed his spelling."[49] Consequently, as it may be assumed of someone acquainted with English as a second language, "the misspelling of 'Addition' on the title page of the second edition, added to the other errors, points to James the Printer as the culprit."[50] The implications of this conclusion recall the tendency in colonial writing noted by Abdul R. JanMohamed, in which the non-Western Other "is cast as no more than a recipient of the negative elements of the self that the European projects onto him."[51] Even if such inventive conjecture were credible, why the "phonetic" errors would have been limited to just the title page and not expressed throughout the imprint, as would be expected given such inferences, is not addressed. Turning to the source of Winship's claim itself, found in his work, *The Cambridge Press, 1638–1692*, closer examination of the passages at issue reveals that his explanation of the source of "this curious error" was based on similarities that he identified with two other imprints: Eliot's *New Testament*, printed in 1680 and a reprint of Baily's *Practice of Piety*, printed in 1685.[52] The association of three texts from among the scores published within that five-year period at Samuel Green's print shop seems far from convincing and hardly provides the degree of authority that has been attributed to it.

That James the Printer's alleged phonetic deficiencies would be relevant to the typesetting of the seventeenth-century text in the first place seems odd, especially since the source in use as a copy-text would be either the previously printed edition or the original manuscript. Surely Winship and the critics citing him are not suggesting that Samuel Green dictated the title to James the Printer, who then unintentionally substituted "addition" for "edition" during the typesetting process as the result of his misperception between the two? Even so, this scenario itself would be taking liberties with Winship's deductions, because there is no evidence tying James the Printer to this hypothetical chain of events, only the assumption that "there had been nobody who is known to have had access to the Press who might be suspected of these verbal idiosyncrasies except the native helper renamed James Printer."[53] The obvious cultural implications of this story are problematic to say the least, especially given the tenuous nature of the linkage between the supposed corruption of the text and the attribution of Printer's culpability, which ironically mirrors the rhetoric of racial contamination and miscegenation that haunts the Indian captivity genre.

Moreover, the dubious claim that Printer is the most likely source of the supposed variants on the title page implies a fundamental misunderstanding of the complex skills and practices employed in the processes of typesetting, printing, and collation brought to bear in the production of printed books in the seventeenth century. A note supplied by Neal Salisbury in his own critical edition of *The Sovereignty and Goodness of God* suggests that the attribution of Ter Amicam, which he translates approximately as "thy three-fold friend," should be read as Per Amicam, "by a friend," as it is rendered in subsequent editions.[54] This example recalls the present discussion about James the Printer's alleged involvement in the text, and I wonder if critics might also want to attribute this error to him as well. Read another way, one is left to ponder if the identification of the author as Rowlandson's three-fold friend could be a veiled indication of this author's different roles in the production of the text. This may seem an unlikely possibility, but no less so than the story of Printer's involvement in the "errors," which have attained a level of acceptance that far exceeds what is justified by the available facts.

Typifying the widespread purchase of linguistic assumptions such as these, Lepore goes on to point out the seemingly obvious "misspelling" in the title of the narrative itself, rendering it awkwardly as, "*The Soveraignty [sic] and Goodness of God*."[55] The reading of "Soveraignty" as a "misspelling" that necessitates an obligatory "[sic]" is made even more conspicuous, and ironic, in light of the declaration that opens Lepore's work, in which she states, "this is a study of war, and of how people write about it."[56] While the claims surrounding the role of James the Printer and his alleged role in contaminating the spelling of words found in *The Soveraignty and Goodness of God* seem to provoke more questions than they answer, such conjecture also fosters a confusing and erroneous understanding of the historical evolution of the English language, which was undergoing a period of intense change during this time. The state of English language as it was conceived and used during the seventeenth century was typified by a conspicuous lack of a standard orthography in regard to both spelling and pronunciation.[57]

One could just as easily claim that because the publication of literary works by female authors was exceedingly infrequent during this time, and even more so in the patriarchal world of colonial New England, as Derounian-Stodola and Levernier confirm,[58] it is presumptuous to assume that Rowlandson's text would be treated in the same way as one produced by a male writer. Aside from Anne Dudley Bradstreet's posthumous collection of verse, published under the title *Several poems compiled with great variety of wit and learning*,[59] little else written by female authors made its way to publication in New England during the period of Puritan rule.[60] Among the factors that contributed to this univocal state of literary affairs is that, as late as 1655, the literacy rate among women in the New England colonies was still well below fifty percent.

The journals of John Winthrop provide much insight into the patriarchal social structure that dominated the Puritan colonies during the seventeenth century. In an entry dated April, 1645, for instance, Winthrop describes an incident in which the Governor of Hartford had brought his wife to Boston for treatment after she "had fallen into a sad infirmity," resulting in "the loss of her understanding and reason."[61] The source of this mysterious ailment was, according to Winthrop, attributed to the woman's preoccupation with "reading and writing," which, he goes on to suggest, could have been avoided "if she had attended her household affaires, and such things as belong to women, and not gone out of her way and calling to meddle in such things as are proper for men, whose minds are stronger."[62] Although such notions were expressed in Winthrop's private journals nearly forty years before Rowlandson's narrative was published, given the obstinate nature of Puritan society, in which women who did not adhere to the standards imposed by the patriarchal leadership were routinely ostracized and punished for their aberrant behavior, it would seem safe to assume that even a woman of Rowlandson's social standing may not have been exempt from such strictures. While deep-seated gender bias and discrimination persisted throughout the seventeenth century—as the Salem witch hysteria indicates—continuing outbreaks of systematic gender suppression and violence suggest that little progress had been made from the time of Winthrop.

In light of these additional historical details, it is only natural that questions concerning the production of the narrative of Rowlandson's captivity would continue to persist. As Carroll observes, "indeterminate authorship is a hallmark of earlier women's captivity narratives; scholars routinely note the difficulty, even impossibility, of ascertaining whether a captive woman actually wrote the text herself or dictated it (with interpolated 'improvements'), or whether another, usually male, hand actually composed the text."[63] Based on the preponderance of the evidence regarding *The Soveraignty and Goodness of God,* it is reasonable to assume that the version eventually published had undergone at least some degree of "correction" and/or "amendment." This conclusion compels us to address the thorny questions of authorship and intent, as well as the degree of outside influence that was imposed upon the text, and ultimately, to confront the even more difficult and fraught question: by whom and for what purposes was *The Soveraignty and Goodness of God* produced?

It seems natural that if there were another "hand" involved in the production of the narrative of Rowlandson's captivity, her husband Joseph Rowlandson, along with Increase Mather, would be among the prime suspects. Considered alongside the previously cited examples in chapter 3—detailing the similarities in word choice, phrasing, and narrative structure apparent in the formulaic openings characterizing the sudden attack by the hostile Indians, as well as the frequent interpolation of Biblical scripture discussed in chapter 2—this information offers compelling circumstantial evidence to support the involvement of the Reverend Increase Mather. Derounian-Stodola has also recognized some of the similarities identified thus far and pointed out additional parallels between the "racist tags" that appear in Rowlandson's narrative and the preface attributed to Mather, as well as a "second narrative anomaly that may indicate the pen of a minister-editor,"[64] inserted into the Twentieth Remove,[65] where a "three-page list of providences . . . interrupts the story at a crucial stage."[66]

Nevertheless, in the face of this expanding catalogue of evidence linking the Rowlandson narrative and Mather's work, Michelle Burnham offers an alternative explanation for the so-called textual idiosyncrasies, claiming that Rowlandson's fractured narrative voice may be attributed to "her altered cultural subjectivity, an alteration produced by the extent and duration of contact with her Algonquian captors."[67] The tenuous nature of Burnham's interpretation is highlighted by the rather perplexing question of why the expression of Rowlandson's altered subjectivity would be confined only to the Twentieth Remove. The fact that the narrative of Rowlandson's captivity is, as Derounian-Stodola notes, "reminiscent of sermon stylistics and ministerial retellings of other captivities such as Cotton Mather's version of Hannah Dustan's" captivity works to undermine Burnham's interpretation and ultimately raises more questions than it answers.[68]

Derounian-Stodola attempts to untangle these narrative threads by focusing on several additional places in the text that prompt questions of authorship. Among these, she focuses on similarities with Cotton Mather's account of Dustan's captivity—first published in 1697—and, more generally, on the language employed in the aforementioned "The Preface to the Reader." The implicit weakness of conventional approaches to the Rowlandson narrative, however, are precisely those that Traister has identified. One of the implications of his argument is that scholarly perceptions regarding the Rowlandson narrative reflect a prevailing set of assumptions that are predicated upon Rowlandson's status as the primary author of the text. Hence, instead of following the textual evidence wherever it may lead, scholars all too often minimize the crucial implications that the aforementioned evidence could have on a reader's acceptance of the text as a valid source of historical knowledge. Derounian-Stodola implements this strategy by isolating the most suspect material to the opening description of the attack and to the Twentieth Remove, which she claims "are at odds with the more realistic and tolerant view the captive has of her individual captors elsewhere in the narrative."[69] As I endeavored to demonstrate in the previous chapter, the similar contentions of Burnham and Breitwieser—that Rowlandson indeed takes "a more realistic and tolerant view" of Native people and culture—is seriously undermined by the consistent use of demonizing rhetoric and descriptive techniques deployed throughout the narrative. Derounian-Stodola's inability to see the text as a unified whole stems from a critical approach in which she divides it into distinctive parts that are marked, on the one hand, by "Rowlandson's distinctive narrative voice," and on the other, with those "reminiscent of sermon stylistics."[70] Through this critical strategy she is able to address the questions raised by the uncanny similarities between Mather's work and the Rowlandson narrative as isolated elements apart from the narrative whole, which seems intended to undermine the possibility of Mather's concealed, but far more substantive, contributions.

Derounian-Stodola shows that Increase Mather had been involved in the affairs of the Rowlandsons since the time of Mary's captivity, when her husband Joseph "asked Mather himself to intercede with the Council to redeem his wife and children."[71] Joseph's intriguing encounter with Mather, coupled with inclusion of the initial description of Rowlandson's ordeal in Mather's aforementioned *A Brief History,* is suggestive of more than just a passing interest in Rowlandson's captivity experience. Despite the stylistic, structural, and philosophical similarities shared by the two accounts and other of Mather's works, however, Derounian-Stodola avers from further speculation and appears content in the belief that Mather had only a minor role in the production of Rowlandson's narrative. His involvement is viewed as functional, and thus innocuous, rather than creative and invested, since, as Derounian-Stodola further claims, "Mather was in a position to facilitate the publication of Rowlandson's narrative at the Boston Press because John Foster, and Samuel Sewell, printed many of his works."[72]

Citing Ter Amicam's preface to Rowlandson's text in support of this view, Derounian-Stodola endorses the conventional claim, as testified to on the title page, that Rowlandson "originally intended her story for private circulation until friends and relatives persuaded her to offer it for public consumption."[73] This line of reasoning is especially problematic when one considers the absence of supporting documentation and the suspicion concerning Mather's direct involvement in the writing of the "preface" and, at the very least, portions of the narrative itself. The validity of this explanation appears even less likely given the fact that Rowlandson's narrative was printed on the press of Samuel Green, not John Foster, which Derounian-Stodola offers forth as one of the reasons for Mather's influence. While criticism of this later point may seem relatively inconsequential, the identification of Foster as Mather's primary printer is misleading.

An inventory of Mather's oeuvre confirms that Green printed far more of his works than did Foster in the years leading up to the publication of *The Soveraignty and Goodness of God*, but given his great influence in New England society at the time, one wonders if such a point even matters. Counted among the most influential members of the Massachusetts Bay Colony throughout his life, and minister of Boston's original North Church, Mather would have had little difficulty getting his works published, regardless of the printer. Although Derounian-Stodola appears to accept at face value the statement found in the "Preface" about the composition and publication of the Rowlandson narrative, she misses the chance to further explore the ostensible motivations that lay behind Mather's anonymity and the related possibility that he may have been disposed to other unattributed contributions as well. A more systematic examination of the explicit similarities between Rowlandson's narrative and the writings of Mather reveals that there exists much more than a tangential relationship between his writings and those contained in the narrative of Rowlandson's captivity. In the section that follows, I attempt to draw critical attention to this issue by highlighting some of the more provocative textual connections that are suggestive of Mather's substantial contributions to the production of *The Soveraignty and Goodness of God.*

Noting the stylistic similarities previously discussed in chapter 3 concerning the dramatic opening of the narrative and the shared use in Rowlandson's account of distinctive racial terminology and specialized ecclesiastical concepts, it is difficult to understand why critics have long been so quick to dismiss the possibility of an outside contributor to the narrative proper. In the description of Metacomet's death and dismemberment at the hands of the English forces led by Benjamin Church, which appears in Mather's *A Brief History*, for example, the following Biblical comparison is employed: "and there he was (Like as Agag was hewed in pieces before the Lord) cut into fourquarters, and is now hanged up as a monument of revenging Justice."[74] In the section that Derounian-Stodola identifies as containing a "second narrative anomaly," in the Twentieth Remove of *The Sovereignty and Goodness of God*, a similar description is used to describe the audacity displayed by Rowlandson's Native captors: "Again, they would say, *This summer that they would knock all the Rougues in the head, or drive them into the Sea, or make them flie the Counntrey*: thinking surely, *Agag*-like, *the bitterness of Death is past*."[75] The mutual use of phrases in reference to Agag, King of the Amalekites, whom Samuel disembodied in retribution for his crimes against "the children of Israel when they came up out of Egypt,"[76] in these examples is provocative to say the least. That the reference is drawn from a Biblical story related to the escape of the Israelites from captivity in Egypt, which as we have already seen was a prevalent theme in the writings and sermons of Puritan ministers, works to further substantiate the involvement of a "ministerial hand."

In another example describing her captors' movements in response to the pursuit of English military forces, found in the Fifth Remove, the following detail is provided: "some carried their decrepit mothers, some carried one, and some another. Four of them carried a great *Indian* upon a Bier, but going through the thick Wood with him, they were hindered, and could make no haste."[77] The footnote provided by Neal Salisbury in his edited critical edition of *The Sovereignty and Goodness of God* offers an explanatory gloss for Rowlandson's distinctive use of the word "Bier," characterizing it as "a rare reference to a New England sachem being carried this way."[78] Readers wondering about the possible source of this "rare" description need look no further than Mather's *An Essay for the Recording of Illustrious Providences*,[79] in which he describes the observance of a ghostly apparition by a Dr. Frith, who while "lying on his Bed, the Chamber doors were thrown open, and a Corps with attending Torches brought to his bed-side upon a Bier; The Corps representing one of his own family."[80] The fact that this distinctive term appears in both *The Soveraignty and Goodness of God* and Mather's work, and could be read as a subtle means of associating Rowlandson's Native captors with the anti-Puritan English government headed by the catholic King Charles II, provides contemporary readers with yet another intriguing instance of intertextual association.

Besides these examples, similarities in vocabulary, usage, and spelling lend further support to the involvement of Increase Mather in the direct production of Rowlandson's text. For example, the frequent use of Latinate abbreviations such as "*viz*" and "*ver. ult.*" in the Rowlandson narrative, as shorthand for "namely" or "that is to say" find common usage in Mather's work and seems incongruous with the work of a lay author.[81] Additionally, in Ter Amicam's "The Preface to the Reader," as well as the captivity narrative itself, there is a correlation in the use of words ending with the letter *l* where a preference for a double *l* is indicated. In many of these cases, this similarity concerns the use of the adjectival suffix *–ful*, which is consistently rendered as *–full* in the "The Preface to the Reader," the captivity narrative proper, and in works such as Mather's *A Brief History*.[82] In the sermon of Joseph Rowlandson appended at the end of Rowlandson's narrative, also printed by Samuel Green, the now standard usage of the suffix *–ful* is instead used. The distinction created by this simple detail would seem to preclude his direct involvement in the writing process of *The Soveraignty and Goodness of God*, as well as the ascription of the other inconsistencies in the text relating to the processes of typesetting and printing, since it seems reasonable to expect that the same conventions would be found in Joseph Rowlandson's sermon, Ter Amicam's "Preface," and the Rowlandson narrative itself, were he the "ministerial hand."

The Third Remove contains a description in which Rowlandson is given a Bible by one of the participants in the raid upon Medfield. Attributing this act of Indian kindness to the work of God, Rowlandson gives thanks, stating, "I cannot but take notice of the wonderfull mercy of God to me in those afflictions, in sending me a Bible."[83] After taking the Bible she asks the anonymous Indian if she would be allowed to read it. "He answered, yes," and then she continues, "it came into my mind to read the 28. *Chap.* of *Deut.*"[84] Within the larger context of the narrative, this incident marks an important turning point in Rowlandson's experience as a captive, signifying the beginning of her psychological and spiritual transformation and her acceptance of God's providential judgment and mercy. Presented as if she had been led to the passage by the very direction of God himself, Rowlandson's voice gives the reader a glimpse into the overwhelming fear and hopelessness she and other captives may have experienced at such times:

> When I read it my dark heart wrought on this manner, *that there was no mercy for me, that the blessings were gone, and the curses come in their room, and that I had lost my opportunity.* But the Lord helped me still to go on reading till I came to *Chap.* 30 the seven first verses, where I found, *There was mercy promised again; if we would return to him by repentance; and though we are scattered from one end of the Earth to the other, yet the Lord would gather us together, and turn all those curses upon our Enemies.*[85]

Through the accounting of events given up to this point in her captivity, Rowlandson is not presented as one with a great familiarity of the Bible. Such is indicated by the sense of surprise in her reaction to the scriptural verses she describes reading at this point, which also suggests a lack of knowledge concerning descriptions of God's punishment for disobedience that are found throughout Deuteronomy and specifically in chapters 28 through 30. In terms of the narrative as a whole, this episode operates on multiple levels of significance. This passage serves essentially as a confessional admission of Rowlandson's sins, which reinforce the similarity of *The Soveraignty and Goodness of God* to the classic Puritan jeremiad. At the same time, it operates as a key metaphorical example that would be comprehensible to her fellow Puritan settlers, who are described as being "scattered from one end of the Earth to the other," ever more alienated from Puritan community as well as the authority and protection of God.[86] From this point in the narrative onward, the Bible that Rowlandson keeps in her possession provides a constant source of solace and serves as the tangible anchor point in the textual explanation for the interpolation of Biblical material into the narrative that unfolds.

When the issue of Biblical interpolation is examined more closely, one finds that a number of the verses used in *The Soveraignty and Goodness of God* were also commonly used in the sermons and histories of both Increase and Cotton Mather. Aside from their presence in the narrative of Rowlandson's captivity, the above-cited selection from Deuteronomy seems to be a particular favorite of Cotton Mather, appearing in both his anonymously published *Humiliations follow'd with Deliverences* (1697),[87] as well as in *A Pastoral Letter to the English Captives in Africa* (1698).[88] Cotton Mather's use of these particular scriptural examples represents a tangible connection between Rowlandson's work and that of the Mathers, which goes beyond what has been previously recognized. Near the end of another of Increase Mather's prefatory works, "To The Reader," this time accompanying his *A Relation of the Troubles which have hapned in New-England, By reason of the Indians there* (1677), he affirms his own purpose of "declaring the works of God,"[89] anticipating the expression of the same sentiment in Rowlandson's narrative published five years later.[90] In addition to the shared use of chapters 28–30 of Deuteronomy, the similar uncited passage from Psalms 46:8, "Come, behold the works of the Lord, what Desolations He has made in the Earth,"[91] which appears near the end of Rowlandson's description of the attack on Lancaster, is utilized in the same uncited manner in Cotton Mather's *Terribilia Dei* (1697), in his description of Indian attacks upon outlying Puritan settlements.[92] The breadth and complexity of the integration of these verses and their skilled application, which is consistent throughout the entirety of *The Soveraignty and Goodness of God*, in addition to the reiteration of themes present in Increase Mather's published sermons and histories, suggests his presence not only as the outside ministerial hand in question, but as the primary author of the narrative itself. Taken as a whole, considering the weight of the evidence presented and the theologically dense composition of the Rowlandson text, this conclusion should not come as a surprise.

In light of this evidence, it could be argued that Rowlandson herself is doubly captive in *The Soveraignty and Goodness of God*, both by the Native forces that attacked Lancaster and also by Increase Mather. It is my hope that this exegesis represents a step toward delivering her from the ideological and paternalistic subjection that Puritan historiography, and perhaps Increase Mather, have relegated her to. From the historical record itself, it is beyond question that Increase Mather had the opportunity, the means, and the motivation to bring this masquerade to fruition. Whether Mather was indeed the author, or another unidentified Puritan figure, the continued recognition of Mary White Rowlandson—a woman to whom no other writings in any form can be attributed and compared—as the true author of this deeply fraught narrative of captivity and war no longer seems tenable. In the absence of conclusive evidence—a veritable literary smoking gun—we are left to guess how this literary charade was ultimately put into practice. Nonetheless, what we do know is that in the six years preceding the publication of Rowlandson's narrative, Increase Mather had already written about the attack on Lancaster and Rowlandson's captivity numerous times, often in language starkly similar to that used in *The Soveraignty and Goodness of God,* and was intent on publicizing and exploiting the experiences of captives for his own benefit, as well as for the broader colonial efforts of Puritan society. As is the case with most widely accepted beliefs, the act of challenging entrenched narratives and introducing new knowledge is often met with resistance and discord. I expect that the same will be the case in this matter. Ultimately, however, the issue of the authorship of *The Soveraignty and Goodness of God* is not about preserving or dismantling the status of an indispensable text in the American canon, or calling into question the reputations of individual scholars and historians. Instead, the conclusions offered have grown out of an earnest desire to present a more full and accurate account of Mary Rowlandson's captivity and the broader context of King Philip's War surrounding it, which, lest we forget, had a devastating effect on Native peoples and communities in colonial New England.

Previous scholars seem to have just scratched the surface in their efforts to address the complexities relating to the production of the Rowlandson narrative. And, indeed, much more work still remains to be done. My effort to concretely connect the Rowlandson text to the writings of Increase Mather, which was not the original purpose of my research, was prompted by questions that emerged from my engagement with the primary documents available to me. The findings outlined above are the result of an investigative process that while being frustrating and tedious at times, reflect the insights that are indebted to the work of scholars such as Fredson Bowers, W. W. Greg and Ronald McKerrow. In the end it seems that the deficiencies in the recent scholarship on the narrative of Rowlandson's captivity lie not in the efforts of historians and scholars, but often in the critical approaches utilized to engage with colonial social and cultural history.[93] This state of affairs testifies to the power and durability of Puritan historiography and literature, whereby the colonial male subjectivity has become fixed as the normative, and thus legitimate, conception of American identity and experience. It seems as though Native people and subjectivities have been marginalized and excluded from colonial discourse for so long that many modern scholars have lost the ability to see them. The lived experiences of Metacomet, as well as Mary Rowlandson and other captives, during this traumatic period of intercultural conflict, however, demand that historians and scholars take a new, more culturally responsive and affirming approach. To do otherwise condemns us to the mistakes and oversights of past generations caught in the hermetic trap and binary logic formed by figures such as Increase and Cotton Mather, and reiterated by historians like George Parker Winship and Perry Miller. A common weakness of such work stems from the application of uncritical heuristic practices that become contingent upon uninterrupted circuits of reference and are further compromised by the complex cultural interplay between the functions of iterability, intertextuality, and literary interpretation.

5

Representing the Native in the Twenty-First Century

"A Strange Fish" Still?

I remember your name, Mary Rowlandson, I think of you now,
How necessary you have become. Can you hear me, telling this
Story with uneasy boundaries, changing you into a woman leaning
against a wall beneath a HANDICAPPED PARKING ONLY *Sign, arrow*
pointing down directly at you? Nothing Changes, neither of us knows
exactly where to stand and measure the beginning of our lives.

—Sherman Alexie, "Captivity"

AS ALEXIE'S WORDS BEAR witness, the events that transpired during the brief period of time between the attack on Lancaster and captivation of Mary Rowlandson in February 1676, and the death of Metacomet in August of the same year, continue to have an influence on the development of American literary and historical discourses. Through the vehicle of *The Soveraignty and Goodness of God*, Mary Rowlandson became a celebrated model of Christian piety and an enduring symbol of American frontier perseverance, with Native people cast in the role of demonic savages. The enduring influence of this depiction is evidenced by Edgar Allan Poe's *The Narrative of Arthur Gordon Pym of Nantucket* (1838), whose title character gives ironic voice to the anxieties of generations of

Americans looking out toward the vast unsettled frontier with a thirst for adventure, attended by the terrifying yet exhilarating fear "of death or captivity among barbarian hordes."[1] Herman Melville's *The Confidence Man* (1857) displays a similar, if not more developed, irony in his treatment of racism against Native people in a story related by one of the many riverboat passengers who inhabit the novel. Articulating the attitudes of the time, he observes: "true it is, scarce a family he knows but some member of it, or connection, has been by Indians maimed or scalped."[2] More recently, we have witnessed the publication of several texts focused on Indian captivity narratives. Jim Fergus's best seller *One Thousand White Women* (1998), Elmore Leonard's *The Tonto Woman* (1998), and Deborah Larsen's *The White* (2002) suggest that the American public's romance with the "tryals" of Indian captivity is far from dead. Suffused with descriptions of "the hardships and terrors of life on the frontier," according to an August 2002 *New York Times* book review, such works continue to resonate with modern readers.[3] Given the more nuanced portrayals of Indian people found in the

Figure 12. Engraving of a "typical" Indian attack on a frontier family, c. 1880s, from the author's private collection.

work of Fergus and Larsen, insofar as both deal with young white female captives who assimilate and adapt by varying degrees to Native culture, we can identify the symptoms of that age-old American malady diagnosed by Renato Rosaldo as "imperialist nostalgia."[4]

The significance and depiction of the life of Metacomet, on the other hand, has ebbed and flowed with the times, at once the demon savage stalking the New England wilderness and, at the same time, a tragic figure that haunts the psyche of an American people grown remorseful over the destruction of Native cultures. In 1820 Robert Charles Sands, with the encouragement of the Reverend James Wallis Eastburn, made his contribution to the nostalgic recuperation of Metacomet's legacy with the epic poem *Yamoyden, A Tale of the Wars of King Philip: in six Cantos.* Operating as an oblique challenge to colonial ideology, Sands evokes the spectral image of Metacomet mourning his failed insurrection against the English: "While unrevenged my kindred lie, / My nation's ghosts indignant cry; / And unatoned, my native lands / Must captive pass to stranger hands."[5] Reinforcing this imagery, Sands furnishes Metacomet with a lament against the frailty of historical memory: "When the last echo shall have died, / That spoke my tribe's expiring pride; / They quenchless font diminished not, / When Metacom shall be forgot."[6] In that same year, Washington Irving published his similarly romanticized sketch of Metacomet titled, "Philip of Pokonoket," as a corrective to what he viewed as the slanders and dishonor heaped upon Metacomet after his death.[7] More famously, John Augustus Stone rendered Metacomet a tragic national hero in his 1829 play *Metamora; or, The Last of the Wampanoags.*[8] Echoing the sentiments exemplified in Cooper's *Last of the Mohicans* (1826), Stone offers forth his own mournful homage to the "vanishing Indian." This body of work was given a new dimension in 1836 by the Pequot writer, William Apess, who became the first Native writer to address the legacy of Metacomet in his *Eulogy on King Philip.*[9]

Aside from John Easton's, *A Relacion of the Indyan Warre* (1675),[10] Washington's, Sands's, Stone's, and Apess's discursive texts are among the earliest in which Metacomet and his cause are sympathetically portrayed. According to Patricia Bizzell, Apess's inclusion of a speech attributed to Metacomet in his *Eulogy on King Philip* represents "the strongest possible challenge to the historical hegemony of his white audience, by allowing Philip a voice and a means of inscribing an Indian narration of the events into the written record for the very first time."[11] While John Easton's account of his meeting with Metacomet marks a significant moment leading up to King Philip's War, it wasn't until the publication of Metacomet's speech in Apess's work that he became knowable to general audiences.

In an article originally published in *The American Scholar*, Jill Lepore, addressing the assertions of scholars such as Bizzell, provocatively reads the proliferation of Native American speeches as a symptom of "how Americans' long-standing admiration for Indian oratory has subjected Indians to a shabby sort of historical ventriloquism."[12] While sympathetic to critics and historians "motivated by the hope of finding more native voices to balance a historical narrative," she calls into question the authenticity of speeches by Native leaders who bear witness to their colonial experiences.[13] Among the speeches attributed to Metacomet, Lepore examines those preserved by John Eliot, John Easton, and William Apess, as well as another found in the notebooks of a Rhode Island senator named Theodore Foster. Lepore provides an account of the rise of the "eloquent savage," positioning Apess at the confluence of a revisionist movement that began with Washington Irving's effort to redeem Metacomet's legacy by claiming him as "an American patriot."[14]

In response to the speech found in Apess's *Eulogy on King Philip*, Lepore remarks, "even Indians succumbed. In 1836 the Pequot Indian minister and activist William Apess gave a speech he attributed to Philip that began, 'Brothers,—You see this vast country before us, which the great Spirit gave to our fathers and us; you see the buffalo and deer that are now our support.' Apess had leaned so heavily on the speeches of western Indians that he neglected to remove the buffalo from the New England landscape."[15] Putting aside Lepore's unfamiliarity regarding the extent of North America's traditional bison range, which extended as far east as present-day New Jersey, Pennsylvania, and New York,[16] and their enduring memory in traditional stories, Lepore dismisses the speech, citing the use of "formulaic conventions" that led John Bougham to mock Forest's melodramatic figure in a parody titled *Metamora:*

Last of the Pollywogs.[17] Just how the derisive ridicule of Metacomet by a non-Native actor more than a decade after Apess's work was published offers any insight into the speech in question is strange to say the least.

The primary weakness in Lepore's analysis, however, is her association of Apess with authors such as Cooper and Stone who contribute to what Vizenor terms "the literature of dominance" on the sole basis of shared themes and subject matter. Taking such ideas to their logical conclusion, I wonder if Lepore would also see, for example, the work of Frederick Douglass as derivative of Richard Hildreth?[18] Instead, William Apess seems to express many of the qualities that Vizenor attributes to postindian warriors, who "hover at last over the ruins of tribal representations and surmount scriptures of manifest manners with new stories: these warriors counter the surveillance and literature of dominance with their own simulations of survivance."[19] William Apess was a crossblood Pequot writer who spoke out against the prejudice and racism he saw and experienced during his life and, like Douglass, did so in emphatic terms. The nature and effects of racism, prejudice, and discrimination is a theme that pervades Apess' work in both subtle and overt ways. A particularly striking example from his own experience is offered in *Eulogy on King Philip:* "About two years ago, I called at an inn in Lexington; and a gentleman present, not spying me to be an Indian; began to say they ought to be exterminated."[20] Always aware "that our reading of the past determines our understanding of the present,"[21] Apess asserts his historical voice in a way that is implicitly contrasted with the hyperbolic style of Puritan historians, stating, "I took it up in our defense, though not boisterous but coolly; and when he came to retire, finding that I was an Indian, he was unwilling to sleep opposite my room for fear of being murdered before morning."[22] The deep irony expressed in this example where a member of a Native community decimated by centuries of systematic violence is met with anti-Indian hatred and terror speaks to the power of the images that pervade Indian captivity narratives and frontier histories. We could do much worse than to consider the words and ideas that Apess has left for us about colonial American history, even if, as Lepore asserts, "since literacy was often the last step in the path toward acculturation, educated Indians may not have been the most authentic spokespeople for their more numerous nonliterate countrymen."[23] The San Carlos Apache artist, Douglas Miles, takes exception to such essentialized cultural equations, stating that characterizations such as Lepore's in which authenticity is measured against acculturation, render modern Native people like him "a cultural ghost living in some no man's land, when this is still my country."[24]

Lepore takes a similar critical stance regarding the example of the speech promoted by Foster, which he claimed "had been made by Philip in 1675, evoking 'the True Reason of this War,' and originally transcribed, he said, by John Borden."[25] After invalidating this source, which Lepore speculates to be a "heavily edited and embellished" version of Easton's account of Metacomet's words,[26] as part and parcel to "the cult of the eloquent savage,"[27] she insists that the image of Metacomet that comes down to us through the literary record is largely one of fictive creation. The assumption regarding the irretrievable absence of Metacomet's authentic voice—one at the center of Lepore's analysis—seems to rest on the implicit privileging of literacy and writing as the exclusive domain of reliable communication. Lepore draws a distinction between Cotton Mather and Metacomet as a case in point, asserting, "Mather's prose is not routinely modernized; his sermons are not rewritten to address contemporary concerns; his exhortations do not appear on billboards. Even eloquent patriots like Patrick Henry, whose words we still cite today, are not willfully modernized or deliberately misquoted. Their words, we believe, exist in time and in space; they are real, historical, written, and thus immutable. As a result, historians can reliably know Cotton Mather and Patrick Henry in ways they cannot know King Philip."[28] This statement is not only dismissive of Native-centered knowledge conveyed through oral tradition and storytelling practices that are assumed to be inaccessible, unstable, and unreliable, but it also displays a perilous faith in written colonial texts. Lest we forget, written words merely stand in for speech, and we all know that both can carry a lie. And as Metacomet's complaint to Easton bears witness, he was well accustomed to the lies of the English. In another way, Lepore also seems to be reiterating the selfsame privileging of presence over absence that my work seeks to address, whereas in her essay, English writing articulates reliable knowledge where Native speech and writing cannot.

The dichotomy between written and oral modes of expression that Lepore implies is taken up in a different manner through the voice of the slave, Florens, in Toni Morrison's *A Mercy* (2008). After being sent on a journey to secure the services of a healer for her sick Mistress, Florens laments, "with the letter I belong and am lawful. Without it I am a weak calf abandon by the herd, a turtle without shell, a minion with no telltale signs but a darkness I am born with, outside, yes, but inside as well and the inside dark is small, feathered and toothy."[29] One is left to question whether or not Metacomet, similarly without a letter, is also left abandoned and forlorn, even despite the words others have deployed in their inadequate attempts to recall his presence. Perhaps distracted by a search for Metacomet's authentic essence, Lepore calls into question every source but one, a little-known letter to the General Court taken down by his scribe, Tom Sancsuik, in 1671, and thereby reduces Metacomet to a veritable nonentity, forever silenced by his lack of an unadulterated voice.

The problem with such assertions is that the very aims of recovering and restoring Native subjectivities to the historical record falls victim to an adherence to a standard of confirmation that is much more rigorous than that applied to documents of the colonial culture. This particular brand of privilege and marginalization is evident in the critical reception of *The Soveraignty and Goodness of God*, which has long held the status of celebrated literary classic and invaluable source of historical and ethnological knowledge. Despite the authority explicitly afforded this text, Lepore's own writing seems to reflect a deeper suspicion about its accessibility. In the section of *The Name of War* concerning Rowlandson's position within the context of King Philip's War and Indian captivity, Lepore struggles to resolve her conclusions in the face of historical indeterminacy as she declares:

> Her words *must have* had a powerful effect on those who read them . . . Like Rowlandson, many colonists had *probably* pledged to die rather than be taken captive by Indians, . . . Still, adult,

> able-bodied, and specially male colonists who offered little resistance to capture *may have* been judged harshly, their easy capitulation seen as a sign not only of weakness but also, *possibly*, of a willingness to abandon English ways. Returning captives were no doubt welcomed back into English society, but some were also *probably* feared and, to a certain extent mistrusted. A few colonists *may have* even believed that having lived among the Indians left a former captive contaminated by the influences of Indian society and Indian culture."[30]

The hesitancy Lepore displays (emphasis mine) in writing about Rowlandson's captivity is reflective of its shadowy and unstable origins.

It is my contention that the words attributed to Metacomet in Easton's *Relacion of the Indyan Warre* and Apess's *Eulogy on King Philip* are of equal or even greater significance to the deeply problematic testimony of Mary Rowlandson, while being infinitely more valuable in terms of their unique contributions to the historical record. It is more than a bit ironic that Metacomet's quoted words, few as they may be, manifest in a greater number of different texts than do Rowlandson's, which are confined to the pages of *The Soveraignty and Goodness of God* and its numerous reprintings. The annulment of writing by and about Metacomet has the effect of short-circuiting the process of historical inclusion through the displacement or erasure of the named subject, effectively confining Native trauma to a perpetual condition of what Cathy Caruth terms "unclaimed experience." Counter-narratives to hegemonic colonial discourses constitute, according to Caruth, "a new mode of reading and of listening that both the language of trauma, and the silence of its mute repetition of suffering, profoundly and imperatively demand."[31] As Vizenor reminds us, "Native American Indian identities are created in stories, and names are essential to a distinctive personal nature, but memories, visions, and the shadows of heard stories are paramount verities of a tribal presence."[32] Any discourse that acts to deny the Native presence inevitably becomes an alibi for the exclusion of historical witnessing of writers and historians responsive to Native subjectivities, revealing the ensconced fissures that lie beneath the surface and retain the capacity to give voice to a conception of history that is multivocal and rhizomatic in nature.

In much of the recent scholarship addressing the colonial period, the portrayals of Native people in New England that appear in the sermons and histories produced by William Bradford and Increase Mather, or in captivity narratives such as *The Soveraignty and Goodness of God,* are most often approached through the narrow context of colonial historiography and Calvinist doctrine, if at all. In the all-too-common turn of Puritan texts, the historical agency of Native people was inscribed with meaning through discourses predicated on the hermeneutics of divine providence, Christian conversion, and redemption that functioned to marginalize and silence Native subjectivities. Unfortunately, far too many contemporary critics seem to abide the authoritative inertia of conventional modes of historical explanation that circumscribe the analysis of colonial North American literary texts. This unfortunate tendency leads invariably to a situation in which scholars find themselves contributing to or deconstructing theoretical lines of thought with only sporadic attention to the corporeal presence of Native people in colonial history.

The collective amnesia concerning Native American historical agency that typifies New England literary discourse, where some of the most brutal practices of extermination and genocide were put into practice and codified into colonial law, is still operant and often pertains to incidents of extreme violence. In May of 1756, for instance, Robert Hunter Morris, the Lieutenant Governor and Commander in Chief of the Province of Pennsylvania, issued a proclamation aimed at the extermination of the Delaware Indians. In this document, Morris authorizes "for the scalp of every male *Indian* enemy, above the age of Twelve Years, produced as Evidence of their being killed, the Sum of *One Hundred and Thirty Pieces of Eight.*"[33] Unfortunately, the practice of offering rewards for the scalps of Native people is not an aberration in American history, as similar measures instituted in Boston (1722); Halifax, Nova Scotia (1749); Philadelphia (1780); and Blue Earth County, Minnesota (1865), tragically attest. In fact, such brutal practices were often inherent to the larger processes of dispossession and deterritorialization that extended into the early twentieth century.

As I have endeavored to show throughout this work, historians and critics alike have displayed a disquieting tendency to reiterate the claims and assumptions of their predecessors, often repackaged in light of the most recent theoretical trends. And while the perspectives critics have taken in regard to *The Soveraignty and Goodness of God* have varied greatly, far too often this preference contributes to the preservation of an historical attitude that is often woefully inadequate and exclusionary. In its fundamental being, this category of historical and literary work is often predicated on the long-standing and systemic neglect of Native subjectivities, unconscious or not, and has come to represent symptoms of the perva-sive nature of intercultural conflict stemming from the struggle over land and resources throughout North America. Our collective failure to systematically address the fundamental issues regarding the persistent encroachment of European and American settlers onto the lands of Native peoples, and the concomitant social pressures brought to bear on affected populations, enables critics to avoid the contentious historical questions raised by these conditions, while evading the potential backlash associated with challenging entrenched narratives, cultural hegemony, and America's exceptionalist inheritance.

The striking timidity of critics and historians to candidly address conflicts over North American land and property, as well as the often attendant issues of racial discrimination, oppression, and cultural hegemony, which were crucial factors that led to the intense hostilities exhibited during King Philip's War, is problematic to say the least. While relatively brief in its duration, this conflict represents but one instance in a long line of similarly treated military engagements that demonstrate the fundamental challenge that the absence of Native subjectivities embodies in the scholarly discourse concerning Indian captivity narratives and American literary discourse in general. The situation that results anticipates the experiences of other marginalized and oppressed groups in American history, whether relating to African American, Asian American, or Latina/o people similarly subjectified. It is important, however, to acknowledge that any such historical or literary texts can only ever possess the power and authority we choose to grant to them.

The development of anticolonial counter-narratives in the form of slave narratives, Indian boarding school narratives, and memoirs detailing the experiences of Japanese Americans confined to internment camps during World War II, to cite but a few examples, illustrate the liberating capacity and subversive promise of written and spoken words. Henry Louis Gates, for instance, describes slave narratives in precisely these terms: "it was only the black slaves in the United States who—once secure and free in the north, and with generous encouragement and assistance of northern abolitionists—created a *genre* of literature that at once testified against their captors and bore witness to the urge of every black slave to be free and literate."[34]

Frederick Douglass's firsthand testimony, the *Narrative of the Life of Frederick Douglass*, works to challenge and overturn the formulaic demonizing binaries endemic to the captivity narrative genre in an angst-ridden description of slave hunters following his escape from bondage: "in writing to a dear friend, immediately after my arrival to New York, I said I felt like one who had escaped a den of hungry lions . . . I was afraid to speak to anyone for fear of speaking to the wrong one, and thereby falling into the hands of money-loving kidnappers, whose business it was to lie in wait for the panting fugitive, as the ferocious beasts of the forest lie in wait for their prey."[35] Clearly, the invocation of demonizing animal imagery represents a direct challenge to the dominant historical and literary discourses that operated to render Native and African American subjectivities voiceless. Commenting on Douglass's mastery of the affective capacities of both oral and written English, Gates further observes, "Douglass tells such a good tale that his text opens itself to all classes of readers, from those who love an adventure story to those who wish to have rendered for them in fine emotional detail the facts of human bondage—what it meant to discover that one was a slave and what one proceeded to do about it, while someone else was simultaneously busy doing all manner of things to keep the slave from imagining himself or herself otherwise."[36]

Articulating another challenge to "the literature of dominance,"[37] the Ojibwa activist Dennis Banks provides testimony to the legacy of Indian boarding schools: "There is one dark day in the lives of

Figure 13. Fugitive slave seized by slave hunter, c. 1880s, from the author's private collection.

all Indian children: the day when they are forcibly taken away from those who love and care for them, from those who speak their language. They are dragged, some screaming and weeping, others in silent terror, to a boarding school where they are to be remade into white kids."[38] Taking this line of thought one step further, the Dinè poet and scholar Laura Tohe reminds us that the colonial ideologies that led to the injustice of the Indian boarding school system did not affect only Native people, but demeans us all: "in the end there are no winners; there are only the victims and the survivors of an inhumane system, whether they are the colonized or the decolonized."[39] In this statement, Tohe reconceptualizes the zero-sum equation made by Aimé Césaire "that colonization . . . dehumanizes even the most civilized man; that colonial activity, colonial enterprise, colonial conquest, which is based on the contempt of the native and justified by that contempt, inevitably tends to change him who undertakes it."[40]

The not-so-conspicuous absence of Native subjectivities that pervades popular and scholarly discourse is especially ironic when we consider just how entangled the captivity narrative form has become in the broader discourse of discovery and conquest, serving as a vehicle for the systematic promulgation of disparaging stereotypes and explicitly racist imagery over the last three and a half centuries. The literary trope of captivity, with its insidious appeal, has not only been used to depict conflicts with Native and other non-Western peoples, but has also been used to demarcate the broader struggle of "civilized" European cultures to subjugate the very landscape itself.

Matthew Teorey, for instance, has shown how the narrative of Ernest Shackleton's expedition to Antarctica, *South* (1920), is characterized as a "captivity in the ice" and has become yet another manifestation of this resilient and versatile literary form.[41] Teorey further observes that the language and imagery used to construct imperialist conceptions of the Other, as with wilderness landscapes, is employed "to explain to contemporary readers that to conquer the 'other' one must simultaneously resist and adapt to its foreignness."[42] Hence, for the captivity narrative to achieve its most extensive influence, it was imperative that such accounts be accepted as factual by the reading public, which in colonial America included even the most educated and learned minds.

It is instructive to be reminded that the governor of the Plymouth settlement and patriarch of the first Thanksgiving, William Bradford, describes the Native people in ways that would become second nature to English colonial discourse, not only in North America, but in Australia and New Zealand as well: "The salvage people, who are cruell, barbarous, and most trecherous, being most furious in their rage, and merciless where they overcome; not being contente only to kill, and take away life, but delight to tormente men in the most bloodie manner that may be; flaying some alive with shells of fishes, cutting of the members and joynts of others by piecemeal, and boiling on the coals, eate the collops of their flesh in their sight whilst they live; with other cruelties horrible to be related."[43] As the evocation of the tropes of barbarism and savagery make clear, English colonists such as Bradford ensured the continued hostility between the settlers and their Native neighbors, while reinforcing their own personal authority and control over the arriving immigrant settlers.

Within the larger conceptual schema, such tactics worked to strengthen and unify the Puritan community through the negation of the Native Other. One of America's most venerable founding fathers, George Washington, responding, nearly 150 years after Bradford, to a report submitted by James Duane regarding ongoing negotiations with Native nations,[44] spoke in similar terms, legitimizing the use animalistic imagery in the depiction of Native people. Arguing for the use of treaty-making as an alternative to the seemingly unending cycles of retributive warfare on the American frontier, Washington promotes the efficacy of his preferred course of action:

> [P]olicy and [economy] point very strongly to the expediency of being upon good terms with the Indians, and the propriety of purchasing their Lands in preference to attempting to drive them by force of arms out of their Country; which as we have already experienced is like driving Wild Beasts of the Forests which will return as soon as the pursuit is at an end and fall perhaps on those that are left there; when the gradual extension of our Settlements will as certainly Cause the Savage as the Wolf to retire; both being beasts of Prey tho' they differ in shape.[45]

To discover just how central the notion of the inherent inferiority of Native people would become to American nationhood, we need look no further than the decisions handed down by the US

Supreme Court. Among precedent-setting Supreme Court decisions alone, the frequent use of demonizing language is nothing short of shocking. In one of the most famous legal decision in the corpus of federal Indian law, *Cherokee Nation v. Georgia* of 1831, Associate Justice William Johnson argued in his concurring opinion that Native nations could not be properly considered as independent sovereigns since they represented an "anomaly unknown to the books that treat of states, and which the law of nations would regard as nothing more than wandering hordes, held together only by ties of blood and habit, and having neither laws or government, beyond what is required of a savage state."[46]

Even in cases where the court issued decisions that recognized the inherent rights of Native people, the language of these decisions was virtually identical, following closely the manner of literary representation common to the Indian captivity narrative, as well as that of works produced by colonial writers such as John Winthrop, William Bradford, and Increase and Cotton Mather. In *Ex Parte Crow Dog* of 1883,[47] the court found that a Brule Lakota man by the name of Crow Dog, who had been charged and convicted of the killing of another Lakota named Spotted Tail, was not subject to Dakota Territorial law because he had already been punished in accordance to Lakota custom. Delivering the majority decision, Justice Stanley Matthews's reasoning reveals the degree to which conceptions of cultural and racial superiority were ingrained in American thought. Among his comments on the authority of the American judicial system in regard to Crow Dog's crime, and the validity of Lakota law, he writes, "it tries them, not by their peers, nor by the customs of their people, nor the law of their land, but by superiors of a different race, according to the law of a social state of which they have an imperfect conception, and which is opposed to the traditions of their history, to the habits of their lives, to the strongest prejudices of their savage nature; one which measures the red man's revenge, by the maxims of the white man's morality."[48] In his influential essay, "Theses on the Philosophy of History," Walter Benjamin declared, "there is no document of civilization which is not at the same time a document of barbarism."[49] Considering the examples cited from Bradford, Washington, and the Supreme Court, it seems that Benjamin's judgment was well justified.

Even in the work of an accomplished historian such as Richard Slotkin, the inclusion of Native subjectivities is far too uncommon, while being virtually nonexistent in the work of other influential historians such as Perry Miller and Samuel Eliot Morison. To cite but one glaring example of the type of cultural blindness that pervades the field, in the preface to Miller's work, *Errand into the Wilderness* (1964), he reveals the intent behind the book as an effort to set down "the massive narrative of the movement of European culture into the vacant wilderness of America."[50] Indeed, the notions of North America as *terra nullius* and *vacuum domicilium* have served as both effectual alibis for English colonialism and essential vehicles for deterritorialization since the seventeenth century. This is to say nothing of the neglect of Native subjectivities in much of the literary scholarship concerning literary descriptions of colonial warfare surveyed throughout this literary excavation.

Puritan writers were simply not equipped with a sufficient knowledge to formulate accurate cultural insights about Native people, nor were they willing to entertain intellectual possibilities that conflicted with their own established theological systems, especially since Native worldviews contrasted so sharply with the colonial order they sought to impose. As the Osage/Cherokee theologian George Tinker has pointed out, even the much-praised Puritan missionary, John Eliot, displayed a combination of "immigrant attitudes of superiority" and contempt for Native religious traditions that rendered him blind to the fundamental nature of Native culture and society.[51] Nevertheless, the lack of knowledge and the cultural blindness displayed by Puritan leaders does not excuse or explain why so many subsequent historians and scholars have obliquely accepted Puritan writings as an accurate and valid reflection of New England Native cultures.

A glance through some popular history books of the nineteenth century provides useful insight into just how widespread and enduring negative views of Native people have been in American discourse. In A. S. Barnes's *A Brief History of the United States*, first published in 1871, for instance, the author expresses the desire to convey "those important events in our history which every American citizen should know" to elementary school students.[52] Barnes goes on to characterize the pre-colonial "progress and education" of Native American people in terms that should now be all too familiar: "he made no advancement, but each son emulated the prowess of his father in the hunt and fight. The hunting ground and the battlefield embraced every thing of real honor or value. So the son was educated to throw the tomahawk, shoot the arrow, and catch fish with a spear. He knew nothing of books, paper, writing, or history."[53] The clear ethnocentric bias displayed in works like Barnes's should not be dismissed as the unfortunate words of the ignorant and uninformed. Instead, these examples serve as revealing anchor points in a persistent and systematic effort to marginalize the beliefs, traditions, and stories of Native people in order to render them historically irrelevant and invisible.

Historical marginalization is one of the primary concerns that Cherokee novelist Thomas King takes up in his comic masterpiece, *Green Grass, Running Water*. Among other historical figures such as Henry Dawes, John Collier, and Elaine Goodale, readers also encounter Mary Rowlandson ironically resurrected as a student in a course on Native American culture. Clearly struggling to make sense of a lecture regarding the experiences of Cheyenne, Kiowa, Comanche, and Arapaho warriors imprisoned at Fort Marion in 1874, "Rowlandson rolled her lips together and slid a pencil under her nose. 'Do we have to know all these guys' names? I mean, will they all be on the test?'"[54] The answer, as any teacher knows, is, "there's always that chance,"[55] but of course we can discern King's irony and understand that the disinterest towards such knowledge is the very root of the problem. The Blackfeet novelist, Stephen Graham Jones, takes an even more sarcastic approach by including Mary Rowlandson in the glossary of his 2003 novel, *The Bird is Gone: A ~~Monograph~~ Manifesto*. Not mentioned anywhere else in the novel, Jones' definition for Rowlandson as "still tied up, and liking it," conveys his sardonic skepticism towards colonial American history and the haunting significance of the Indian captivity narrative in American literature.[56]

Spurred on by King's and Jones's use of irony and satire, we can understand the predicament that emerges from the detached approach to Indian captivity narratives that many contemporary literary scholars have taken, displaying little interest in addressing the problematic issues of colonial oppression that is irreducible in the subject matter. Indeed, many seem content to explore theoretical concerns that engender the negation of Native subjectivities in deference to abstract philosophical concepts and highly specified historic experiences in which Native people have occupied little space. While scholars specializing in postcolonial and subaltern studies have begun to show increased interest in analyzing the effects of European, British, and American colonialism, and its lasting effects on the Indigenous inhabitants of North and South America, the field remains largely focused on colonial discourses emanating from Asia and Africa.[57] And while Native scholars such as Taiaiake Alfred, Jodi Byrd, Jeff Corntassel, Dale Turner, and Robert Warrior have all contributed to the dialogue between indigeneity and subaltern studies, there is still much work to be done in assessing Native American experience and its vital significance to Euro-American colonial discourse.[58]

As long as colonial mythologies such as those propagated by Indian captivity narratives continue to endure, Native subjects will continue to be presented through what Bhabha terms, "an arrested, fetishistic mode of representation within the field of identification."[59] It is a much rarer case indeed for a Native person to be represented as a captive of Euro-American military forces in a manner similar to what authors of captivity narratives depicted as the "tryals" and "sufferings" of settlers such as Mary Rowlandson, Quintin Stockwell, and Hannah Dustan, to name but a few. Colonial discourses have combined to classify Native cultures as barbarous and pagan, while the rhetoric of the Indian captivity narrative has contributed much to the marginalization of Native peoples through the negation of their historical voices. The intellectual apparatus behind the Indian captivity narrative, however, is challenged by the legacy of European colonialism, in which explorers frequently transported Native captives back to Europe where they would be displayed for a curious public, eager for a glimpse at the "savage" of North America. Practically every early explorer from Christopher Columbus, Amerigo Vespucci, and John Cabot to Hernándo Cortez, Vasca N´uñez de Balboa, and Juan Ponce de Leon was known to have abducted Native people as specimens and curiosities for the purpose of display and slavery.

Although documentation concerning the ultimate fate of those who survived the arduous journey across the Atlantic to England

and Europe is naturally scarce, the relative lack of information regarding these experiences does not mitigate the enormous suffering caused by this practice.[60] An enigmatic passage by an anonymous witness from *The Great Chronicle of London* (1502) describes an encounter with three Native captives "clothid in Beastis skynnys," presented to the Court by John Cabot: "noo man cowed undyrstand theym, and in theyr demeanure lyke to bruyt bestis whom the kyng kept a time aftyr. Of which upon ii yeris passed afftyr I sawe ii of theym apparaylyd afftyr Inglysh men in Westmynstyr paleys, which at that tyme I cowed not discern From Inglysh men tyll I was lernyd what men they were, But as For speech I hard noon of theym uttyr oon word."[61] Ironically, the sense of alienation and inscrutable silence attributed to these witnesses came to be seen as one of the defining characteristics of Native people in historical texts over the ensuing centuries.

Despite the supposed inability of Native captives to articulate accounts of their removes and give voice to their own experiences in foreign lands, nonetheless it seems that the very presence of these exoticized Native people had an indelible effect on those who encountered them. In English literature, one needs only to turn to the work of William Shakespeare to discover the enduring spectral presence of Native captives in Europe. In his tragicomic play, *The Tempest*, a text suffuse with colonial overtones, after catching a glimpse of the monstrous Caliban, the jester Trinculo ponders, "what have we here, a man or a fish? Dead or alive?—A fish, he smells like a fish; a very ancient and fish-like smell; a kind of not-of-the-newest-poor-john. A strange fish! Were I in England now, as once I was, and had but a fish painted, not a holiday-fool but would give a piece of silver. There would this monster make a man. Any strange beast there makes a man. When they will not give a doit to relieve a lame beggar, they will lay out ten to see a dead Indian."[62] Through the association of Caliban with the carnivalesque spectacle of traveling exhibitions of Native people common throughout the sixteenth and seventeenth centuries in England, Trinculo completes the circuit by inextricably linking the tyranny of abject representation to the exigencies of the colonial project.[63] Shakespeare's dramatic, and subversive, inscription of the colonial gaze of the Other brings the vital issue of representation and subjectivity into clearer focus. Analyzing the crucial issue of Native American representation and the axiomatic regime of power relations that define colonial systems of classification is just one way that contemporary scholars and writers can challenge the harmful stereotypes that typify conventional views of the past and continue to shape perceptions in the present.

The enduring influence of the captivity narrative form is nowhere more apparent than in the proliferation of images that have emerged from Iraq and Afghanistan following their invasion as the focal point on the War on Terror. Beginning with the March 2003 capture of Jessica Lynch and six other American soldiers of the US Army's 507th Maintenance Company in the Iraqi city of Nasiriyah, scenes of captive Americans flanked by menacing ranks of Iraqi soldiers and masked insurgents became a common fixture of the American media's coverage of the war. The deeply problematic nature of Native representation in American culture was placed in stark relief by the revelation that the code name assigned to Osama bin Laden by the US military was the name of a Native leader who, like Metacomet, took up arms to defend his homeland against colonial incursions in the nineteenth century: Geronimo, or Goyahkla, as he was known to the Chiricahua Apache. As thoughtless as this choice may have been, the ongoing demonization of Native American historical figures invokes the association of Native as savage and savage as terrorist in a way that reinforces the negation implicit in colonial discourse. This association echoes in the announcement in which the legacy of frontier history and cultural negation continues to haunt contemporary Native people: "The first round, a 5.56-mm. bullet, struck bin Laden in the chest. As he fell backward, the SEAL fired a second round into his head, just above his left eye. On his radio, he reported, 'For God and country—Geronimo, Geronimo, Geronimo.' After a pause, he added, 'Geronimo E.K.I.A.'—enemy killed in action."[64]

In a 2007 op-ed published in the *New York Times*, Susan Faludi noted the oblique relationship between the captivity narrative of Mary Rowlandson and this recent conflict, inscribing the coordinated terrorist attacks of September 11, 2001, within the same context as the Native assault on Lancaster in 1676: "In the weeks and months after 9/11, many commentators described the 'dream-like' mindset that the disaster had induced. They attributed our fugue to the 'unimaginable' unreality of the event. Nothing like this had ever happened before. But essential to our understanding of what that attack means to our national psyche is a recognition that it did happen before, over and over."[65] I wonder if Faludi, in her call for Americans to reclaim our "abandoned resolve," was aware of the implicit irony of her historical analogy as she associates the actions of Al-Qaeda with those of Native Americans led by Metacomet, who were desperately fighting to defend *their* homelands and ways of life.

Lepore similarly circumscribes the Native resistance to Puritan incursions led by Metacomet within the ready-made context created by colonial writers, whereby Native people are always already reduced to the status of aggressor. The questions and answers she poses in her introduction to *The Name of War* are revealing of the subtle cultural bias that continues to impair our understanding of colonial history: "But what really happened? Did the Puritans conquer? Did Metacom rebel? Did one Indian brother fight another? Did King Philip wage a war? Yes, yes, yes, and yes again."[66] The ease with which Lepore answers these questions is indicative of a conception of history in which the prescribed roles of sovereign and subdued, citizen and exile, are already fixed.

Faludi presents a similar view on this matter in *The Terror Dream* (2007), in which she asks, "what if the deepest psychological legacy of our original war on terror wasn't the pleasure we now take in dominance but the original shame that domination seeks desperately to conceal."[67] By referring to the Puritan campaigns against the original Native inhabitants of North America as "our original war on terror," Faludi reinforces a prevailing strain of historical understanding that is inextricably linked to the legacy of American exceptionalism, which she nonetheless seems intent on challenging. Her indecision calls to mind Philip Deloria's discussion of expectation and anomaly in the way Native people have been viewed in America.[68] It's as if Americans are simply not equipped with a language or conceptual framework that can comprehend Native people outside of their own self-perpetuating Manichean dualisms. As Faludi's words makes clear, the fear and loathing invoked by the horrific images of modern terrorism reaches to the core of America's national psyche and extends renewed meaning to the age-old struggle between the forces of good and evil, civilization and savagery, and Christian and pagan—recalling again a time, a place, and a world where the very fate of civilization is put into peril by savages who lurk in the dark and howling wilderness, waiting to descend anew upon unsuspecting settlements.

Afterword

"To the Victor Belong the Spoils": An Afterword on Colonialist History

GEORGE E. TINKER
(WAZHAZHE/OSAGE NATION)

WE INDIANS DARE NEVER forget "history is written by the winners." Some say this is a generalized adaptation of a quote that is attributed to Napoleon: "History is the version of past events that people have decided to agree upon." This is no less true of literary history or the history of a scholarly tradition in academic discourse; and as Edward Said demonstrated in his ground-breaking book, *Orientalism*, it is much the same dynamic that we have experienced under colonialism, whether we are dealing with literatures, histories, anthropologies, or comparative studies of colonized people. As we weigh who exactly the people in power are that have decided to agree upon the particular parameters of how to talk about past events (i.e., talk about the colonized *us*), the initial quote comes back into focus.

Especially under european colonialism—the specter that has haunted most of the globe since that famous series of proclamations by european christian popes (called "papal bulls") from 1452 to 1493, giving much of the world to either Portugal or Spain—it is the colonial conquerors who get the privilege of writing history, assuring us that the history they write is "*wie es eigentlich gewesen*," as it actually happened, a lingering reminder of Leopold von Ranke's simplistic romantic-era historiography of two centuries back. Yet Ranke's simplistic historiography still reigns supreme, it seems, when colonialist historians are writing about American Indian subjects, who are allowed very little voice or subjectivity of their own. So we are too often stuck with the colonizer's narrative, history as it actually happened in the colonialist historian's imaginary, histories and narratives in which we, the colonized, are typically silenced and stereotyped if not outright demonized even yet today.

In *Buried in Shades of Night*, Billy J. Stratton has written a superb postcolonial historiography, a new and wonderful account of puritan colonialist history associated with the english invasion and occupation of the land they renamed New England. Within this critique he focuses our attention on the so-called "captivity narrative" titled *The Soveraignty and Goodness of God*, long attributed to Mary Rowlandson as a personal memoir of her experiences. His is a very different reading of the Rowlandson text, however, and a different telling of the historical narrative that dominates the usual colonialist histories. Stratton eloquently argues that a particular narrative of the european (i.e., english) invasion of north America is deeply embedded in *The Soveraignty and Goodness of God*, one that continues, at least implicitly, to validate the invasion and conquest right up to our contemporary moment. Stratton's most pressing concern is the persistent and clear tendency of virtually all writers who write about this puritan period to completely circumvent or erase Native subjectivity in their telling of this history.

In his incisive argument with regard to Rowlandson and her purported text, Stratton brings what we might identify as the force of Said to bear on his reading of puritan literature. It becomes clear in this reading of the scholarly interpretive traditions around "Rowlandson" that scholars have a version of history that they have implicitly decided to agree upon. And that contemporary version does not have room for the voices of American Indians but invariably builds on the larger colonial narrative and succeeding colonialist histories. When interpretations of *The Soveraignty and Goodness of God* continue to presuppose that it was actually written by Mary Rowlandson as an accurate personal memory of her time as a captive of the Wampanoag Confederacy, they implicitly if not explicitly conceive of the colonialist invaders as victims and the victims as perpetrators. In a curious but pronounced reversal, these scholars implicitly defend the invaders (with their lies, propaganda, theft of land, and perpetual wars of conquest) over the actual injured parties, the original Natives of the land, whose defense of homeland against the christian invader is effectively ignored and erased. Whether it is modern (White) feminists who have a vested interest in celebrating the first publication by a woman in north America (utterly ignoring the racist content of *The Soveraignty and Goodness of God* in their analyses) or more serious scholars of the puritan american tradition who simply cave in to telling the version of past events that has become customary, the actual voices of Indian folk are systematically excluded. Indian subjectivity is erased.

It would seem that, once the historical narrative has been established in the colonialist public consciousness, it becomes very difficult to imagine an even slightly different telling of the story, let alone one that is wholly other. As a result, *The Soveraignty and Goodness of God* continues to be read so convincingly as objective history ("wie es eigentlich gewesen"). Since it became entrenched very early in puritan New England and in London as trustworthy historical narrative, it has been blithely accepted by successive interpreters over time, so that even today the authenticity of this text remains largely unquestioned by contemporary interpreters, who continue to presume Rowlandson's authorship and to recite the text's narrative as a true and factual history.

Stratton elegantly demonstrates that much of this *scholarship* is little more than what Indian folk might call a White lie, only this White lie is anything but trivial. Based on Stratton's detailed and exhaustive analysis, it seems clear that, rather than having been written by Rowlandson, the text was deeply influenced if not actually written as self-justifying propaganda by an influential puritan minister-polemicist who persistently engaged in what had already become stereotypical demonization of the colonized Other. Rather than Rowlandson's being the first text written in America by a female writer, it now seems much more likely to have been ghostwritten by the Reverend Increase Mather (an associate of Rowlandson's minister husband), exploiting Rowlandson's name to underscore his own production of puritan propaganda, which argued a consistent justification for christian war-making and conquest. If true, as I believe it is based on the available evidence, Mather exploits the experiences and memory of Mary Rowlandson as a screen, concealing his authorship in order to create the illusion of an ally in his own nefarious self-justification for christian conquest in the Metacomet War—usually called King Philip's War in puritan propaganda. If there is any actual history embedded in *The Sovereignty and Goodness of God*, it is a history of the intellectual and sociopolitical excesses of puritan colonialism and propaganda in north America rather than a history of the events that occurred during this puritan war of conquest. In other words, we might say this foundational colonial text was dripping with masculine english testosterone.

While his argument seems not only plausible but entirely probable, Stratton's book has already irritated some of the entrenched "puritan America" guild of scholars, who have made a habit of erasing Indian voice and Indian subjectivity in their telling of the puritan America story for so long that they can no longer even recognize themselves in a coherent critique. Overall, Stratton's critique of the vast literary and historical literature written about *The Sovereignty and Goodness of God* is certainly compelling. His analysis shies away from critiquing neither the mainstream colonialist historians nor the more contemporary, more liberal interpretations of this text. Indeed, he demonstrates quite presciently that even many of the most recent scholars who address this text fall into the same old intractable patterns of literary interpretation. This text certainly moves beyond contemporary writers such as Jill Lepore and even Michelle Burnham, two of my own favorites, challenging them to deal with Native subjectivity in their scholarship and to respond with new historical creativity. Stratton's critique is developed in such a systematic way that even those contemporaries he critiques should not but recognize its significance and validity. Ultimately, then, the greatest gifts of Stratton's book are its close reading of the texts and the development of a useful historiography, generating a particularly new literary history of puritan north America as conceived from a postcolonial vantage point. While the themes of this work span historical and literary concerns, Stratton's sophisticated analysis makes it much more than the sum of these discourses.

Buried in Shades of Night deals (postcolonially) with early forms of european/english (i.e., puritan) literary production emerging from north America soon after the onset of invasion and conquest. As a result, Stratton's text represents both a provocative critique of the captivity narrative genre and an exceptional historiographic analysis of the period (within the parameters of puritan writings and the historical events they disclose).

Stratton demonstrates that contemporary scholars, rooted in their own academic social imaginary, continue to participate, implicitly at least, in the deconstruction and erasure of the societies of the aboriginal owners of the land. Language has been intentionally erased by the colonizer, cultural practices have been seriously suppressed and eroded, and indigenous self-identity has been shamelessly and self-consciously attacked by the colonizer. Values, including scholarly values, have been replaced with a paradigm that continues to rely upon the inequity of the participants. It is, as Albert Memmi (in his historic *Colonizer and Colonized*) describes it, making "the colonized feel like a foreigner in his own country" (107). The erasure of Native subjectivity in modern historical treatments of puritan New England and particularly of the Rowlandson narrative finds yet another resonance in Memmi: "[The colonized] is in no way a subject of history any more. Of course, he carries its burden, often more cruelly than others, but always as an object" (92).

We American Indians who remain on this continent and have not forgotten the voices of our ancestors have come to expect contemporary colonial scholars to continue to produce colonial scholarship—whether they recognize themselves in the category of colonialist or not. Most, of course, are good-hearted people who have engaged long careers in academia without paying much attention to the aboriginal owners of this land and have seen no reason to begin to do so at this late date. After a while, it is easier to recite the old lies than to put creative energy in the hard research and theoretical reflection that Stratton calls us to. Indeed, we are still engaged in the process of recovering our own subjectivity and agency and, particularly, the historical subjectivities of those ancestors that the colonialists persistently tell us are no longer recoverable.

While erasure of the Native and Native subjectivity seems to have worked well enough for the colonial project up to the present, they, and by "they" I mean to include especially the professional academic scholars and critics of the euro-settler class, have much to learn about us and about their own history. But then they would have to listen to us and open themselves to our stories. Billy J. Stratton has given settler scholars some very clear direction in this stunning volume. wita wathonthakithe, wali we'-a-hno^{n}.

Notes

Introduction

1. See, for instance, John Winthrop's famous address, "A Modell of Christian Charity" (in *The Puritans: A Sourcebook of Their Writings*, vol. 1, revised edition, ed. Perry Miller and Thomas H. Johnson, New York: Harper and Row, 1963), delivered to the passengers of the *Arbella*, during their transatlantic voyage to Massachusetts Bay; as well as Increase Mather's *The Mystery of Israel's Salvation . . . Being the substance of several sermons preached By Increase Mather, M.A. Teacher of a Church in Boston in New England* (London, 1669); and William Hubbard's *The happiness of a people in the wisdome of their rulers . . . Preached at Boston, May 3d, 1676, being the day of election there* (Boston: John Foster, 1676). A sampling from some of the less well-known texts includes Nathaniel Morton's *New-Englands memoriall (1669) . . . published for use and benefit of present and future generations* (Cambridge, MA: S. G. and M. J. for John Vsher, 1669); Jonathan Mitchel's *Nehemiah on the vvall in troublesom times* (1671); and Elias Burling's *A call to back-sliding Israel* (1694) *. . . or his testimony for the crucified Jesus, our alone advocate in heaven* (New York: William Bradford, 1694).

2. This edition and translation, printed from 1560 to 1644, was produced by a group of Calvinist scholars and designed to challenge the legitimacy of the Catholic *Book of Common Prayer*, which, according to reformists such a John Calvin and John Knox, corrupted the word and intention of God.

3. Emory Elliott, *The Cambridge Introduction to Early American Literature* (Cambridge: Cambridge University Press, 2002), 9.

4. John Winthrop, "A Modell of Christian Charity," 195.

5. The phrase "howling wilderness" traces back to Deuteronomy 32:10 of the King James Bible, which states of Moses, "He found him in a desert land, and in the waste howling wilderness; he led him about, he instructed him, he kept him as the apple of his eye." The earlier translation, created by the English scholar William Tyndale, uses the similar phrase, "rorynge wildernesse." In the later example, and those that came to saturate Puritan texts, the perception of the wilderness as a dark foreboding place absent of God is apparent.

6. Winthrop, "A Modell of Christian Charity," 199.

7. Roy Harvey Pearce, *The Savages of America: A Study of the Indian and the Idea of Civilization*, rev. ed. (Baltimore: Johns Hopkins Press, 1965), 20.

8. Increase Mather, *A Brief History of the Warr with the Indians in New-England, (From June 24, 1675. when the first English-man was murdered by the Indians, to August 12, 1676. when Philip, alias Metacomet, the principal Author and Beginner of the Warr, was slain.) Wherein the grounds, Beginning, and Progress of the Warr, is summarily expressed. Together With A Serious Exhortation to the Inhabitants of that Land* (Boston: Printed and sold by John Foster, 1676), 1.

9. Edward Johnson, *A history of New-England. From the English planting in the yeere 1628. untill the yeere 1652. Declaring the form of their government, civill, military, and ecclesiastique. Their wars with the indians, their troubles with the Gortonists, and other heretiques. Their manner of gathering of churches, the commodities of the country, and description of the principall towns and havens, with the great encouragements to increase trade betwixt them and old England. With the names of all their governours, magistrates, and eminent ministers* (London: printed for Nath. Brooke, 1653), 24, 26.

10. William Bradford, *Of Plymouth Plantation: 1620–1647* (1856), ed. Samuel Eliot Morison (New York: Random House, 1981), 302.

11. See Francis Jennings, *The Invasion of America: Indians, Colonialism, and the Cant of Conquest* (Chapel Hill: University of North Carolina Press, 1975).

12. William S. Simmons, *Spirit of the New England Tribes* (Hanover, NH: University Press of New England, 1986), 3.

13. Homi Bhabha, *The Location of Culture* (New York: Routledge, 1994), 85.

14. George Armstrong Custer, *Wild Life on the Plains and the Horrors of Indian Warfare* (St. Louis: Sun Publishing, 1874). This work was also reprinted in 1883, 1886, and five times in 1891 following the events culminating in the Wounded Knee Massacre.

15. Wilcomb E. Washburn, ed., *The Garland Library of Narratives of North American Indian Captivities*, 111 vols. (New York: Garland, 1975–1983).

16. Annette Kolodny, "Review Essay," *Early American Literature* 14 (1979): 232.

17. Widely recognized by scholars as the first American novel, Susanna Rowson's *Charlotte: A Tale of Truth* was published in London 1791, but not in North America until 1794.

18. Roy Harvey Pearce, "The Significance of the Captivity Narrative," *American Literature* 19 (1947–48), 1.

19. Pearce, "Significance of the Captivity," 2.

20. It was not, however, the first captivity narrative written about events that took place in North America. See, for example, Cabeza de Vaca, *La Relacion* (1542); George Best, *A True Discourse* (1578); and Pierre-Esprit Radisson, *The Relation of my Voyage, being in Bondage in the Land of Irokoits*, written in 1665, but not published until 1858.

21. The unabridged title is *The Soveraignty and Goodness of God, Together with the Faithfulness of His Promises Displayed: Being a Narrative of the Captivity and Restauration of Mrs. Mary Rowlandson; Commended by Her, to All that desires to Know the Lords Doings to, and Dealings with Her; Especially to her Dear Children and Relations, The Second Edition Corrected and Amended, Written by Her Own hand for Her Private Use, and Now Made Publick at the Earnest Desire of Some Friends, and for the Benefit of the Afflicted* (Cambridge: Printed by Samuel Green, 1682). The first edition is no longer extant. Although the title's spelling is often modernized, I use the abbreviation, *The Soveraignty and Goodness of God*, throughout this work as a means of retaining the stylistic uniqueness and specificity of the original.

22. Known among his own people, the Wampanoag Pokanoket, as Metacomet, Metacom, and/or Pometacon, he was commonly referred to as King Philip by the English. Metacomet rose to the position of sachem in 1662 after the death of his elder brother, Wamsutta, also known as Alexander, who had himself assumed the sachemship the year before upon the death of their father, Massasoit. Massasoit is best known to non-Natives for providing critical aid to the fledgling Puritans during the early years of the Plymouth colony, granting him a prominent place in the mythico-historical complex of colonial New England.

23. Mather, *Brief History*, 46.

24. The use of such terminology, dating to the earliest English texts in colonial North America, helped to associate Native people with animals and define them as dangerous predators.

25. The Anishinaabe scholar, Gerald Vizenor, coined this term to describe the ways in which Native people have endeavored to resist colonialism, stating, "the character of survivance creates a sense of native presence over absence, nihility, and victimry. Native survivance is an active sense of presence over absence, deracination, and oblivion; survivance is the continuation of stories, not a mere reaction, however pertinent," 1. For applications of this concept, see Vizenor's *Survivance: Narratives of Native Presence* (Lincoln: University of Nebraska Press, 2008).

26. William Apess, *Eulogy on King Philip*, in *A Son of the Forest and Other Writings*, ed. Barry O'Connell (Amherst: University of Massachusetts Press, 1992), 132.

27. David Mitchell and Melissa Hearn, "Colonial Savages and Heroic Tricksters: Native Americans in the American Tradition," *Journal of Popular Culture* 32, no. 4 (1999), 114.

28. According to Thomas J. Holmes's short-title catalogue of Mather's work (*Increase Mather His Works: Being a Short-Title Catalogue of the Published Writings That can be Ascribed to Him*, Cleveland: William Gwinn Mather, 1930), over the course of his career, Mather authored 175 distinct texts, excluding the numerous reprints also printed during his lifetime.

29. Kathryn Zabelle Derounian-Stodola and James Arthur Levernier, *The*

Indian Captivity Narrative, 1550–1900 (New York: Twayne, 1993), 98. One result of the project was Mather's *An essay for the recording of illustrious providences* (1684), which, along with accounts of the miraculous recovery from injuries, the survival of shipwrecks, and other accidents, were also included descriptions of Indian captivity.

30. See Jacques Derrida's "Signature Event Context" in his *Margins of Philosophy* (Chicago: University of Chicago Press, 1982), 307–30, for an insightful explication of the function and consequences of iterability in regard to contextualization, interpretation, and representation.

31. Ibid., 315–16.

32. The captivity narrative of Mary Rowlandson was first published at Boston in an edition that is no longer extant. Before the year was out two more editions were printed on the press of Samuel Green in Cambridge, Massachusetts Colony, and another published in London by Joseph Poole.

33. For a detailed elaboration of these terms see, Gilles Deleuze and Félix Guattari, *A Thousand Plateaus: Capitalism and Schizophrenia*, trans. Brian Massumi (Minneapolis: University of Minnesota Press, 1987), 140–62.

34. At its most basic, the literature of dominance is comprised of those texts that function to delimit and redefine Native peoples and cultures as fabrications, simulations, and fakes in the Euro-American imagination. The proliferation of such texts and the images Native people that they contain contribute to, if not initiate, the "annihilation of tribal cultures" (9). See Vizenor's *Manifest Manners: Narratives on Postindian Survivance* (Lincoln: Bison Books, 1994), 9–15.

35. Vizenor, *Manifest Manners*, 8.

Chapter 1

1. See Paul Virilio and Sylvere Lotringer, *Pure War* (1983, repr., New York: Semiotext(e), 1997).

2. Virilio and Lotringer, *Pure War*, 152.

3. Jean-Philippe Mathy, "The Atlantic as Metaphor," *Atlantic Studies* 1 (2004): 109.

4. Gilles Deleuze and Félix Guattari, *A Thousand Plateaus: Capitalism and Schizophrenia*, trans. Brian Massumi (1980; repr., Minneapolis: University of Minnesota Press, 1987), 6.

5. Ibid., 4–5.

6. Mathy, "Atlantic as Metaphor," 107.

7. Aimé Césaire, *Discourse on Colonialism*, trans. Joan Pinkham (1955; repr., Monthly Review Press, 1972), 21.

8. Enrique Dussel, *The Invention of the Americas: Eclipse of "the Other" and the Myth of Modernity*, trans. Michael D. Barber (1992; repr., New York: Continuum, 1995), 17.

9. See, for example, James Hartman, "Providence Tales and the Indian Captivity Narrative: Some Transatlantic Influences on Colonial Puritan Discourse," *Early American Literature* 32 (1997): 66–81; as well as Linda Colley's *Captives* (New York: Pantheon, 2002).

10. Kathryn Zabelle Derounian-Stodola, ed., "Introduction," *Women's Indian Captivity Narratives* (1998; repr., New York: Penguin Books, 2010), xi.

11. Rafia Zafar, "Capturing the Captivity: African Americans Among the Puritans," *MELUS* 17, no. 2 (1991–92): 19.

12. Brian McGinty, *The Oatman Massacre: A Tale of Desert Captivity and Survival* (Norman: University of Oklahoma Press, 2005), 161.

13. Mary Rowlandson, *The Sovereignty and Goodness of God*, ed. Neal Salisbury (1682; repr., Boston: Bedford/St. Martins, 1997). Originally titled *The Soveraignty and Goodness of God*, passages quoted from this text are taken from Salisbury's critical edition of the second edition printed by Samuel Green at Cambridge, unless otherwise indicated.

14. Jill Lepore, *The Name of War: King Philip's War and the Origins of American Identity* (New York: Vintage, 1998), 125.

15. Branka Arsić, "Mary Rowlandson and the Phenomenology of Patient Suffering," *Common Knowledge* 16 (2009): 248.

16. Although several other scholars have written on this topic, my discussion concerning the publication history and title page of Rowlandson editions is gleaned from Charles Evans's definitive *American Bibliography. A Chronological Dicitonary of All Books, Pamphlets and Periodical Publications Printed in the United States of America from the Genesis of Printing in 1639 Down to and Including the Year [1800]*, 13 vols. (Chicago: The Blakely Press for the Author, 1943–1955); available in digitized form as *Early American Imprints, Series I. Evans (1632–1800)* via Readex.

17. Greg Sieminski, "The Puritan Captivity Narrative and the Politics of the American Revolution," *American Quarterly* 42 (1990): 35.

18. See Joseph Willard, "Notes," in *Mary Rowlandson's Narrative of the Captivity and Removes of Mrs. Mary Rowlandson: Who was Taken by the Indians at the Destruction of Lancaster, in 1676* (Lancaster: Carter, Andrews, and Co., 1828).

19. This example is from the 1773 edition published in New London, Connecticut, by Timothy Green. The title pages for editions published in 1770, 1771, 1791, 1793, 1795, 1796, and 1800 in New England also include this descriptive subtitle.

20. See Increase Mather's *An essay for the recording of illustrious providences* (Boston: Samuel Green, 1684), 39–57; and Cotton Mather's, *Magnalia Christi Americana* (London: Thomas Parkhurst, 1702), Book VII, 90–91.

21. June Namias, *White Captives: Gender and Ethnicity on the American Frontier* (Chapel Hill: University of North Carolina Press, 1993), 29.

22. Virilio and Lotringer, *Pure War*, 27.

23. Deleuze and Guattari, *Thousand Plateaus*, 11.

24. Richard Slotkin, *Regeneration Through Violence: The Mythology of the American Frontier, 1600–1860* (1973; repr., New York: Harper Perennial, 1992), 5.

25. Deleuze and Guattari, *Thousand Plateaus*, 11.

26. Increase Mather uses this distinction in the opening paragraph of his work, *A Brief History of the Warr with the Indians in New-England (From June 24, 1675. when the first English-man was murdered by the Indians, to August 12, 1676. when Philip, alias Metacomet, the principal Author and Beginner of the Warr, was slain.) Wherein the grounds, Beginning, and Progress of the Warr, is summarily expressed. Together With A Serious Exhortation to the Inhabitants of that Land* (Boston: Printed and sold by John Foster, 1676), in reference to property owners who accept the doctrine of divine providence, whereby God had given them, "for a rightful Possession," the land of the Indians, 1.

27. Richard G. Cole, "Sixteenth-Century Travel Books as a Source of European Attitudes Toward Non-White and Non-Western Culture," *Proceedings of the American Philosophical Society* 116, no. 1 (1972): 60.

28. The fall of Constantinople was viewed as among the most cataclysmic events to befall Christendom in the fifteenth century. The sheer number of texts that make reference to this event testifies to its religious and historical significance. Detailed descriptions appear in the works of English writers such as William Caxton, John Mandeville, William Tyndale, and Edward Hall, as well as in the work of European writers such as Guillaume Caoursin, Desiderius Erasmus, Sebastian Brandt, Jacques de Bourbon, and Jean Froissart, to name but a few of the better known examples.

29. Deleuze and Guattari, *Thousand Plateaus*, 7.

30. William Caxton, *The Cronycles of Englond* (London: William Caxton, 1482), P5v.

31. See also, Sir John Mandeville's *Here begynneth a lytell treatyse or booke named Johan Mau[n]deuyll knyght born in Englonde . . .* (Westminster: Wynken de Worde, 1499); Ranulf Higden's *Tabula* (London: Wynken de Worde, 1502); John Frith's *A disputacio of purgatorye . . .* (Antwerp: S. Cock, 1531); and Robert Fabyan's *Fabyans cronycle newly printed . . .* (London: William Rastell, 1533).

32. Caxton, *Cronycles of Englond*, Y4r.

33. Cole, "Sixteenth-Century Travel Books," 59.

34. Homi Bhabha, *The Location of Culture* (London, Routledge, 1994), 73.

35. Abdul R. JanMohamad, "The Economy of the Manichean Allegory: The Function of Racial Difference in Colonialist Literature," in *"Race," Writing, and Difference*, ed. Henry Louis Gates Jr. (Chicago Illinois: University of Chicago Press, 1986), 82.

36. Roslyn L. Knutson, "Elizabethan Documents, Captivity Narratives, and the Market for Foreign History Plays," *English Literary Renaissance* 26 (1996): 77.

37. Thomas Becon, *The new pollecye of warre wherin is declared not only how*

[ye]mooste cruell tyraunt the great Turke may be ouer come, but also all other enemies of the Christen publique weale, lately deuised by Theodore Basille (London: Iohn Maylerre for Iohn Gough, 1542), G4v.

38. *The Estate of Christians, liuing vnder the subiection of the Turke. And also the warres betweene the Christians and the turke, beginning 1592. and continuing till the end of 1593* (London: John Wolfe, 1595), 2, 3.

39. Nabil Matar, "English Accounts of Captivity in North Africa and the Middle East: 1577–1625," *Renaissance Quarterly* 54 (2001): 553.

40. Matar, "English Accounts," 561.

41. Anthony Munday, *The admirable Deliverance of 266 Christians by Iohn Reynard Englishman from the captiuitie of the Turkes, who had been gally slaues many years in Alexandria. The number of the seueralll nations that were captiues follow in the next page* (London: Thomas Dawson, 1608), B1r.

42. Rowlandson, *Sovereignty and Goodness*, 70.

43. Hayden White defines emplotment as "the encodation of the facts contained in the chronicle as components of specific *kinds* of plot structures," *Tropics of Discourse: Essays in Cultural Criticism* (Baltimore: Johns Hopkins University Press, 1978), 83.

44. For the period spanning from 1501 to 1600, Göllner arrived at the astonishing total of 2,463 surviving imprints published in Europe and England. See *his two volume work, Tvrcica: Die europäishen Turkendrucke des XVI* (Budapest and Berlin: Editura Academiei R.P.R., 1961).

45. G. V. Scammell, "The New Worlds and Europe in the Sixteenth Century," *Historical Journal* 12 (1969): 394.

46. Paul Baepler, "The Barbary Captivity Narrative in Early America," *Early American Literature* 30 (1995): 91.

47. Colonel Rigby, "Englishmen in Captivity in Eastern Africa," *Proceedings of the Royal Geographical Society of London* 10 (1865–1866): 114.

48. Ibid.

49. Ellen G. Friedman, "Christian Captives as 'Hard Labor' in Algiers, 16th–18th Centuries," *The International Journal of African Historical Studies* 13 (1980): 617n.

50. Paul Baepler, "White Slaves, African Masters," *Annals of the American Academy of Political and Social Science* 588 (2003): 90.

51. Paul Baepler, "Barbary Captivity," 96.

52. Linda Colley, *Captives* (New York: Pantheon Books, 2002), 13.

53. Edward W. Said, *Orientalism* (1978; repr., New York: Vintage, 1994), 58.

54. White, *Tropics of Discourse*, 121.

55. Homi Bhabha, "Signs Taken for Wonders," in *The Post Colonial Studies Reader*, ed. Bill Ashcroft, Gareth Griffiths, and Helen Tiffin (New York: Routledge, 1997), 29–35.

56. Said, *Orientalism*, 58.

57. Bhabha, *Location of Culture*, 66.

58. Ibid.

59. Ibid.

60. Jacques Derrida, "Signature Event Context," in *Margins of Philosophy*, trans. Alan Bass (1972; repr., Chicago Illinois: University of Chicago Press, 1982), 313.

61. Ibid., 311.

62. Jean Baudrillard, *Simulacra and Simulation*, trans. Shelia Faria Glaser (1981; repr., Ann Arbor Michigan: University of Michigan Press, 1994), 6.

63. Hans Staden, *Geschichte eines Landes, gelegen in der Neuen Welt, America genannt, yon Hans Staden aus Homburg in Hessen* (Marburg, 1557). A new edition and translation of this work was published as *Hans Staden's True History: An Account of Cannibal Captivity in Brazil* by Duke University Press in 2008.

64. Peter Hulme, "Columbus and the Cannibals," in *The Post-Colonial Studies Reader*, ed. Bill Ashcroft, Gareth Griffiths, and Helen Tiffin (New York: Routledge, 1997), 365.

65. Ibid., 365.

66. Ibid., 366.

67. Tzvetan Todorov, *The Morals of History*, trans. Alyson Waters (1991; repr., Minneapolis: Minnesota: University of Minnesota Press, 1995), 106.

68. Hulme, "Columbus and the Cannibals," 366.

69. Accounts of the attack on Lancaster and Rowlandson's captivity are found in Hubbard's *A Narrative of the Troubles with the Indians in New-England* . . . (1677), as well as in Mather's work, *A Brief History of the Warr with the Indians in New-England*, which was published in both Boston and London in 1676.

70. Virilio and Lotringer, *Pure War*, 53.

71. Jill Lepore, *The Name of War: King Philip's War and the Origins of American Identity* (New York: Vintage, 1999), 23.

72. Virilio and Lotringer, *Pure War*, 92.

73. Rowlandson, *Sovereignty and Goodness*, 69.

74. Ibid.

75. Ibid., 70.

76. Arsić makes a similar observation and cites John Demos's description of practices common to Algonquin ritualistic feasts found in his work, *The Unredeemed Captive: A Family Story from Early America* (New York: Knopf, 1994), 149.

77. Rowlandson, *Sovereignty and Goodness*, 71.

78. Ibid., 76.

79. Deleuze and Guattari, *Thousand Plateaus*, 13.

80. Rowlandson, *Sovereignty and Goodness*, 77–78.

81. Ibid., 77.

82. Ibid., 87.

83. Ibid.

84. Arsić, "Mary Rowlandson and the Phenomenology," 261–62.

85. Colin Ramsey, "Cannibalism and Infant Killing: A System of 'Demonizing' Motifs in Indian Captivity Narratives," *Clio* 24, no.1 (1994): 55.

86. Ramsey, "Cannibalism," 55.

87. Ibid., 59.

88. An episode from season 2 titled "Durant, Nebraska," for example, begins with an archetypal Native raid on a frontier settlement in which a white woman—signified as an ex-captive bearing facial tattoos similar to those described in the narrative of Olive Oatman—witnesses a brutal assault carried out by Cheyenne.

89. Bartolomé de Las Casas, *A Short Account of the Destruction of the Indies*, trans. and ed. by Nigel Griffin (1552; repr., New York: Penguin, 1992). Las Casas frequently stresses the eyewitness nature of his observations throughout this text: 5, 9, 12, 15,16, 19, 23, 29.

90. Lepore makes a similar argument about the propagandistic function of English translations of Las Casas's work in *The Name of War*, 8–11.

91. Deleuze and Guattari, *Thousand Plateaus*, 4.

92. Las Casas, *Short Account*, 11.

93. Rabassa, *Writing Violence*, 34

94. Francis Knight, *A relation of seaven yeares slaverie under the Turkes of Argeire* (London: T. Cotes, for Michael Sparke Junior, 1640), 2.

95. Rowlandson, *Sovereignty and Goodness*, 70.

Chapter 2

1. Richard Hakluyt, in his *The principle nauigations* . . . , 2 vols. (London: George Bishop, Ralph Newberie, and Robert Barker, 1599), testifies to the reputation of Spanish soldiers, stating that "if we consider what wars they be that haue made their name so terrible, we shal find them to haue bin none other then against the barbarous *Moores*, the naked *Indians*, and the vnarmed *Netherlanders*," 135.

2. See Daniel Defoe's *A New Voyage Round the World* (Chester: W. Cooke, 1725), in which the author advances the idea of an English colony in South America. For a critical analysis of this text, see Kathryn Rummell's "Defoe and the Black Legend: The Spanish Stereotype in *A New Voyage Round the World*," *Rocky Mountain Review of Language and Literature* 52 (1998): 13–28.

3. William Bradford, *History of Plymouth Plantation*, ed. Charles Deane (Boston: Privately Printed, 1856), 25, 26–27.

4. José Rabasa, *Writing Violence on the Northern Frontier: The Historiography of Sixteenth-Century New Mexico and Florida and the Legacy of Conquest* (Durham, NC: Duke University Press, 2000), 28–29.

5. See John Winthrop's "Modell of Christian Charity," in *The Puritans: A Sourcebook of Their Writings*, rev. ed., vol. 1, ed. Perry Miller and Thomas H. Johnson (New York: Harper and Row, 1963), 199.

6. Howard Mumford Jones, "The Colonial Impulse: An Analysis of the 'Promotion' Literature of Colonization," *Proceedings of the American Philosophical Society* 90 (1946): 131.

7. Emory Elliot, *The Cambridge Introduction to Early American Literature* (Cambridge: University of Cambridge Press, 2002), 36.

8. Following its initial publication, additional editions were printed in London by William Jones in 1634, as well as at Boston on the press of Samuel Green in 1684.

9. Deborah L. Madsen, *American Exceptionalism* (Jackson: University of Mississippi Press, 1998), 23.

10. John Cotton, *God's Promise to his Plantation. As it was delivered in a Sermon* (London: Printed by William Jones, 1630), 1.

11. Julia Kristeva, *Revolution in Poetic Language*, trans. Margaret Waller (1974; repr., New York: Columbia University Press, 1984), 59–60.

12. Cotton, *God's Promise*, 3.

13. Ibid., 4.

14. John Winthrop, *The Journal of John Winthrop, 1630–1649*, ed. Richard S. Dunn, James Savage, Laetitia Yeandle (Cambridge: Belknap Press of Harvard University Press, 1996), 283–84.

15. Cotton, *God's Promise*, 4.

16. Richard Shelly Hartigan, "Saint Augustine on War and Killing: The Problem of the Innocent," *Journal of the History of Ideas* 27 (1966): 198.

17. Robert A. Williams, Jr., *The American Indian in Western Legal Thought: The Discourses of Conquest* (Oxford: Oxford University Press, 1990), 30.

18. Williams, *American Indian*, 197.

19. See Robert Williams, *American Indian*, 30–50, for an in-depth account of the evolution of this concept and its application from the Middle Ages through the seventeenth century.

20. Cotton, *God's Promise*, 4.

21. Bradford, *History of Plymouth Plantation*, 78.

22. Gayatri Chakravorty Spivak, "Can the Subaltern Speak?," in *Marxism and the Interpretation of Culture,* ed. Cary Nelson and Lawrence Grossberg (Urbana: University of Illinois Press, 1988), 305.

23. Bradford, *Of Plymouth Plantation,* 78.

24. Perry Miller, "History," in *The Puritans: A Sourcebook of Their Writings*, rev. ed., vol. 1, ed. Perry Miller and Thomas H. Johnson (New York: Harper and Row, 1963), 89.

25. Molly Farrell, "'Beyond My Skil': Mary Rowlandson's Counting," *Early American Literature* 47 (2012): 60.

26. Increase Mather, *A Brief History of the Warr with the Indians of New-England* (Boston: John Foster, 1676), 23.

27. Increase Mather, *A Brief History*, 12, and see also 20, 25, 27.

28. Rowlandson, *Sovereignty and Goodness*, 71.

29. Ibid.

30. In *The Sovereignty and Goodness of God*, the captivity experience of Mary Rowlandson is structured through the use of twenty sections titled "removes." These denote Rowlandson's initial "removal" from Lancaster following the attack and transport into the wilderness in the company of her Native captors, culminating some eleven weeks later in her ransom.

31. Rowlandson, *Sovereignty and Goodness*, 75.

32. Ibid.

33. Ibid., 109.

34. Ibid., 80, 108–9.

35. William Bradford and Edward Winslow, *Mourt's Relation*, in *A Journal of the Pilgrims at Plymouth: Mourt's Relation*, ed. Dwight B. Heath (1622; repr., New York: Corinth Books, 1963), 20.

36. Bradford and Winslow, *Mourt's Relation*, 20–28.

37. Ibid., 21, 27–28.

38. Cotton, *God's Promise*, 5.

39. Mather, *Brief History*, 1–2.

40. Edward H. Davidson, "John Cotton's Biblical Exegesis: Method and Purpose," *Early American Literature* 17, no. 2 (1982): 119.

41. Cotton, *God's Promise*, 8.

42. Mather, *Brief History*, 1.

43. Marilyn C. Wesley, "Moving Targets: The Travel Text in *A Narrative of the Captivity and Restauration of Mrs. Mary Rowlandson*," *Essays in Literature* 23, no.1 (1996): 43.

44. Ibid.

45. Kathryn Zabelle Derounian-Stodola and James Levernier, *The Indian Captivity Narrative, 1550–1900* (New York: Twayne Publishers, 1993), 100.

46. Hayden White, *Tropics of Discourse: Essays in Cultural Criticism* (Baltimore: Johns Hopkins University Press, 1978), 59, italics in original.

47. Cotton, *God's Promise*, 8–9.

48. Ibid., 10.

49. Rowlandson, *Sovereignty and Goodness*, 69.

50. Ibid., 70.

51. Increase Mather, *A Relation of the Troubles in New-England* (Boston: John Foster), A4r.

52. Mather, *Brief History*, 6.

53. Cotton, *God's Promise*, 17.

54. Rowlandson, *Soveraignty and Goodness*, 68.

55. See ibid., 71, 79, 86, 91, 102.

56. Ibid., 74.

57. Joseph Rowlandson, *The Possibility of God's Forsaking a People that have been visibly near & dear to him together with the misery of a people thus forsaken, set forth in a sermon preached at Weathersfield, Nov. 21. 1678. Being a day of fast and humiliation* (Boston: Printed for John Ratcliffe and John Griffin, 1682), 156.

58. Rowlandson, *Sovereignty and Goodness*, 71. Mather also uses this same phrase in the context of winning souls in the introduction to his *Brief History*, A3v.

59. Michelle Burnham, "The Journey Between: Liminality and Dialogism in Mary White Rowlandson's Captivity Narrative," *Early American Literature* 28 (1993): 65.

60. For reasons that are unclear, the Scriptures cited in the preface as well as those integrated into Rowlandson's narrative seem to be based on a variant of the *King James Bible* that was first published in 1609, and not the Geneva edition, which Puritans held to be the most valid translation of the Bible available. Interestingly, in the Twelfth Remove Rowlandson says that her "mistress" came upon her as she was reading her Bible and "snatched it hastely" out of her hand and threw it outside, 340. After this, it is stated that Rowlandson ran out to retrieve it and then hid it away in her "pocket," 340. The significance of this detail is that one feature of the Geneva edition was that it was the first Bible published in a pocket-size edition; so if this is, indeed, the version Rowlandson possessed, then the citations in her text should match, and yet they do not.

61. Rowlandson, *Sovereignty and Goodness*, 84.

62. King James Bible, Psalms 55:22.

63. Rowlandson, *Sovereignty and Goodness*, 89–90.

64. Ibid., 90.

65. King James Bible, 2 Thess. 3:2.

66. See, for example, Dawn Henwood's essay, "Mary Rowlandson and the Psalms: The Textuality of Survival," *Early American Literature* 32, no. 2 (1997): 169–87; and Denise Kohn and Margaret Campbell, "The Captive Female as Biblical Hero: Rowlandson, Rhetoric, and the Psalms," *The Explicator* 69 (2011): 125–28.

67. Cotton, *God's Promise*, 14.

68. Ibid.

69. Ibid.

70. Mather, *Brief History*, 24.

71. Edward Said, *Culture and Imperialism* (New York: Knopf, 1993), 7.

72. Rowlandson, *Sovereignty and Goodness*, 101.

73. Ives Goddard and Kathleen Bragdon, *Native Writings in Massachusett*, 2 vols., (Philadelphia: American Philosophical Society, 1988), 14.

74. Francis Jennings, *The Invasion of America: Indians, Colonialism, and the Cant of Conquest* (New York: W. W. Norton, 1976), 180.

75. Jill Lepore, *The Name of War: King Philip's War and the Origins of American Identity* (New York: Vintage, 1998), xvi.

76. Samuel G. Drake, "Prefatory by the Editor," in *The History of King Philip's War by the Rev. Increase Mather, D.D. Also, A History of the Same War by the Rev. Cotton Mather* (Albany: J. Munsell, 1862), ix, xxviii.

77. Kathryn Derounian-Stodola, “The Indian Captivity Narratives of Mary Rowlandson and Olive Oatman: Case Studies in the Continuity, Evolution, and Exploitation of Literary Discourse,” *Studies in the Literary Imagination* 27 (1994): 33–46.

78. Craig S. Womack, *Red on Red: Native American Literary Separatism* (Minneapolis: University of Minnesota Press, 1999), 11–12

79. Jennings, *Invasion of America*, 178.

80. Howard Zinn, *The Peoples History of the United States*, 1980 (New York: Harper Books, 1999), 16.

Chapter 3

1. For book-length studies, see June Namias’s *White Captives: Gender and Ethnicity on the American Frontier* (Chapel Hill: University of North Carolina Press, 1993); Mitchell Breitwieser’s *American Puritanism and the Defense of Mourning: Religion, Grief, and Ethnology in Mary White Rowlandson’s Captivity Narrative* (Madison: University of Wisconsin Press, 1990); Pauline Turner Strong’s *Captive Selves, Captivating Others: The Politics and Poetics of Colonial American Captivity Narratives* (Boulder, CO: Westview Press, 1999); and Susan Howe’s *The Birth-Mark: Unsettling the Wilderness in American Literary History* (Middletown, CT: Wesleyan University Press, 1993). Among the recent critical work positioning the Rowlandson narrative within discussions of more theoretical concerns are Bryce Traister’s “Mary Rowlandson and the Invention of the Secular” (*Early American Literature* 42 [2009]); Jordan Stein’s “Mary Rowlandson’s Hunger and the Historiography of Sexuality” (*American Literature* 81 [2009]); Branka Arsić’s “Mary Rowlandson and the Phenomenology of Patient Suffering” (*Common Knowledge* 16 [2009]); and Sidonie Smith’s “Reading the Posthuman Backward: Mary Rowlandson’s Doubled Witnessing” (*Biography* [Winter 2012]).

2. For an enlightening discussion of this genre see, Paul J. Lindholdt’s “The Significance of the Colonial Promotion Tract” in *Early American Literature and Culture: Essays Honoring Harrison T. Meserole*, ed. Kathryn Zabelle Derounian-Stodola (Newark: University of Delaware Press, 1992), 57–72.

3. The use of title pages as support for the truth claims of literary narratives, far from being exclusive to Rowlandson’s text or even the Indian captivity genre, was a common feature of English and American literary production from the sixteenth century and well into the twentieth. In the discursive genres of seventeenth-century promotion and travel literature, a similar narrative strategy is also apparent. Texts such as Robert Johnson’s *A True Declaration of the estate of the Colonie in Virginia* (1610), Edward Winslow’s *Good News from New England: or a true Relation of things very remarkable at the Plantation of Plymouth* (1624), and William Strachey’s *A true repertory of the wracke, and*

redemption of Sir Thomas Gate Knight (1625), offer but three representative examples of this narrative strategy in English colonial discourse.

4. Increase Mather, *A Brief History of the Warr with the Indians in New-England* (Boston: John Foster, 1676), A3.

5. Mather, *A Brief History*, A3.

6. Jill Lepore, *The Name of War: King Philip's War and the Origins of American Identity* (New York: Vintage, 1998), 48.

7. See also the 1760 edition of Elizabeth Hanson's captivity narrative published in London, *An Account of the Captivity of Elizabeth Hanson . . . by Samuel Bownas*, 2nd ed. (London: Samuel Clark, 1760).

8. Mather, *A Relation of the Troubles which have hapned in New-England* (Boston: John Foster, 1677), A2r.

9. Yael Ben-Zvi, "Ethnology and the Production of Foreignness in Indian Captivity Narratives," *American Indian Quarterly* 32 (2008): x.

10. Ibid. For an in-depth discussion of Chamberlain's role in the Johnson narrative, see, Lorrayne Carroll, "'Affecting History': Impersonating Women in the Early Republic," *Early American Literature* 39 (2004), as well as her manuscript, *Rhetorical Drag: Gender Impersonation, Captivity, and the Writing of History* (Kent, OH: The Kent State University Press, 2007).

11. John Bunyan, *The pilgrim's progress from this world to that which is to come* (Boston: Samuel Green, 1681), 166 [unpaginated].

12. Horace Engdahl, "Philomena's Tongue: Introductory Remarks on Witness Literature," in *Witness Literature: Proceedings of the Nobel Centennial Symposium*, ed. Horace Engdahl (River Edge, NJ: World Scientific, 2002), 3.

13. Ter Amicam, "The Preface to the Reader," in *The Soveraignty and Goodness of God*, ed. Neal Salisbury (1682; repr., Boston, Bedford/St. Martins, 1997), 65.

14. Jacques Derrida, "Signature Event Context," *Margins of Philosophy*, trans. Alan Bass (1972; repr., Chicago: University of Chicago Press, 1982), 315.

15. Frederick Lewis Weis, Preface to *The Narrative of the Captivity and Restoration of Mrs. Mary Rowlandson: The Lancaster Edition* (1903; repr., Boston: Houghton Mifflin Company, 1930), v.

16. Mark Ludwig, Introduction to *The Captive: An Early American Classic*, by Mary Rowlandson (Tucson, AZ: American Eagle, 1990), v.

17. Frederick Drimmer, Introduction to *Captured by Indians: 15 Firsthand Accounts, 1750–1870*, ed. Frederick Drimmer (1961; repr., New York: Dover, 1985), 10.

18. Ibid., 10–11.

19. Ibid., 11.

20. Derrida, "Signature Event Context," 320.

21. Kathryn Zabelle Derounian-Stodola and James Levernier, *The Indian Captivity Narrative, 1550–1900* (New York: Twayne Publishers, 1993), 94.

22. Richard VanDerBeets, Introduction to *Held Captive by Indians:*

Selected Narratives 1642–1836, ed. Richard VanDerBeets (Knoxville: University of Tennessee Press, 1973), xii.

23. Ibid.

24. Roy Harvey Pearce, "The Significances of the Captivity Narrative," *American Literature* 19 (1947–48): 1.

25. Derrida, "Signature Event Context," 320.

26. According to the modern calendar, before the eighteenth century the new year began on March 25.

27. Rowlandson, *Sovereignty and Goodness*, 68.

28. Phillips D. Carleton, "The Indian Captivity," *American Literature* 15 (1943): 171.

29. Hayden White, *Tropics of Discourse: Essays in Cultural Criticism* (Baltimore: Johns Hopkins University Press, 1978), 81 (italics in original).

30. Ibid., 94.

31. Ibid., 83.

32. Ibid.

33. Rowlandson, *Sovereignty and Goodness of God*, 68.

34. Ibid., 69.

35. Ibid., 70.

36. See Michel Foucault's *Power/Knowledge: Selected Interviews and Other Writings, 1972–1977*, ed. Colin Gordon (New York: Pantheon Books, 1980), for a discussion on the relationship between epistemological truth and social power.

37. Ibid., 133.

38. In the preface that accompanies the Rowlandson narrative, however, the author identifies members of the Narragansett and Nipmucs as responsible for the attack, 63–64.

39. Rowlandson, *Sovereignty and Goodness of God*, 68.

40. Ibid., 69.

41. Molly Farrell, "'Beyond My Skil': Mary Rowlandson's Counting," *Early American Literature* 47 (2012): 67.

42. Homi K. Bhabha, *The Location of Culture* (New York: Routledge, 1994), 72.

43. June Namias, *White Captives*, 22.

44. Rowlandson, *Sovereignty and Goodness*, 68.

45. Mather, *A Brief History*, 22.

46. Increase Mather, *An Essay for the Recording of Illustrious Providences* (Boston: Samuel Green, 1684), 39.

47. Samuel G. Drake, "Prefatory by the Editor," *The History of King Philip's War by the Rev. Increase Mather, D.D. also, A History of the Same War, By the Rev. Cotton Mather, D.D.*, ed. Samuel G. Drake (Albany: J. Munsell, 1862), xxvii.

48. Cotton Mather, *Magnalia Christi Americana: Or, The Ecclesiastical History of New-England, From Its First Planting in the Year 1620. unto the Year*

of our Lord, 1698. In Seven Books (London: Thomas Parkhurst, 1702), Book VII, 68.

49. Pearce, "Significances of the Captivity Narrative," 3.

50. Mather, *Magnalia Christi*, Book VII, 90.

51. Derrida, "Signature Event Context," 320–21.

52. Mather, *A Relation*, 64.

53. Francis Jennings, *The Invasion of America: Indians, Colonialism, and the Cant of Conquest* (Chapel Hill: University of North Carolina Press, 1975), 146.

54. See chapter two of Simmons's work, *Spirit of the New England Tribes* (Hanover, NH: University Press of New England, 1986), 10–36.

55. Increase Mather, *An Historical Discourse Concerning the Prevalency of Prayer* (Boston: J. Foster, 1677), 5.

56. Michael G. Hall, *The Last American Puritan: The Life of Increase Mather, 1639–1723* (Middletown, CT: Wesleyan University Press, 1988), 5–6.

57. Rowlandson, *Sovereignty and Goodness*, 70.

58. Hayden White, *Tropics of Discourse: Essays in Cultural Criticism* (Baltimore: Johns Hopkins University Press, 1978), 84.

59. Francis Jennings, in *The Invasion of America*, referred to King Philip's War as the "second war of Puritan conquest," owing to its roots in the repeated incursions of English settlers on Native lands, 178–79.

60. White, *Tropics of Discourse*, 98.

61. Rowlandson, *Sovereignty and Goodness*, 71.

62. Alice Morse Earle, *The Sabbath in Puritan New England* (New York: Charles Scribner's Sons, 1891), 251.

63. Virilio and Lotringer, *Pure War*, 40.

64. William Haller, Jr., *The Puritan Frontier: Town-Planting in New England Colonial Development, 1630–1660* (New York: Columbia University Press, 1951), 14–16.

65. Ibid., 14.

66. Eric B. Schultz and Michael J. Tougias, *King Philip's War: The History and Legacy of America's Forgotten Conflict* (Woodstock, VT: Countryman, 1999), 20.

67. Ebenezer W. Pierce, *Indian History, Biography and Genealogy: Pertaining to the Good Sachem Massasoit of the Wampanoag Tribe, and His Descendants* (North Abington, MA: Zerviah Gould Mitchell, 1878), 56.

68. Robert B. Caverly, *The Heroism of Hannah Duston, Together with the Indian Wars of New England* (Boston: B. B. Russell, 1875), 206.

69. Ter Amicam, "Preface to the Reader," 64.

70. Also variously referred to as James Quinapaug, or Quannapaquait in other texts.

71. George Madison Bodge, *Soldiers in King Philip's War Being a Critical Account of that War with a Concise History of the Indian Wars of New England from 1620–1677* (Boston: By the Author, 1906), 352.

72. Marion Fuller Safford, *The Story of Colonial Lancaster (Massachusetts)* (Rutland, VT: Tuttle, 1937), 32.

73. Ibid.

74. Bodge, *Soldiers in King Philip's War*, 352.

75. Mary Pray, "A Letter to the Governor of Rhode Island," in *Further Letters on King Philip's War* (Providence: E. L. Freeman Co., 1923), 23.

76. Michelle Burnham, "The Journey Between: Liminality and Dialogism in Mary White Rowlandson's Captivity Narrative," *Early American Literature* 28 (1993): 61.

77. Mather, *Brief History*, 7.

78. Ibid., 71n. Bodge, however, lists the number of casualties from the first attack upon Lancaster at seven, 352.

79. Shelia McIntyre, "'I Heare it so Variously Reported': News-letters, Newspapers, and the Ministerial Network in New England, 1670–1730," *The New England Quarterly* 71 (1998): 595.

80. Rowlandson, *Sovereignty and Goodness*, 83.

81. Mitchell Breitwieser, *American Puritanism and the Defense of Mourning*, 146.

82. Ibid.

83. Ibid., 5.

84. Ibid., 146.

85. Ibid., 148.

86. Ibid.

87. Ibid., 148–49.

88. Burnham, "Journey Between," 64.

89. Gerald Vizenor, *Manifest Manners: Narratives on Postindian Survivance* (1994; repr., Lincoln: University of Nebraska Press, 1999), 8.

90. Burnham, "Journey Between," 64.

91. Ibid.

92. Benjamin Thompson, "New England's Crisis" (1676), in *So Dreadful a Judgment: Puritan Responses to King Philip's War, 1676 1677*, ed. Richard Slotkin and James K. Folsom (Middletown, CT: Wesleyan University Press, 1978), 218.

93. Schultz and Tougias, *King Philip's War*, 290.

94. Increase Mather, *A Brief History of the Warr with the Indians in New-England . . . Together With A Serious Exhortation to the Inhabitants of that Land* (Boston: Printed and sold by John Foster, 1676), 46.

95. Ibid.

96. See Rowlandson, *Sovereignty and Goodness*, 88, 89, 93–94, 101, 103, 105, 106, 107, 108, and 109.

97. Breitwieser, *American Puritanism*, 146.

98. Rowlandson, *Sovereignty and Goodness*, 97.

99. As with other orations attributed to Native American leaders, the importance lies not strictly in the ability to determine the precision of the words

spoken, which with all oral traditions are open to ambiguity, but in the accuracy of the events and historical context that such words describe, and in this case the validity of Metacomet's complaint is confirmed. See Ebenezer Pierce's *Indian History, Biography and Genealogy*, 56–59.

100. William Apess, *Eulogy on King Philip, as Pronounced at the Odeon, In Federal Street, Boston, By The Rev. William Apess, An Indian, January 8, 1836*, 2nd ed. (Boston: Published by the Author, 1837), 27–28.

101. Jill Lepore, "Wigwam Words," *The American Scholar* 70 (2001): 108.

102. John Easton, "A Relacion of the Indyan Warre, by Mr. Easton, of Road Isld., 1675," in *Narratives of the Indian Wars: 1675–1699*, ed. Charles H. Lincoln (New York: Charles Scribner's Sons, 1913), 11.

103. Ibid., 10.

104. Pierce, *Indian History*, 57.

105. John Easton, "A Relacion of the Indyan Warre, By Mr Easton, of Rhoade Isld., 1675," in *The Present State of New-England, with Respect to the Indian VVar* (N.S. London: Dorman Newman, 1675).

106. Ibid., 17.

107. Russell Bourne, *The Red King's Rebellion: Racial Politics in New England 1675–1678* (New York: Atheneum, 1990), 12.

108. Ibid., 18.

109. Apess, *Eulogy on King Philip*, 5.

Chapter 4

1. George Selement, "Publication and the Puritan Minister," *The William and Mary Quarterly* 37 (1980): 220.

2. Ibid., 222.

3. Ibid., 222, 226.

4. Kathryn Zabelle Derounian, "The Publication, Promotion, and Distribution of Mary Rowlandson's Indian Captivity Narrative in the Seventeenth Century," *Early American Literature* 23, no. 3 (1988): 239.

5. Ibid., 244.

6. Ibid., 246.

7. W. W. Greg, "The Rationale of the Copy-Text," in *Bibliography and Textual Criticism: English and American Literature 1700 to the Present*, ed. O. M. Brack, Jr., and Warner Barnes (Chicago: University of Chicago Press, 1969), 44.

8. Ibid., 46–47.

9. Paraphrased in ibid., 46.

10. See Gary Ebersole's *Captured By Texts: Puritan to Postmodern Images of Indian Captivity* (Charlottesville: University Press of Virginia, 1995), 44–47.

11. Derounian, "Publication, Promotion, and Distribution," 240.

12. Ibid., 240.

13. Kathryn Zabelle Derounian-Stodola, "The Indian Captivity Narratives of Mary Rowlandson and Olive Oatman: Case Studies in the Continuity, Evolution, and Exploration of Literary Discourse," *Studies in the Literary Imagination* 27 (1994): 41.

14. Bryce Traister, "Mary Rowlandson and the Invention of the Secular," *Early American Literature* 42 (2009): 334.

15. Michel Foucault, "What is an Author?," in *The Foucault Reader*, trans. Josué V. Harari, ed. Paul Rabinow (1979; repr., New York: Pantheon Books, 1984), 103.

16. Brian McGinty, *The Oatman Massacre: A Tale of Desert Captivity and Survival* (Norman: University of Oklahoma Press, 2005), 162.

17. Lorrayne Carroll, "'Affecting History': Impersonating Women in the Early Republic," *Early American Literature* 39 (2004): 511.

18. Ibid., 511.

19. Anne Kusener Nelsen, "King Philip's War and the Hubbard-Mather Rivalry," *The William and Mary Quarterly* 27 (1970): 615.

20. William Hubbard, *A Narrative of the Troubles with the Indians in New-England, from the first planting thereof in the year 1607, to the present year 1677. But chiefly of the late Troubles in the two last eyars, 1675. and 1676. To which is added a Discourse about Warre with the Pequods in the year 1637* (Boston: by John Foster, 1677), T2v.

21. Ibid., T2v.

22. Perry Miller, *The New England Mind: From Colony to Providence*, 1953 (Boston: Beacon Press, 1961), 20.

23. Michelle Burnham, "Anne Hutchinson and the Economics of Antinomian Selfhood in Colonial New England," *Criticism* 39 (1997): 337.

24. Miller, *New England Mind*, 20.

25. Ibid., 21.

26. Increase Mather, *A Brief History of the Warr with the Indians in New-England, Together With A Serious Exhortation to the Inhabitants of that Land* (Boston: Printed and sold by John Foster, 1676), 25.

27. David Levin, "Forms of Uncertainty: Representation of Doubt in American Histories," *New Literary History* 8 (1976): 59.

28. Joseph Rowlandson, *The possibility of God's forsaking a people, that have been visibly near & dear to him together with the misery of a people thus forsaken, set forth in a sermon preached at Weathersfield, Nov. 21. 1678. Being a day of fast and humiliation* (Boston: Printed for John Ratcliffe and John Griffin, 1682).

29. Nelsen, "Hubbard-Mather Rivalry," 620.

30. Increase Mather, *Heavens Alarm to the World* (Boston: John Foster, 1681), C2r.

31. Increase Mather, *A Relation of the Troubles which have hapned in New-England By reason of the Indians there* (Boston: John Foster, 1677), 76.

32. Ter Amicam, "Preface to the Reader," *The Soveraignty and Goodness of God*, ed. Neal Salisbury (1682; repr., Boston, Bedford/St. Martins, 1997), 67.

33. This acknowledgement suggests an evolution in her thought from the previous claim, that "Mather's impact on the work came after its composition," found in her 1988 essay, "The Publication, Promotion, and Distribution of Mary Rowlandson's Indian Captivity Narrative in the Seventeenth Century." She challenges David Minter's speculation, supported by the work of David A. Richards, "which argues that Increase Mather encouraged Rowlandson to write the narrative, sponsored its publication, and supplied its preface."

According to Teresa Toulouse, "Commentators have often used David Richards's 1967 unpublished Yale College honors thesis, '"The Memorable Preservations': narratives of Indian captivity in the Literature and Politics of Colonial New England, 1675–1725," as support for the claim of Mather's authorship of the preface, "But Richards nowhere makes this claim; he does point out that the arguments advanced in the preface were certainly shared and disseminated by Mather." See Toulouse, "Female Captivity and 'Creole' Male Identity in the Narratives of Mary Rowlandson and Hannah Swarton," in *Creole Subjects in the Colonial Americas*, eds. Ralph Bauer and Jose Antonio Mazzotti (University of North Carolina Press, 2009), 321n.

34. Derounian-Stodola, "Indian Captivity Narratives," 41.

35. Lorrayne Carroll, *Rhetorical Drag: Gender Impersonation, Captivity, and the Writing of History* (Kent, OH: The Kent State University Press, 2007), 248.

36. Increase Mather, "To the Reader," in Samuel Willard, *Covenant-keeping the way to blessedness* (Boston: James Glen, for Samuel Sewall, 1682), A4–A12.

37. Mather, *Brief History*, 15–16.

38. Rowlandson, *Sovereignty*, 105.

39. Ter Amicam, "Preface to the Reader," 67.

40. Levin, "Forms of Uncertainty," 61.

41. Ibid., 60.

42. Richard Slotkin and James K. Folsom, eds., *So Dreadful a Judgment: Puritan Responses to King Philip's War, 1676–1677* (Middletown, CT: Wesleyan University Press, 1978), 302.

43. See David L. Greene's study on the life of Mary Rowlandson in the years following her captivity, "New Light on Mary Rowlandson," *Early American Literature* 20 (1985): 24–37.

44. Ebersole, *Captured By Texts*, 19.

45. Derounian, "Publication, Promotion, and Distribution," 252.

46. The identification of Diebold's research as a "Yale dissertation" seems a subtle effort to assign more authority than this unpublished source may merit. See Robert K. Diebold, "A Critical Edition of Mrs. Mary Rowlandson's Captivity Narrative" (PhD diss., Yale University, 1972).

47. Jill Lepore, *The Name of War: King Philip's War and the Origins of American Identity*, 126.

48. Ibid., 295n.

49. Derounian, "Publication, Promotion, and Distribution," 245.

50. Ibid.

51. Abdul R. JanMohamad, "The Economy of the Manichean Allegory: The Function of Racial Difference in Colonialist Literature," in *"Race," Writing, and Difference*, ed. Henry Louis Gates Jr. (Chicago: University of Chicago Press, 1986), 85–86.

52. George Parker Winship, *The Cambridge Press, 1638–1692: A Reexamination of the Evidence Concerning The Bay Psalm Book and the Eliot Indian Bible as well as other Contemporary Books and People* (Philadelphia: University of Pennsylvania Press, 1945), 342.

53. Ibid.

54. Salisbury, Note to *Sovereignty and Goodness of God by Mary Rowlandson with Related Documents*, ed. Neal Salisbury (New York: Bedford/St. Martin's, 1997), 68n.

55. Lepore, *Name of War*, 125.

56. Ibid., ix.

57. See Albert H. Marckwardt's *American English* (New York: Oxford University Press, 1980), 11–22.

58. Kathryn Zabelle Derounian-Stodola and James Arthur Levernier, *The Indian Captivity Narrative, 1550–1900*, 98–99.

59. Anne Dudley Bradstreet, *Several poems compiled with great variety of wit and learning* (Boston: John Foster, 1678).

60. While Bradstreet's other work, *The tenth muse lately sprung up in America*, was published at London in 1650, it never made it to press in the Massachusetts Bay Colony, lending additional support to the idea that works authored by women would not have been treated like those of male authors. Another noted exception is Sarah Goodhue's posthumously published work, *Copy of a valedictory and monitory writing left by Sarah Goodhue* (New London, CT, 1681).

61. John Winthrop, "From the Journal," in *The English Literatures of America: 1500–1800*, ed. Myra Jehlen and Michael Warner (New York: Routledge, 1997), 315.

62. Ibid.

63. Carroll, "Affecting History," 511.

64. Derounian-Stodola, "Indian Captivity Narratives," 41.

65. Rowlandson, *Sovereignty and Goodness*, 104–6.

66. Derounian-Stodola, "Indian Captivity Narratives," 41.

67. Michelle Burnham, "The Journey Between: Liminality and Dialogism in Mary White Rowlandson's Captivity Narrative," *Early American Literature* 28 (1993): 61.

68. Derounian-Stodola, "Indian Captivity Narratives," 41.

69. Ibid.

70. Ibid.

71. Derounian, "Publication, Promotion, and Distribution," 241.

72. Ibid., 242.

73. Ibid.

74. From Mather's *Brief History*, quoted in Strong, *Captive Selves*, 94.

75. Rowlandson, *Sovereignty and Goodness*, 106.

76. See the King James Bible, 1611 edition, 1 Samuel 15, for the account of this incident.

77. Rowlandson, *Sovereignty and Goodness*, 78–79.

78. Salisbury, *Sovereignty and Goodness of God*, 78n.

79. Although Mather's text wasn't published until 1684, Salisbury points out that Mather had begun the initial research for this work as early as 1670.

80. Increase Mather, *An Essay for the Recording of Illustrious Providences* (Delmar, NY: Scholars' Facsimiles & Reprints, 1977), A3v.

81. See Rowlandson, *Sovereignty and Goodness*, 74, 76, 77, 88, 104, and 111.

82. In "The Preface to the Reader" there are three instances of the adjective suffix *-full*, "wonderfull," "unmercifull," and "awfull," as well as four additional examples of words spelled with double *l*, where a single *l* is now common. In the Rowlandson narrative, this same adjective-suffix usage is found sixteen times, with an additional ten instances of other double *l* usage.

83. Rowlandson, *Sovereignty and Goodness*, 76.

84. Ibid.

85. Ibid., 77.

86. Ibid.

87. Cotton Mather, *Humiliations follow'd with Deliverences* (Boston: B. Green and J. Allen for Samuel Philips, 1697), 4.

88. Cotton Mather, *A Pastoral Letter To The English Captives, In Africa From New-England* (Boston: B. Green and J. Allen, 1698), 15.

89. Increase Mather, *A Relation of the Troubles which have hapned in New-England* (Boston: Printed and sold by John Foster, 1677), A2v.

90. Rowlandson, *Sovereignty and Goodness*, 82.

91. Ibid., 70.

92. Cotton Mather, *Terribilia Dei.: Remarkable Judgements of God* (Boston: B. Green and J. Allen, 1697), 31.

93. A particularly fraught analysis is that of Sidonie Smith's "Reading the Posthuman Backward: Mary Rowlandson's Doubled Witnessing," published in the Winter 2012 issue of *Biography* (137–52). Smith takes a rather novel approach to *The Soveraignty and Goodness of God* in this essay by attempting to read it through the lens of posthumanism. In addition to containing a baffling variety of factual inaccuracies—which include the identification of the raiding party as a "band of Wampanoag Indians" that "took Mary Rowlandson of Deerfield . . . captive," in addition to confusing the publishing history in which the London edition, *A True History of the Captivity & Restoration of Mrs. Mary Rowlandson*, is attributed as the Boston edition and *The Soveraignty and Goodness of God* as being published in "Cambridge, England"—while the analysis offered seems theoretically over-signified to say the least (142). Representative

of the effort to address the question of what a posthumanist analysis can "tell us about the social action of Puritan narratives of captivity" is Smith's claim that "it is a disembodied, spiritual posthumanity of self-erasing representation, mediated by the Word that *The True Relation* (Smith's abbreviation for the title of Rowlandson's narrative) inscribes" (144). The laborious decontextualization of the Rowlandson text, and lack of attention paid to Native subjectivities that is evident throughout this essay, seems symptomatic of a broader tendency to treat texts as an assembly of syntactic units that can be detached from their historical contexts and effectively read through practically any theoretical concept or perspective.

Chapter 5

1. Edgar Allan Poe, *The Narrative of Arthur Gordon Pym of Nantucket* (1838; repr., New York: Penguin, 1986), 57.

2. Herman Melville, *The Confidence Man: His Masquerade* (1857; repr., New York: Norton, 1971), 129.

3. Michiko Kakutani, "Adoptive Daughter of the Hills and Valleys," *New York Times*, August 6, 2002, E6.

4. Renato Rosaldo, *Culture and Truth: The Remaking of Social Analysis* (New York: Beacon, 1989), 69.

5. Robert C. Sands, *The Writings of Robert C. Sands, in Prose and Verse. With a Memoir of the Author. In Two Volumes*, vol. 1 (New York: Harper and Brothers, 1834), 282.

6. Sands, *Writings of Robert C. Sands*, 292.

7. Washington Irving, "Philip of Pokonoket: An Indian Memoir" in *The Sketch-Book of Geoffrey Crayon, Gent*, 1820, rev. ed. (New York: G. P. Putnam's Sons, 1884), 429.

8. Although Stone's play premiered at New York's Park Theatre, December 15, 1829, the manuscript was presumed lost and not published until 1941, after being discovered at the University of Utah. As Janet Black notes in her unpublished dissertation, "Staging Captivity: *Metamora* and American Identity" (PhD diss., University of Denver, 2002), after its opening, the play continued to garner popular success over the next thirty years, with performances frequent in New York, Buffalo, Philadelphia, Boston, Cincinnati, Louisville, Natchez, and New Orleans.

9. William Apess, *Eulogy on King Philip as Pronounced at the Odeon, In Federal Street, Boston, By The Rev. William Apess, An Indian, January 8, 1836*, 2nd ed. (Boston: Published by the Author, 1837).

10. John Easton, *A Relacion of the Indyan Warre, By Mr Easton, of Rhoade Isld., 1675*, in *The Present State of New-England, with Respect to the Indian VVar* (London: Dorman Newman, 1675).

11. Patricia Bizzell, "The 4th of July and the 22nd of December: The Function of Cultural Archives in Persuasion, as Shown by Frederick Douglass

and William Apess," *College Composition and Communication* 48 (February 1997): 56.

12. Jill Lepore, "Wigwam Words," *The American Scholar* 70 (2001): 98.

13. Ibid., 108.

14. Ibid., 101.

15. Ibid.

16. William T. Hornaday, *The Extermination of the American Bison* (Washington, D.C.: Government Printing Office, 1889), 375–86.

17. Lepore, "Wigwam Words," 101.

18. Richard Hildreth was a nineteenth-century novelist, historian, and journalist whose novel, *The Slave: Memoirs of Archy Moore* (1836) is considered among the first anti-slavery novels in American letters.

19. Gerald Vizenor, *Manifest Manners: Narratives on Postindian Survivance* (Lincoln: Bison Books, 1994), 5.

20. William Apess, *Eulogy on King Philip* (1837; repr., Amherst: University of Massachusetts Press, 1997), 133.

21. Anne Marie Dannenberg, "'Where, Then, Shall We Place the Hero of the Wilderness?': William Apess's *Eulogy on King Philip* and Doctrines of Racial Destiny," in *Early Native American Writing: New Critical Essays* (Cambridge, UK: Cambridge University Press, 1996), 67.

22. Apess, *Eulogy*, 133.

23. Lepore, "Wigwam Words," 106.

24. Douglas Miles, Personal Communication, April 3, 2013.

25. Lepore, "Wigwam Words," 102.

26. Ibid., 104.

27. Ibid., 107.

28. Ibid., 105.

29. Toni Morrison, *A Mercy* (New York: Alfred A. Knopf, 2008), 115.

30. Lepore, *Name of War*, 129, emphasis mine. In fact, throughout the whole of this work, Lepore uses the qualifiers possibly, probably, may have, might have, and must have, over one hundred times.

31. Cathy Caruth, *Unclaimed Experience: Trauma, Narrative, and History* (Baltimore: Johns Hopkins University Press, 1996), 9.

32. Vizenor, *Manifest Manners*, 56.

33. Robert Hunter Morris, "A Proclamation," *The Pennsylvania Gazette*, May 6, 1756, 1.

34. Henry Louis Gates, Jr., Introduction to *The Classic Slave Narratives*, ed. Henry Louis Gates, Jr. (New York: Signet Books, 1987), 1.

35. Frederick Douglass, *Narrative of the Life of Frederick Douglass* (1845; repr., New Haven: Yale University Press, 2001), 74–75.

36. Gates, "Introduction," 6.

37. See Vizenor, *Manifest Manners*, 9–15.

38. Dennis Banks, *Ojibwa Warrior: Dennis Banks and the Rise of the American Indian Movement* (Norman: University of Oklahoma Press, 2005), 24.

39. Laura Tohe, *No Parole Today* (Albuquerque: West End Press, 1999), xii.

40. Aimé Césaire, *Discourse on Colonialism*, trans. Joan Pinkham (1955; repr., Monthly Review Press, 1972), 20.

41. Matthew Teorey, "Sir Ernest Shackleton's Miraculous Escape from Antarctica as Captivity Narrative: 'The Grip of the Ice,'" *English Literature in Transition, 1880–1920* 47 (2004): 275.

42. Ibid., 273.

43. William Bradford, *Bradford's History "Of Plimouth Plantation"* (Boston: Wright and Potter Printing, 1898), 33–34.

44. James Duane was at the time the head of the Committee of Indian Affairs and a delegate to the Continental Congress.

45. George Washington, "Letter: George Washington to James Duane," in *Cases and Materials on Federal Indian Law*, ed. David Getches, Charles F. Wilkinson, and Robert A. Williams, Jr. (St. Paul, MN: West Group, 1998), 85.

46. David Getches, Charles F. Wilkinson, and Robert A. Williams, Jr., eds., *Cases and Materials on Federal Indian Law* (St. Paul, MN: West Group, 1998), 109.

47. Among other major Supreme Court cases, similar sentiments can also be found in: *United States v. Kagama*, 1886 (118 U.S. 375, 6 S.Ct. 1109, 30 L.Ed. 228) and *Tee-Hit-Ton Indians v. United States*, 1955 (348 U.S. 272, 75 S.ct. 313, 99 L.ed.314.), to cite just two of the most blatant examples.

48. Getches, *Cases and Materials*, 156.

49. Walter Benjamin, "Theses on the Philosophy of History," in *Illuminations*, trans. Harry Zohn, ed. Hannah Arendt (1955, repr., New York: Schocken, 1968), 256.

50. Perry Miller, quoted in Jane Tompkins, "Indians," in *"Race," Writing, and Difference*, ed. Henry Louis Gates, Jr. (Chicago: University of Chicago Press, 1986), 59–77.

51. George E. Tinker, *Missionary Conquest: The Gospel and Native American Cultural Genocide* (Minneapolis: Fortress Press, 1993), 21–22.

52. A. S. Barnes, *A Brief History of the United States* (1871; repr., New York: American, 1885), 1.

53. Ibid., 12.

54. Thomas King, *Green Grass, Running Water* (New York: Houghton Mifflin, 1993), 18–19.

55. Ibid., 19.

56. Stephen Graham Jones, *The Bird is Gone: A ~~Monograph~~ Manifesto* (Tallahasse, FL: FC2, 2003), 168.

57. Although several book-length studies have been published in which scholars have sought to extend the ideas developed in Said's *Orientalism* from an array of cultural, historical, and geographical stances, North American colonialism vis-à-vis Native American culture has only recently began to receive attention. See, for example, Ashcroft, Griffiths, and Tiffin, *The Empire Writes Back* (1990); Gayatri Chakravorty Spivak, *The Post-Colonial Critic* (1990); Homi Bhabha, *The Location of Culture* (1994); Anne McClintock, *Imperial Leather* (1995); Bart Moore-Gilbert, *Postcolonial Theory* (1997); Phillip Darby,

The Fiction of Imperialism (1998); Ania Loomba, *Colonialism/Postcolonialism* (1998); and Robert Young's *Poscolonialism* (2001).

58. See Taiaiaike Alfred and Jeff Corntassel, "Being Indigenous: Resurgences Against Contemporary Colonialism," in *Government and Opposition: An International Journal of Comparative Politics* 40 (2005): 597–614; Jodi A. Byrd and Michael Rothenberg, "Between Subalternity and Indigeneity," *Interventions: International Journal of Postcolonial Studies* 13 (2011): 1–12; Dale A. Turner, *This Is Not A Peace Pipe* (Toronto: University of Toronto Press, 2006); and Robert Warrior, "'Native Critics in the World': Edward Said and Nationalism," in *American Indian Literary Nationalism*, ed. Robert Warrior, Jace Weaver, and Craig Womack (Albuquerque: University of New Mexico Press, 2006), 179–223.

59. Homi Bhabha, *Location of Culture* (New York: Routledge, 1994), 76.

60. See Alden Vaughn, *Transatlantic Encounters: American Indians in Britain, 1500–1776* (Cambridge, UK: Cambridge University Press, 2006), for a rich discussion of transatlantic Native experiences between New England and the Britain.

61. "The Great Chronicle of London," in *The English Literatures of America: 1500–1800,* ed. Myra Jehlen and Michael Warner (New York: Routledge, 1997), 42.

62. William Shakespeare, *The Tempest*, in *The Norton Shakespeare Based on the Oxford Edition,* ed. Stephen Greenblatt et al. (New York: W. W. Norton, 1997), 2.2, 3078.

63. While not going as far as critics such as John Gillies and Eric Cheyfitz in claiming Caliban as an analog to Native American people, Stephen Greenblatt distinguishes Caliban for his subversion of European hegemony through the mastery of Prospero's own language and reason (35).

64. Nicolas Schmidle, "Getting Bin Laden," *The New Yorker*, August 8, 2011, accessed February 24, 2013. http://www.newyorker.com/reporting/2011/08/08/110808fa_fact_schmidle?currentPage=all.

65. Susan Faludi, "America's Guardian Myths," *New York Times,* September 7, 2007.

66. Lepore, *The Name of War: King Philip's War and the Origins of American Identity* (New York: Vintage, 1998), xv.

67. Susan Faludi, *The Terror Dream: Myth and Misogyny in an Insecure America* (New York: Picador, 2008), 277.

68. See especially the introduction to Philip Deloria's *Indians in Unexpected Places* (Lawrence: University of Kansas Press, 2004), 3–14.

References

Alexie, Sherman. *First Indian on the Moon.* Brooklyn: Hanging Loose Press, 1993.

Alfred, Taiaiaike, and Jeff Corntassel. "Being Indigenous: Resurgences Against Contemporary Colonialism." *Government and Opposition: An International Journal of Comparative Politics* 40 (2005): 597–614.

Apess, William. *Eulogy on King Philip, as Pronounced at the Odeon. In Federal Street, Boston, By The Rev. William Apess, An Indian, January 8, 1836.* 2nd ed. Boston: William Apess, 1837.

———. *Eulogy on King Philip, as Pronounced at the Odeon, in Federal Street Boston (1836).* In *A Son of the Forest and Other Writings.* Edited by Barry O'Connell. Amherst: University of Massachusetts Press, 1992.

Apocalypto. Directed by Mel Gibson. Performed by Rudy Youngblood, Dalia Hernández, and Raoul Trujillo. Touchstone Pictures, 2006.

Armstrong, Nancy, and Leonard Tennenhouse. "The American Origins of the English Novel." *American Literary History* 4 (1992): 386–410.

Arsić, Branka. "Mary Rowlandson and the Phenomenology of Patient Suffering." *Common Knowledge* 16 (2009): 247–75.

Ashcroft, Bill, Gareth Griffiths, and Helen Tiffin, eds. *The Empire Writes Back: Theory and Practice in Post-Colonial Literatures.* New York: Routledge, 1990.

Askew, Anne. *The first examinacio of Anne Askew latelye martired in Smythfelde, by the Romyshe popes vpholders, wyth the elucydacyon of Iohan Bale.* Imprynted at Marpurg in the lande of Hessen. London: Printed by Nicholas Hill, 1546.

At a Court Held at Boston in New-England the 29th of March, 1677. By the Council. Edward Rawson. Secr.' Broadside. Boston, 1677.

Baepler, Paul. "The Barbary Captivity Narrative in Early America." *Early American Literature* 30, no. 2 (1995): 90–120.

———. "White Slaves, African Masters." *Annals of the American Academy of Political and Social Science* 588 (2003): 90–111.

Banks, Dennis. *Ojibwa Warrior: Dennis Banks and the Rise of the American Indian Movement.* Norman: University of Oklahoma Press, 2005.

Barnes, A. S. *A Brief History of the United States.* 1871. New York: American, 1885.

Baudrillard, Jean. *Simulacra and Simulation.* Translated by Shelia Faria Glaser. Ann Arbor: University of Michigan Press, 1994.

Becon, Thomas. *The new pollecye of warre wherin is declared not only how [ye] mooste cruell tyraunt the great Turke may be ouer come, but also all other enemies of the Christen publique weale, lately deuised by Theodore Basille.* London: Iohn Maylerre for Iohn Gough, 1542.

Benjamin, Walter. *Illuminations.* 1955. Translated by Harry Zohn. Edited by Hannah Arendt. New York: Schocken, 1968.

Ben-Zvi, Yael. "Ethnology and the Production of Foreignness in Indian Captivity Narratives." *American Indian Quarterly* 32 (2008): ix–xxxi.

Best, George. *A True Discourse of the late voyages of discouerie, for the finding of a passage to Cathaya, by the Northvveast, vnder the conduct of Martin Frobisher Generall deuided into three bookes. In the first wherof is shewed, his first voyage . . . Also, there are annexed certayne reasons, to proue all partes of the worlde habitable, with a generall mappe adioyned. In the second, is set out his second voyage . . . In the thirde, is declared the strange fortunes which hapned in the third voyage . . . VVith a particular card therevnto adioyned of Meta Incognita.* London: Henry Bynnyman, 1578.

Bhabha, Homi. *The Location of Culture.* London: Routledge, 1994.

———. "Signs Taken for Wonders." In *The Post Colonial Studies Reader*, edited by Bill Ashcroft, Gareth Griffiths, and Helen Tiffin, 29–35. New York: Routledge, 1997.

Bizzell, Patricia. "The 4th of July and the 22nd of December: The Function of Cultural Archives in Persuasion, as Shown by Frederick Douglas and William Apess." *College Composition and Communication* 48 (February 1997): 44–60.

Black, Janet. "Staging Captivity: *Metamora* and American Identity." PhD diss., University of Denver, 2002.

Bodge, George Madison. *Soldiers in King Philip's War Being a Critical Account of that War with a Concise History of the Indian Wars of New England from 1620–1677.* Boston: By the Author, 1906.

Bourne, Russell. *The Red King's Rebellion: Racial Politics in New England 1675–1678.* New York: Atheneum, 1990.

Bradford, William. *Bradford's History "Of Plimouth Plantation." From the original manuscript. With a report of the proceedings incident to the return of the manuscript to Massachusetts.* Boston: Wright and Potter Printing Co., 1898.

———. *History of Plymouth Plantation*, edited by Charles Deane. Boston: Privately Printed, 1856.

———. *Of Plymouth Plantation: 1620–1647.* 1856. Edited by Samuel Eliot Morison. New York: Modern Library, 1981.

Bradford, William, and Edward Winslow. *Mourt's Relation.* 1622. In *A Journal of the Pilgrims at Plymouth: Mourt's Relation*, edited by Dwight B. Heath. New York: Corinth Books, 1963.

Bradstreet, Anne Dudley. *The tenth muse lately sprung up in America or severall poems, compiled with great variety of vvit and learning, full of delight. Wherein especially is contained a compleat discourse and description of the four elements, constitutions, ages of man, seasons of the year. Together with an exact epitomie of the four monarchies, viz. The Assyrian, Persian, Grecian, Roman. Also a dialogue between Old England and New, concerning the late troubles. With divers other pleasant and serious poems. By a gentlewoman in those parts.* Printed at London: for Stephen Bowtell at the signe of the Bible in Popes Head-Alley, 1650.

———. *Several poems compiled with great variety of wit and learning, full of delight wherein especially is contained a compleat discourse, and description of the four elements, constitutions, ages of man, seasons of the year, together with an exact epitome of the three by a gentlewoman in New-England.* Boston: Printed by John Foster, 1678.

Breitwieser, Mitchell. *American Puritanism and the Defense of Mourning: Religion, Grief, and Ethnology in Mary White Rowlandson's Captivity Narrative.* Madison: University of Wisconsin Press, 1990.

Bunyan, John. *The pilgrim's progress from this world to that which is to come, delivered under the similitude of a dream wherein is discovered the manner of his setting out, his dangerous journey, and safe arrival at the desired countrey.* Boston: Samuel Green, 1681.

Burling, Elias. *A call to back-sliding Israel and may be as a necessary word of caution and admonition to the inhabitants of East and West-Jarsey, Pennsilvania, &c. as a remembrancer to them to call to mind their former state, and whence they are fallen. With some short account of my leaving a second time that party of them called Quakers, which have condemned G. Keith, and all that own him, or his testimony for the crucified Jesus, our alone advocate in heaven.* New York: William Bradford, 1694.

Burnham, Michelle. "Anne Hutchinson and the Economics of Antinomian Selfhood in Colonial New England." *Criticism* 39 (1997): 337–58.

———. "The Journey Between: Liminality and Dialogism in Mary White Rowlandson's Captivity Narrative." *Early American Literature* 28, no. 1 (1993): 60–75.

Byrd, Jodi A., and Michael Rothenberg. "Between Subalternity and Indigeneity." *Interventions: International Journal of Postcolonial Studies* 13 (2011): 1–12.

Carleton, Phillips D. "The Indian Captivity." *American Literature* 15 (1943): 169-80.

Carroll, Lorrayne. "'Affecting History': Impersonating Women in the Early Republic." *Early American Literature* 39 (2004): 511–52.

———. *Rhetorical Drag: Gender Impersonation, Captivity, and the Writing of History.* Kent, OH: Kent State University Press, 2007.

Caruth, Cathy. *Unclaimed Experience: Trauma, Narrative, and History.* Baltimore: Johns Hopkins University Press, 1996.

Castillo, Bernal Diaz del. *The Conquest of New Spain.* Translated by J. M. Cohen. New York: Penguin, 1963.

———. *Historia verdadera de la conquista de la Nueva Espana.* 2 vols. 1584. Edited by Miguel Léon Portilla. Madrid: Historia, 1984.

Caverly, Robert B. *The Heroism of Hannah Duston, Together with The Indian Wars of New England.* Boston: B. B. Russell, 1875.

Caxton, William. *The Cronycles of Englond.* London: William Caxton, 1482.

Césaire, Aimé. *Discourse on Colonialism.* 1955. Translated by Joan Pinkham. Monthly Review Press, 1972.

Cheyfitz, Eric. *The Poetics of Imperialism: Translation and Colonization from 'The Tempest' to 'Tarzan.'* Philadelphia: University of Pennsylvania Press, 1997.

Chipman, Donald E. "In Search of Cabeza de Vaca's Route Across Texas: An Historiographical Survey." *Southwestern Historical Quarterly* 91 (1997): 127–48.

Church, Thomas. *The Entertaining History of King Philip's War: Which Began in the Month of June, 1675, As Also of Expeditions More Lately Made against the Common Enemy, and Indian Rebels in the Eastern Parts of New-England; with Some Account of the Divine Providence Towards Col. Benjamin Church.* 1716. Newport, Rhode-Island: Solomon Southwick, 1772.

Cole, Richard G. "Sixteenth-Century Travel Books as a Source of European Attitudes Toward Non-White and Non-Western Culture." *Proceedings of the American Philosophical Society* 116, no.1 (1972): 59–67.

Colley, Linda. *Captives.* New York: Pantheon Books, 2002.

Conforti, Joseph A. *Imagining New England: Explorations of Regional Identity from the Pilgrims to the Mid-Twentieth Century.* Chapel Hill: University of North Carolina Press, 2001.

Cooper, James Fennimore. *Last of the Mohicans: A Narrative of 1757.* 2 vols. Philadelphia: H.C. Carey & I. Lea, 1826.

Cotton, John. *God's Promise to His Plantation.* London: Printed by William Jones, 1630.

Custer, George Armstrong. *Wild Life on the Plains and The Horrors of Indian Warfare.* St. Louis: Sun Publishing, 1874.

Da Pian del Carpine, Giovanni. *Historia Mongalorum quos nos Tartaros appellamus: Friar Giovanni di Plano Carpini's Account of His Embassy to the Court of the Mongol Khan.* 1330–1331. Translated by Erik Hildinger. Boston: Branden Publishing Co., 1996.

Dannenberg, Anne Marie. "'Where, Then, Shall We Place the Hero of the Wildernes?' William Apess's *Eulogy on King Philip* and Doctrines of Racial Destiny." In *Early Native American Writing: New Critical Essays,* edited by Helen Jaskowski, 66–82. Cambridge, UK: Cambridge University Press, 1996.

Darby, Phillip. *The Fiction of Imperialism: Reading Between International Relations and Postcolonialism.* London: Cassell, 1998.

Davidson, Edward H. "John Cotton's Biblical Exegesis: Method and Purpose." *Early American Literature* 17, no. 2 (1982): 119–38.

Defoe, Daniel. *A New Voyage Round the World.* Chester: W. Cooke, 1725.

Deleuze, Gilles, and Félix Guattari. *A Thousand Plateaus: Capitalism and Schizophrenia.* 1980. Translated by Brian Massumi. Minneapolis: University of Minnesota Press, 1987.

Deloria, Philip J. *Indians in Unexpected Places.* Lawrence: University of Kansas Press, 2004.

Demos, John. *The Unredeemed Captive: A Family Story from Early America.* New York: Knopf, 1994.

Derounian, Kathryn Zabelle. "The Publication, Promotion, and Distribution of Mary Rowlandson's Indian Captivity Narrative in the Seventeenth Century." *Early American Literature* 23 (1988): 239–61.

Derounian-Stodola, Kathryn Zabelle. "The Indian Captivity Narratives of Mary Rowlandson and Olive Oatman: Case Studies in the Continuity, Evolution, and Exploitation of Literary Discourse." *Studies in the Literary Imagination* 27 (1994): 33–46.

———, ed. "Introduction." In *Women's Indian Captivity Narratives,* edited by Kathryn Zabelle Derounian-Stodola (1998), xi–xxviii. New York: Penguin Books, 2010.

Derounian-Stodola, Kathryn Zabelle, and James Arthur Levernier. *The Indian Captivity Narrative: 1550–1900.* New York: Twayne Publishers, 1993.

Derrida, Jacques. "Signature Event Context." In *The Margins of Philosophy.* 1972. Translated by Alan Bass. Chicago: University of Chicago Press, 1982.

Diebold, Robert Kent. "A Critical Edition of Mrs. Mary Rowlandson's Captivity Narrative." PhD diss., Yale University Press, 1972.

Douglass, Frederick. *Narrative of the Life of Frederick Douglass.* 1845. New Haven: Yale University Press, 2001.

Drake, Samuel G. "Prefatory by the Editor." *The History of King Philip's War by the Rev. Increase Mather, D. D. also, A History of the Same War, By the Rev. Cotton Mather, D. D.* Albany: J. Munsell, 1862.

Drimmer, Frederick. Introduction to *Captured by Indians: 15 Firsthand Accounts, 1750–1870.* 1961. Edited by Frederick Drimmer. New York: Dover, 1985.

Dussel, Enrique. *The Invention of the Americas: Eclipse of "the Other" and the Myth of Modernity.* 1992. Translated by Michael D. Barber. New York: Continuum, 1995.

Earle, Alice Morse. *The Sabbath in Puritan New England.* Charles Scribner's Sons: New York, 1891.

Easton, John. "A Relacion of the Indyan Warre, By Mr Easton, of Rhoade Isld., 1675." In *The Present State of New-England, with Respect to the Indian VVar Wherein is an Account of the true Reason thereof (as far as can be Judged by Men): Together with most of the Remarkable Passages that have happened from the 20th of June, till the 10th of November, 1675 / Faithfully*

Composed by a Merchant of Boston, and Communicated to his Friend in London. N. S. London: Printed for Dorman Newman, 1675.

———. "A Relacion of the Indyan Warre, by Mr. Easton, of Road Isld., 1675." In *Narratives of the Indian Wars: 1675–1699*. Edited by Charles H. Lincoln. New York: Charles Scribner's Sons, 1913.

Ebersole, Gary. *Captured By Texts: Puritan to Postmodern Images of Indian Captivity*. Charlottesville: University Press of Virginia, 1995.

Elliot, Emory. *The Cambridge Introduction to Early American Literature*. Cambridge: Cambridge University Press, 2002.

Engdahl, Horace. "Philomena's Tongue: Introductory Remarks on Witness Literature." In *Witness Literature: Proceedings of the Nobel Centennial Symposium*, edited by Horace Engdahl. River Edge, NJ: World Scientific Publishing, 2002.

The Estate of Christians, liuing vnder the subiection of the Turke. And also the warres betweene the Christians and the turke, beginning 1592. and continuing till the end of 1593. London: John Wolfe, 1595.

Evans, Charles. *American Bibliography. A Chronological Dicitonary of All Books, Pamphlets and Periodical Publications Printed in the United States of America from the Genesis of Printing in 1639 Down to and Including the Year [1800]*. Chicago: The Blakely Press, for the Author, 1943–1955.

Fabyan, Robert. *Fabyans cronycle newly printed wyth the cronycle, actes, and dedes done in the tyme of the reygne of the moste excellent prynce kynge Henry the vii. father vnto our most drad souerayne lord kynge Henry the .viii. To whom be all honour, reuere[n]ce, and ioyfull contynaunce of his prosperous reygne, to the pleasure of god and weale of this his realme amen*. London: William Rastell, 1533.

Faludi, Susan. "America's Guardian Myths." *New York Times*, September 7, 2007.

———. *The Terror Dream: Myth and Misogyny in an Insecure America*. New York: Picador, 2008.

Farrell, Molly. "'Beyond My Skil': Mary Rowlandson's Counting." *Early American Literature* 47 (2012): 59–87.

Fergus, Jim. *One Hundred White Women: The Journals of Mary Dodd*. New York: St. Martin's Press, 1998.

Fickes, Michael. "'They Could Not Endure That Yoke': The Captivity of Pequot Women and Children after the War of 1637." *The New England Quarterly* 73 (2000): 58–81.

Foucault, Michel. *Power/Knowledge: Selected Interviews and Other Writings, 1972–1977*. Edited by Colin Gordon. New York: Pantheon Books, 1980.

———. "What is an Author?" In *The Foucault Reader*. Edited by Paul Rabinow. Translated by Josué V. Harari. 1979. Reprint, New York: Pantheon Books, 1984.

Friedman, Ellen G. "Christian Captives as 'Hard Labor' in Algiers, 16th–18th Centuries." *The International Journal of African Historical Studies* 13 (1980): 616–32.

Frith, John. *A disputacio of purgatorye made by Ioh[a]n Frith which is deuided in to thre bokes. The first boke is an answere vnto Rastell, which goeth aboute to proue purgatorye by naturall phylosophye. The seconde boke answereth vnto Sir Thomas More, which laboureth to proue purgatorye by scripture. The thirde boke maketh answere vnto my lorde of Rochestre which most leaneth vnto the doctoures. Assertionis Lutheranae confutatio.* Antwerp: S. Cock, 1531.

Gates, Henry Louis, Jr. Introduction to *The Classic Slave Narratives*, edited by Henry Louis Gates Jr., 1–14. New York: Signet Books, 1987.

Gates, Henry Louis, Jr., and Kwame Anthony Appiah, eds. *"Race," Writing, and Difference.* Chicago: University of Chicago Press, 1986.

The General Laws and Liberties of the Massachusetts Colony, Revised and Reprinted. Cambridge, MA: Printed by Samuel Green, for John Usher of Boston, 1672.

Getches, David, Charles F. Wilkinson and Robert A. Williams, Jr., eds. *Cases and Materials on Federal Indian Law.* St. Paul, MN: West Group, 1998.

Gillies, John. "Shakespeare's Virginian Masque." *English Literary History* 53 (1986): 673–707.

Gnaphaeus, Gulielmus. *A myrrour or glasse from them that be syke in payne. Translated out of Dutche in English.* Prynted in Southwarke: By Iames Nicolson, for Ian Gough cum priuilegio Regali, 1536.

Goddard, Ives, and Kathleen Bragdon. *Native Writings in Massachusett.* 2 vols. Philadelphia: American Philosophical Society, 1988.

Göllner, Carl. *Tvrcica: Die europäishen Turkendrucke des XVI. Jahrhunderts.* 2 vols. Budapest and Berlin: Editura Academiei R.P.R., 1961.

Goodhue, Sarah. *Copy of a valedictory and monitory writing left by Sarah Goodhue.* New London, CT: 1681.

"The Great Chronicle of London." 1502. In *The English Literatures of America: 1500–1800*, edited by Myra Jehlen and Michael Warner. New York: Routledge, 1997.

Greenblatt, Stephen. *Learning to Curse: Essays in Early Modern Culture.* 1990. New York: Routledge, 2007.

Greene, David L. "New Light on Mary Rowlandson." *Early American Literature* 20 (1985): 24–37.

Greg, W. W. "The Rationale of the Copy-Text." In *Bibliography and Textual Criticism: English and American Literature 1700 to the Present*, edited by O.M. Brack, Jr., and Warner Barnes, 41–58. Chicago: University of Chicago Press, 1969.

Gyles, John. *Memoirs of Odd Adventures, Strange Deliverances, etc., in the Captivity of John Gyles, Esq., Commander of the Garrison on St. George River, in the District of Maine. Written by Himself.* Boston: S. Knefland and T. Green, 1736.

Hakluyt, Richard. *The principle nauigations, voyages, traffiques and discoueries of the English nation made by sea or ouer-land, to the remote and farthest distant quarters of the earth, at any time within the compasse of these 1600.*

yeres: deuided into three seuerall volumes, according to the positions of the regions, whereunto they were directed. The first volume containeth the worthy discoueries, &c. of the English . . . The second volume comprehendeth the principall nauigations . . . to the south and south-east parts of the world . . . By Richard Hakluyt preacher, and sometime student of Christ-Church in Oxford. 2 vols. London: George Bishop, Ralph Newberie, and Robert Barker, 1599.

Hall, Michael G. *The Last American Puritan: The Life of Increase Mather 1639–1723.* Middletown, CT: Wesleyan University Press, 1988.

Haller, William, Jr. *The Puritan Frontier: Town-Planting in New England Colonial Development, 1630–1660.* New York: Columbia University Press, 1951.

Hanson, Elizabeth. *An Account of the Captivity of Elizabeth Hanson, Now or Late of Kachecky, in New-England: Who, with Four of her Children and Servant-Maid,was taken captive by the Indians, and carried into Canada. Setting Forth The various remarkable Occurrences, sore Trials, and wonderful Deliverances which befel them after their Departure, to the Time of their Redemption. Taken in Substance from her own Mouth, by Samuel Bownas.* 2nd ed. London: Samuel Clark, 1760.

———. *An Account of the Captivity of Elizabeth Hanson, Now or Late of Kachecky, in New-England: Who, with Four of her Children and Servant-Maid, was taken captive by the Indians, and carried into Canada. Setting forth The various remarkable Occurrences, sore Trials, and wonderful Deliverances which befell them after their Departure, to the Time of their Redemption. Taken in Substance from her own Mouth, by Samuel Bownas.* 1728. London: James Phillips, 1782.

Hartigan, Richard Shelly. "Saint Augustine on War and Killing: The Problem of the Innocent." *Journal of the History of Ideas* 27 (1966): 195–204.

Hartman, James. "Providence Tales and the Indian Captivity Narrative: Some Transatlantic Influences on Colonial Puritan Discourse." *Early American Literature* 32 (1997): 66–81.

Hell on Wheels. Durant, Nebraska. Directed by Adam Davidson. Performed by Anson Mount, Dominique McElligott, Helmer Twoyoungmen, and Lisa Christie. American Movie Classics, 2012.

Henwood, Dawn. "Mary Rowlandson and the Psalms: The Textuality of Survival." *Early American Literature* 32, no. 2 (1997): 169–87.

Higden, Ranulf. *Tabula.* London: Wynken de Worde, 1502.

Holmes, Thomas J. *Increase Mather His Works: Being a Short-Title Catalogue of the Published Writings That can be Ascribed to Him.* Cleveland: William Gwinn Mather, 1930.

Hornaday, William T. *The Extermination of the American Bison.* Washington, D.C.: Government Printing Office, 1889.

Howe, Susan. *The Birth-Mark: Unsettling the Wilderness in American Literary History.* Middletown, CT: Wesleyan University Press, 1993.

Hubbard, William. *The happiness of a people in the wisdome of their rulers directing and in the obedience of their brethren attending unto what Israel ougho [*sic*] to do recommended in a sermon before the Honourable Governour and Council, and the respected Deputies of Mattachusets [*sic*] colony in New-England. : Preached at Boston, May 3d, 1676, being the day of election there.* Boston: John Foster, 1676.

———. *A Narrative of the Troubles with the Indians in New-England from the first planting thereof in the year 1607. to this present year 1677. But chiefly of the late Troubles in the two last years, 1675. and 1676. To which is added a Discourse about the Warre with the Pequods inn the year 1637.* Boston: John Foster, 1677.

Hulme, Peter. "Columbus and the Cannibals." In *The Post-Colonial Studies Reader*, edited by Bill Ashcroft, Gareth Griffiths, and Helen Tiffin, 365–69. New York: Routledge, 1997.

JanMohamad, Abdul R. "The Economy of the Manichean Allegory: The Function of Racial Difference in Colonialist Literature." In "*Race*," *Writing, and Difference*, edited by Henry Louis Gates Jr., 78–106. Chicago: University of Chicago Press, 1986.

Jennings, Francis. *The Invasion of America: Indians, Colonialism, and the Cant of Conquest.* New York: W. W. Norton, 1976.

Johnson, Edward. *A history of New-England. From the English planting in the yeere 1628. untill the yeere 1652. Declaring the form of their government, civill, military, and ecclesiastique. Their wars with the indians, their troubles with the Gortonists, and other heretiques. Their manner of gathering of churches, the commodities of the country, and description of the principall towns and havens, with the great encouragements to increase trade betwixt them and old England. With the names of all their governours, magistrates, and eminent ministers.* London: Printed for Nathanial Brooke, 1653.

Jones, Howard Mumford. "The Colonial Impulse: An Analysis of the 'Promotion' Literature of Colonization." *Proceedings of the American Philosophical Society* 90 (1946): 131–61.

Jones, Stephen Graham. *The Bird is Gone: A ~~Monograph~~ Manifesto.* Tallahassee: FC2, 2003.

Kakutani, Michiko. "Adoptive Daughter of the Hills and Valleys." *New York Times*, August 6, 2002, E6.

King, Thomas. *Green Grass, Running Water.* New York: Houghton Mifflin, 1993.

Knight, Francis. *A relation of seaven yeares slaverie under the Turkes of Argeire, suffered by an English captive merchant Wherein is also conteined all memorable passages, fights, and accidents, which happined in that citie, and at sea with their shippes and gallies during that time. Together with a description of the sufferings of the miserable captives under that mercilesse tyrannie. Whereunto is added a second booke conteining a discription of Argeire, with its originall, manner of government, increase, and present flourishing estate.* London: T. Cotes, for Michael Sparke Junior, 1640.

Knutson, Roslyn L. "Elizabethan Documents, Captivity Narratives, and the Market for Foreign History Plays." *English Literary Renaissance* 26 (1996): 75–113.

Kohn, Denise and Margaret Campbell. "The Captive Female as Biblical Hero: Rowlandson, Rhetoric, and the Psalms." *The Explicator* 69 (2011): 125–28.

Kolodny, Annette. "Review Essay." *Early American Literature* 14 (1979): 228–35.

Kristeva, Julia. *Revolution in Poetic Language.* 1974. Translated by Margaret Waller. New York: Columbia University Press, 1984.

Larsen, Deborah. *The White.* New York: Knopf, 2002.

Las Casas, Bartolomé de. "Brevíssima relacíon de la detruycíon de las Indias." 1552. In *Obras Completas,* vol. 11, edited by J. B. Lassegue. Madrid: Editorial Alianza, 1992.

———. *A Short Account of the Destruction of the Indies.* 1552. Translated and edited by Nigel Griffin. New York: Penguin Books, 1992.

———. *The Spanish colonie, or Briefe chronicle of the acts and gestes of the Spaniardes in the West Indies, called the newe world, for the space of xl. yeeres: written in the Castilian tongue by the reuerend Bishop Bartholomew de las Cases or Casaus, a friar of the order of S. Dominicke. And nowe first translated into english, by M.M.S.* Imprinted at London: Thomas Dawson for William Brome, 1583.

———. *The tears of the Indians being an historical and true account of the cruel massacres and slaughters of above twenty millions of innocent people, committed by the Spaniards in the islands of Hispaniola, Cuba, Jamaica, &c. : as also in the continent of Mexico, Peru, & other places of the West-Indies, to the total destruction of those countries / written in Spanish by Casaus, an eye-witness of those things; and made English by J.P.* London: Printed by J.C. for Nath. Brook, 1656.

Leonard, Elmore. *The Tonto Woman and Other Western Stories.* New York: Delacorte, 1998.

Lepore, Jill. *The Name of War: King Philip's War and the Origins of American Identity.* New York: Vintage, 1998.

———. "Wigwam Words." *The American Scholar* 70, no. 1: 97–108.

Levin, David. "Forms of Uncertainty: Representation of Doubt in American Histories." *New Literary History* 8 (1976): 59–74.

Lindholdt, Paul J. "The Significance of the Colonial Promotion Tract." In *Early American Literature and Culture: Essays Honoring Harrison T. Meserole,* edited by Kathryn Zabelle Derounian-Stodola, 57–72. Newark: University of Delaware Press, 1992.

Loomba, Ania. *Colonialism/Postcolonialism.* New York: Routledge, 1998.

Ludwig, Mark. "Introduction." In Mary Rowlandson, *The Captive: An Early American Classic.* Tucson: American Eagle Publications, 1990.

Madsen, Deborah L. *American Exceptionalism.* Jackson: University of Mississippi Press, 1998.

Mandeville, Sir John. *Here begynneth a lytell treatyse or booke named Johan Mau[n]deuyll knyght born in Englonde in the towne of saynt Albone [and] speketh of the wayes of the holy londe towarde Jherusalem, [and] of marueyles of Ynde [and] of other dyuerse cou[n]trees.* Westminster: Wynken de Worde, 1499.

Marckwardt, Albert H. *American English.* New York: Oxford University Press, 1980.

Martin, Joel. *Sacred Revolt: The Muskogee's Struggle for a New World.* Boston: Beacon, 1991.

Matar, Nabil. "English Accounts of Captivity in North Africa and the Middle East: 1577–1625." *Renaissance Quarterly* 54 (2001): 553–72.

Mather, Cotton. *Humiliations follow'd with Deliverences: A Brief Discourse on the Matter and Method, Of that Humiliation which would be an Hopeful Symptom of our Deliverance from Calamity. Accompanied and Accomodated with A . . . Narrative Of a Nota'le Deliverance lately Received by some English Captives, From the Hands of Cruel Indians. And some Improvement of that narrative. Whereto is added A Narrative of Hannah Swarton, containing a great many wonderful passages, relating to her Captivity and Deliverance.* Boston: Printed by B. Green and J. Allen for Samuel Philips, 1697.

———. *Terribilia Dei.: Remarkable Judgements of God, on several sorts of offenders, in several scores of instances; among the people of New-England. Observed, collected, related, and improved; in two sermons, at Boston-lecture in the month of July 1697.* Boston: Printed by B. Green and J. Allen, 1697.

———. *A Pastoral Letter To The English Captives, In Africa From New-England.* Boston: Printed by B. Green and J. Allen, 1698.

———. *Magnalia Christi Americana: Or, The Ecclesiastical History of New-England, From Its First Planting in the Year 1620. unto the Year of our Lord, 1698.* In *SevenBooks.* London: Thomas Parkhurst, 1702.

Mather, Increase. *The Mystery of Israel's Salvation explained and applyed: or, A discourse concerning the general conversion of the Israelitish nation Wherein is shewed, 1. That the twelve tribes shall be saved. 2. When this is to be expected. 3. Why this must be. 4. What kind of salvation the tribes of Israel shall partake of (viz.) a glorious, wonderful, spiritual, temporal salvation. Being the substance of several sermons preached By Increase Mather, M.A. Teacher of a Church in Boston in New England.* London, 1669.

———. *A Brief History of the Warr With the Indians in Nevv-England, (From June 24, 1675. when the first English-man was murdered by the Indians, to August 12, 1676. when Philip, alias Metacomet, the principal Author and*

Beginner of the Warr, was slain) Wherein the Grounds, Beginning, and Progress of the warr, is summarily expressed. Together With A Serious Exhortation to the Inhabitants of that Land. Boston: Printed and Sold by John Foster, 1676.

———. *A Brief History of the War with the Indians of New England From June 24. 1675. (when the first Englishman was Murdered by the Indians) to August 12. 1676. when Philip, alias Metacomet, the principal Author and Beginner of the War, was slain.* London: for Richard Chiswell, 1676.

———. "To The Reader." In *A Brief History of the Warr with the Indians in New-England.* Boston: John Foster, 1676.

———. *An historical discourse concerning the prevalency of prayer wherein is shewed that New-Englands late deliverance from the rage of the heathen, is an eminent answer of prayer.* Boston: J. Foster, 1677.

———. *A Relation of the Troubles which have hapned in New-England, By reason of the Indians there: from the year 1614 to the year 1675. Wherein the frequent Conspiracyes of the Indians to cutt off the English, and the wonderfull providence of God in disappointing their devices, is declared: Together with an Historical Discourse concerning the Prevalency of Prayer; shewing that New Englands late deliverance from the Rage of the Heathen is an eminent Answer of Prayer.* Boston: Printed and sold by John Foster, 1677.

———. *Heavens Alarm to the World. Or a Sermon wherein is shewed, that fearful sights and signs in heaven are the presages of great calamities at hand.* Boston: John Foster, 1681.

———. "To the Reader." In Samuel Willard, *Covenant-keeping the way to blessedness.* Boston: James Glen, for Samuel Sewall, 1682.

———. *An essay for the recording of illustrious providences wherein an account is given of many remarkable and very memorable events which have hapned this last age, especially in New-England.* Boston: Samuel Green for Joseph Browning, 1684.

———. *An Essay for the Recording of Illustrious Providences.* 1684. Delmar, NY: Scholars' Facsimiles and Reprints, 1977.

———. *Narrative of the Captivity of Quintin Stockwell who was taken at Deerfield, in Massachusetts, by a Party of Indians, in the Year 1677; Communicated in his own words, and Originally Published by the Eminent Dr. Increase Mather, in the Year 1684, in Indian Captivities or Life in the Wigwam.* Edited by Samuel G. Drake. 1851. Reprint, New York: AMS Press, 1975.

Mather, Increase, and Cotton Mather. *The History of King Philip's War by the Rev. Increase Mather, D.D. also, A History of the Same War, By the Rev. Cotton Mather, D.D.* 1862. Edited by Samuel G. Drake. Facsimile reprint, Bowie, MD: Heritage Books, 1990.

Mathy, Jean-Philippe. "The Atlantic as Metaphor." *Atlantic Studies* 1 (2004): 107–17.

McClintock, Anne. *Imperial Leather: Race, Gender and Sexuality in the Colonial Contest.* New York: Routledge, 1995.

McGinty, Brian. *The Oatman Massacre: A Tale of Desert Captivity and Survival.* Norman: University of Oklahoma Press, 2005.

McIntyre, Shelia. "'I Heare it so Variously Reported': News-letters, Newspapers, and the Ministerial Network in New England, 1670–1730." *The New England Quarterly* 71 (December 1998): 593–614.

Melville, Herman. *The Confidence Man: His Masquerade.* 1857. New York: Norton, 1971.

Miles, Douglas. Personal Communication. April 3, 2013.

Miller, Perry. *The New England Mind: From Colony to Providence.* 1953. Boston: Beacon Press, 1961.

The Missing. Directed by Ron Howard. Performed by Tommy Lee Jones, Cate Blanchet, and Eric Schweig. Imagine Entertainment, 2003.

Mitchel, Jonathan. *Nehemiah on the vvall in troublesom times.* Cambridge, MA: S. G. (Samuel Green) and M. J. (Marmaduke Johnson), 1671.

Mitchell, David, and Melissa Hearn. "Colonial Savages and Heroic Tricksters: Native Americans in the American Tradition." *Journal of Popular Culture* 32, no. 4 (1999): 101–18.

Moore-Gilbert, Bart. *Postcolonial Theory: Contexts, Practices, Politics.* London: Verso, 1997.

Morris, Robert Hunter. "A Proclamation." *The Pennsylvania Gazette*, May 6, 1756.

Morrison, Toni. *A Mercy.* New York: Alfred A. Knopf, 2008.

Morton, Nathaniel. *New-Englands memoriall or, A brief relation of the most memorable and remarkable passages of the providence of God manifested to the planters of New-England in America with special reference to the first colony thereof, called New-Plimouth : as also a nomination of divers of the most eminent instruments deceased, both of church and common-wealth, improved in the first beginning and after-progress of sundry of the respective jurisdictions in those parts, in reference unto sundry exemplary passages of their lives, and the time of their death / published for use and benefit of present and future generations.* Cambridge, MA: S. G. (Samuel Green) and M. J. (Marmaduke Johnson) for John Vsher, 1669.

Munday, Anthony. *The admirable Deliverance of 266 Christians by Iohn Reynard Englishman from the captiuitie of the Turkes, who had been gally slaues many years in Alexandria. The number of the seueralll nations that were captiues follow in the next page.* London: Thomas Dawson, 1608.

Namias, June. *White Captives: Gender and Ethnicity on the American Frontier.* Chapel Hill: University of North Carolina Press, 1993.

Nelsen, Anne Kusener. "King Philip's War and the Hubbard-Mather Rivalry." *The William and Mary Quarterly* 27 (1970): 615–29.

Nuñez Cabeza de Vaca, Alvar. *Adventures in the Unknown Interior of America.* 1542. Translated and edited by Cyclone Covey. Albuquerque: University of New Mexico Press, 2002.

Ochino, Bernardino. *A tragoedie or dialoge of the vniuste vsurped primacie of the Bishop of Rome and of all the iust abolishyng of the same, made by master*

Barnardine Ochine an Italian, [and] translated out of Latine into Englishe by Master Iohn Ponet Doctor of Diuinitie, neuer printed before in any language. Imprynted at London: [By N. Hill] for Gwalter Lynne, 1549.

Pearce, Roy Harvey. *The Savages of America: A Study of the Indian and the Idea of Civilization.* Baltimore: Johns Hopkins Press, Revised Edition 1965.

———. "The Significances of the Captivity Narrative." *American Literature* 19 (1947–48): 1–20.

Pierce, Ebenezer W. *Indian History, Biography and Genealogy: Pertaining to the Good Sachem Massasoit of the Wampanoag Tribe, and His Descendants.* North Abington, MA: Zerviah Gould Mitchell, 1878.

Poe, Edgar Allan. *The Narrative of Arthur Gordon Pym of Nantucket.* 1838. New York: Penguin, 1986.

Pray, Mary. "A Letter to the Governor of Rhode Island." In *Further Letters on King Philip's War.* Providence: Printed for the Society by the E.L. Freeman Co. from the original MSS. in the Archives of the Commonwealth of Massachusetts, 1923.

Rabasa, José. *Writing Violence on the Northern Frontier: The Historiography of Sixteenth-Century New Mexico and Florida and the Legacy of Conquest.* Durham, NC: Duke University Press, 2000.

Radisson, Peter Espirit. *Radisson's Voyages. Voyages of Peter Espirit Radisson, Being an Account of His Travels and Experiences Among the North American Indians, From 1652 to 1684.* Edited by Gideon D. Scull. London, 1858.

Ramsey, Colin. "Cannibalism and Infant Killing: A System of 'Demonizing' Motifs in Indian Captivity Narratives." *Clio* 24 (1994): 55–68.

Rigby, Colonel. "Englishmen in Captivity in Eastern Africa." *Proceedings of the Royal Geographical Society of London* 10 (1865–1866): 113–16.

Rosaldo, Renato. *Culture and Truth: The Remaking of Social Analysis.* New York: Beacon, 1989.

Rowlandson, Joseph. *The possibility of God's forsaking a people, that have been visibly near & dear to him together with the misery of a people thus forsaken, set forth in a sermon preached at Weathersfield, Nov. 21. 1678. Being a day of fast and humiliation.* Boston: Printed for John Ratcliffe and John Griffin, 1682.

Rowlandson, Mary White. *The Soveraignty and Goodness of God, Together with the Faithfulness of His Promises Displayed: Being a Narrative of the Captivity and Restauration of Mrs. Mary Rowlandson; Commended by Her, to All that desires to Know the Lords Doings to, and Dealings with Her; Especially to her Dear Children and Relations, The Second Edition Corrected and Amended, Written by Her Own hand for Her Private Use, and Now Made Publick at the Earnest Desire of Some Friends, and for the Benefit of the Afflicted.* Cambridge: Printed by Samuel Green, 1682.

———. *A True History of the Captivity & Restoration of Mrs. Mary Rowlandson, A Minister's Wife in New-England. Wherein is set forth the Cruel and*

Inhumane Usage she underwent amongst the Heathens, for Eleven Weeks time: and her Deliverance from them. Written by her own Hand, for her Private Use: And now made Publick at the earnest Desire of some Friends, for the Benefit of the afflicted. London by Joseph Poole, 1682.

———. *A Narrative of the Captivity, Sufferings and Removes of Mrs. Mary Rowlandson, Who was taken Prisoner by the Indians with several others, and treated in the most barbarous and cruel Manner by these vile Savages: With many other remarkable Events during her Travels. Written by her own Hand, for her private Use, and now made public at the earnest Desire of some Friends, and for the Benefit of the afflicted.* Boston: John Boyle, 1773.

———. *A Narrative of the Captivity, Sufferings, and Removes of Mrs. Mary Rowlandson: Who Was Taken Prisoner by the Indians, with Several Others, and Treated in the Most Barbarous and Cruel Manner, by Those Vile Savages: with Many Other Remarkable Events During Her Travels.* New London, Conn: Timothy Green, 1773.

———. *The Narrative of the Captivity and Restoration of Mrs. Mary Rowlandson: The Lancaster Edition.* 1682. 1903. Edited by Frederick Lewis Weis. Boston: Houghton Mifflin Company, 1930.

———. *The Sovereignty and Goodness of God by Mary Rowlandson with Related Documents.* 1682. Edited by Neal Salisbury. New York: Bedford/St. Martin's, 1997.

Rowlandson, Mary, and John Williams. *Captivity and Deliverance of Mr. John Williams, Pastor of the Church in Deerfield, and Mrs. Mary Rowlandson, of Lancaster, Who Were Taken, Together With Their Families and Neighbors, By the French and the Indians, and Carried Into Canada. Written By Themselves.* Brookfield: Printed by Hori Brown, 1811.

Rowson, Susanna. *Charlotte: A Tale of Truth.* 2 vols. London, William Lane 1791.

———. *Charlotte: A Tale of Truth.* 2 vols. Philadelphia: D. Humphreys, for M. Carey, 1794.

Rummell, Kathryn. "Defoe and the Black Legend: The Spanish Stereotype in *A New Voyage Round the World.*" *Rocky Mountain Review of Language and Literature* 52 (1998): 13–28.

Safford, Marion Fuller. *The Story of Colonial Lancaster.* Rutland, VT: Tuttle Publishing, 1937.

Said, Edward W. *Culture and Imperialism.* New York: Knopf, 1993.

———. *Orientalism.* 1978. Reprint, New York: Vintage Books, 1994.

Salisbury, Neal. "Note." *The Sovereignty and Goodness of God by Mary Rowlandson with Related Documents.* 1682. Edited by Neal Salisbury. New York: Bedford/St. Martin's, 1997.

Saltonstall, Nathaniel. *A New and Further Narrative of the State of New-England, By N.S., 1676*, in *Narratives of the Indian Wars, 1675–1699.* 1676. In *Narratives of the Indian Wars, 1675–1699*, edited by Charles H. Lincoln, 77–99. New York: Scribner's, 1913.

Sands, Robert C. *The Writings of Robert C. Sands, in Prose and Verse. With a Memoir of the Author. In Two Volumes.* Vol. 1. New York: Harper and Brothers, 1834.

Scammell, G. V. "The New Worlds and Europe in the Sixteenth Century." *The Historical Journal* 12 (1969): 389–412.

Schultz, Eric B., and Michael J. Tougias. *King Philip's War: The History and Legacy of America's Forgotten Conflict.* Woodstock, VT: The Countryman Press, 1999.

Selement, George. "Publication and the Puritan Minister." *The William and Mary Quarterly* 37, no. 2 (1980): 219–41.

Shakespeare, William. *The Tempest.* In *The Norton Shakespeare Based on the Oxford Edition.* Edited by Stephen Greenblatt et al. New York: W. W. Norton, 1997.

Sieminski, Greg. "The Puritan Captivity Narrative and the Politics of the American Revolution." *American Quarterly* 42 (1990): 35–56.

Simmons, William S. *Spirit of the New England Tribes.* Hanover, NH: University Press of New England, 1986.

Slotkin, Richard. *Regeneration Through Violence: The Mythology of the American Frontier, 1600–1860.* 1973. New York: Harper-Perennial, 1992.

Slotkin, Richard, and James K. Folsom, eds. *So Dreadful a Judgment: Puritan Responses to King Philip's War, 1676–1677.* Middletown, CT: Wesleyan University Press, 1978.

Smith, Sidonie. "Reading the Posthuman Backward: Mary Rowlandson's Doubled Witnessing." *Biography* 35 (2012): 137–52.

Spivak, Gayatri Chakravorty. "Can the Subaltern Speak?" In *Marxism and the Interpretation of Culture*, edited by Cary Nelson and Lawrence Grossberg, 271–313. Urbana: University of Illinois Press, 1988.

Staden, Hans. *Geschichte eines Landes, gelegen in der Neuen Welt, America genannt, yon Hans Staden aus Homburg in Hessen.* Marburg, 1557.

Stein, Jordan. "Mary Rowlandson's Hunger and the Historiography of Sexuality." *American Literature* 81 (2009): 469–95.

Stone, John Augustus. *Metamora; or, The Last of the Wampanoags: an Indian tragedy in five acts.* 1829. In *Metamora and other plays.* Edited by E. R. Page. Princeton, NJ: Princeton University Press, 1941.

Strong, Pauline Turner. *Captive Selves, Captivating Others: The Politics and Poetics of Colonial American Captivity Narratives.* Boulder, CO: Westview Press, 1999.

Teorey, Matthew. "Sir Ernest Shackleton's Miraculous Escape from Antarctica as Captivity Narrative: 'The Grip of the Ice.'" *English Literature in Transition, 1880–1920* 47 (2004): 273–91.

Ter Amicam. "The Preface to the Reader." In *The Sovereignty and Goodness of God, Together with the Faithfulness of His Promises Displayed, Being a Narrative of the Captivity and Restauration of Mrs. Mary Rowlandson. Commended by Her, to All that Desires to Know the Lords Doings to, and*

Dealings with Her. Especially to Her Dear Children and Relations, The Second Addition Corrected and Amended. Written Down By Her Own Hand for Her Private Use, and Now Made Publick at the Earnest Desire of Some Friends, and for the Benefit of the Afflicted. 1682. Edited by Neal Salisbury. Boston, Bedford/ St. Martins, 1997.

Thornton, Russell. *American Indian Holocaust and Survival: A Population History Since 1492.* Norman: University of Oklahoma Press, 1987.

Tinker, George E. *Missionary Conquest: The Gospel and Native American Cultural Genocide.* Minneapolis: Fortress Press, 1993.

Todorov, Tzvetan. *The Morals of History.* 1991. Translated by Alyson Waters. Minneapolis: University of Minnesota Press, 1995.

Tohe, Laura. *No Parole Today.* Albuquerque: West End Press, 1999.

Tompkins, Jane. "Indians." In *"Race," Writing, and Difference*, edited by Henry Louis Gates, Jr, 59–77. Chicago: University of Chicago Press, 1986.

Tompson, Benjamin. "New England's Crisis." 1676. In *So Dreadful a Judgment: Puritan Responses to King Philip's War, 1676–1677*, edited by Richard Slotkin and James K. Folsom. Middletown, CT: Wesleyan University Press, 1978.

Toulouse, Teresa. "Female Captivity and 'Creole' Male Identity in the Narratives of Mary Rowlandson and Hannah Swarton." In *Creole Subjects in the Colonial Americas*, edited by Ralph Bauer and Jose Antonio Mazzotti, 313–33. University of North Carolina Press, 2009.

Traister, Bryce. "Mary Rowlandson and the Invention of the Secular." *Early American Literature* 42, no. 2 (2009): 323–54.

Turner, Dale A. *This Is Not A Peace Pipe.* Toronto: University of Toronto Press, 2006.

Tyler, Royall. *The Algerine Captive; or, the Life and Adventures of Doctor Updike Underhill: Six Years Prisoner Among the Algerines.* Walpole, NH: D. Carlisle, Jr., 1797.

Tyndale, William. *The obedie[n]ce of a Christen man and how Christe[n] rulers ought to governe, where in also (if thou marke diligently) thou shalt fynde eyes to perceave the crafty conveyance of all iugglers.* Antwerp: J. Hoochstraten, 1528.

VanDerBeets, Richard. Introduction to *Held Captive by Indians: Selected Narratives 1642–1836*, edited by Richard VanDerBeets. Knoxville: University of Tennessee Press, 1973.

Vaughn, Alden. *Transatlantic Encounters: American Indians in Britain, 1500–1776.* Cambridge, UK: Cambridge University Press, 2006.

Virilio, Paul, and Sylvere Lotringer. *Pure War.* 1983. New York: Semiotext(e), 1997.

Vizenor, Gerald. *Manifest Manners: Narratives on Postindian Survivance.* Lincoln: Bison Books, 1994.

———. *Survivance: Narratives of Native Presence.* Lincoln: University of Nebraska Press, 2008.

Warrior, Robert A. "'Native Critics in the World': Edward Said and Nationalism." In *American Indian Literary Nationalism*, edited by Robert Warrior, Jace Weaver, and Craig Womack, 179–223. Albuquerque: University of New Mexico Press, 2006.

Washburn, Wilcomb E., ed. *The Garland Library of Narratives of North American Indian Captivities.* 111 vols. New York: Garland Publishing, 1975–1983.

Washington, George. "Letter: George Washington to James Duane." In *Cases and Materials on Federal Indian Law,* edited by David Getches, Charles F. Wilkinson, and Robert A. Williams, Jr. St. Paul, MN: West Group, 1998.

Weis, Frederick Lewis. Preface to *The Narrative of the Captivity and Restoration of Mrs. Mary Rowlandson: The Lancaster Edition*, by Mary White Rowlandson. 1903. Reprint, Boston: Houghton Mifflin Company, 1930.

Wesley, Marilyn C. "Moving Targets: The Travel Text in 'A Narrative of the Captivity and Restauration of Mrs. Mary Rowlandson.'" *Essays in Literature* 23, no. 1: 42–58.

White, Hayden. *Tropics of Discourse: Essays in Cultural Criticism.* Baltimore: Johns Hopkins University Press, 1978.

Willard, Joseph. Notes to *Narrative of the Captivity and Removes of Mrs. Mary Rowlandson: Who was Taken by the Indians at the Destruction of Lancaster, in 1676*, by Mary Rowlandson. Lancaster: Carter, Andrews, and Co., 1828.

William of Rubrek (Willem van Ruysbroeck), *The Journey of William of Rubruck to the Eastern Parts of the World, 1253–55, As Narrated by Himself, With Two Accounts of the Earlier Journey of John of Pian de Carpine.* 1233–1255. Translated by William Woodville Rockhill. London: Hakluyt Society, 1900.

Williams, Robert A., Jr. *The American Indian in Western Legal Thought: The Discourses of Conquest.* Oxford: Oxford University Press, 1990.

Winship, George Parker. *The Cambridge Press 1638–1692: A Reexamination of the Evidence Concerning The Bay Psalm Book and the Eliot Indian Bible as well as other Contemporary Books and People.* Philadelphia: University of Pennsylvania Press, 1945.

Winthrop, John. *A declaration of former passages and proceedings betwixt the Englishand the Narrowgansets, with their confederates wherein the grounds and justice of the ensuing warre are opened and cleared.* Cambridge, MA: Printed by Stephen Daye, 1645.

———. "A Modell of Christian Charity." In *The Puritans: A Sourcebook of Their Writings*, vol. 1, edited by Perry Miller and Thomas H. Johnson. Revised edition. New York: Harper and Row, 1963.

———. *The Journal of John Winthrop, 1630–1649.* Edited by Richard S. Dunn, James Savage, and Laetitia Yeandle. Cambridge: Belknap Press of Harvard University Press, 1996.

———. "From the Journal." In *The English Literatures of America: 1500–1800*, edited by Myra Jehlen and Michael Warner, 308–14. New York: Routledge, 1997.

Womack, Craig S. *Red on Red: Native American Literary Separatism*. Minneapolis: University of Minnesota Press, 1999.

Zafar, Rafia. "Capturing the Captivity: African Americans Among the Puritans." *MELUS* 17 (2): 19–35.

Zinn, Howard. *The Peoples History of the United States.* 1980. New York: Harper Books, 1999.

Index

About the Author

BILLY J. STRATTON EARNED a PhD in American Indian studies from the University of Arizona, with a specialization in Native American literature and critical theory. He serves as an assistant professor in the Department of English and faculty advisor to the Native Student Alliance at the University of Denver, where he teaches courses on twentieth- and twenty-first-century American and Native American literature and Indigenous studies. His broader research interests include transatlantic studies, postcolonial theory, ecocritism, the literature of trauma, film studies, Southern gothic literature, and the literature of the American West. His scholarship has appeared in *Wičazo Ša Review*; *Weber: The Contemporary West*; *Arizona Quarterly*; and *Rhizomes*. In addition, Dr. Stratton was awarded a Fulbright Senior Lecturer assignment in the American Studies program at Julius-Maximilians-Universität Würzburg, in Würzburg, Germany.